S0-AWZ-124

References for the Rest of Us

COMPUTER BOOK SERIES FROM IDG

Are you intimidated and confused by computers? Do you find that traditional manuals are overloaded with technical details you'll never use? Do your friends and family always call you to fix simple problems on their PCs? Then the *"...For Dummies"™* computer book series from IDG is for you.

"...For Dummies" books are written for those frustrated computer users who know they aren't really dumb but find that PC hardware, software, and indeed the unique vocabulary of computing make them feel helpless. *"...For Dummies"* books use a lighthearted approach, a down-to-earth style, and even cartoons and humorous icons to diffuse computer novices' fears and build their confidence. Lighthearted but not lightweight, these books are a perfect survival guide to anyone forced to use a computer.

Already, hundreds of thousands of satisfied readers agree. They have made *"...For Dummies"* books the #1 introductory level computer book series and have written asking for more. So if you're looking for the most fun and easy way to learn about computers look to *"...For Dummies"* books to give you a helping hand.

IDG BOOKS

MORE INTERNET FOR DUMMIES™

by John R. Levine
and Margaret Levine Young

Foreword by Ted Nelson

IDG
BOOKS

IDG Books Worldwide, Inc.
An International Data Group Company

San Mateo, California ◆ Indianapolis, Indiana ◆ Boston, Massachusetts

MORE Internet For Dummies

Published by
IDG Books Worldwide, Inc.
An International Data Group Company
155 Bovet Road, Suite 310
San Mateo, CA 94402

Library of Congress Catalog Card No.: 94-77183

ISBN: 1-56884-164-7

Printed in the United States of America

10 9 8 7 6 5 4 3 2

1B/QX/RS/ZU

Distributed in the United States by IDG Books Worldwide, Inc.

Distributed in Canada by Macmillan of Canada, a Division of Canada Publishing Corporation; by Computer and Technical Books in Miami, Florida, for South America and the Caribbean; by Longman Singapore in Singapore, Malaysia, Thailand, and Korea; by Toppan Co. Ltd. in Japan; by Asia Computerworld in Hong Kong; by Woodslane Pty. Ltd. in Australia and New Zealand; and by Transword Publishers Ltd. in the U.K. and Europe.

For general information on IDG Books in the U.S., including information on discounts and premiums, contact IDG Books at 800-762-2974 or 415-312-0650.

For information on where to purchase IDG Books outside the U.S., contact Christina Turner at 415-312-0633.

For information on translations, contact Marc Jeffrey Mikulich, Foreign Rights Manager, at IDG Books Worldwide; Fax Number 415-286-2747.

For sales inquiries and special prices for bulk quantities, write to the address above or call IDG Books Worldwide at 415-312-0650.

For information on using IDG Books in the classroom, or ordering examination copies, contact Jim Kelly at 800-434-2086.

is a registered trademark of
IDG Books Worldwide, Inc.

About the Authors

John Levine and Margaret Levine Young were members of a computer club in high school (this was before high school students, or even high schools, *had* computers). They came in contact with Theodor H. Nelson, the author of *Computer Lib* and the inventor of hypertext, who fostered the idea that computers should not be taken seriously. He showed us that everyone can understand and use computers.

John wrote his first program in 1967 on an IBM 1130 (a computer roughly as powerful as your typical modern digital wristwatch — only more difficult to use). His first exposure to UNIX was while hanging out with friends in Princeton in 1974; he became an official UNIX system administrator at Yale in 1975. John began working part-time for Interactive Systems, the first commercial UNIX company, in 1977 and has been in and out of the UNIX biz ever since. He used to spend most of his time writing software, but now he mostly writes books because it's more fun. He also teaches some computer courses and publishes and edits an incredibly technoid magazine called *The Journal of C Language Translation.* He has a B.A. and a Ph.D. in computer science from Yale University.

Margy has been using small computers since the 1970s. She graduated from UNIX on a PDP/11 to Apple DOS on an Apple II to MS-DOS and UNIX on a variety of machines. She has done all kinds of jobs that involve explaining to people that computers aren't as mysterious as they might think, including managing the use of PCs at Columbia Pictures, teaching scientists and engineers what computers are good for, and writing computer manuals. She has been president of NYPC, the New York PC Users' Group.

Margy has written several computer books, including *Understanding Javelin PLUS* (John also wrote part of it) and *The Complete Guide to PC-File.* She has a degree in computer science from Yale University.

Welcome to the world of IDG Books Worldwide.

IDG Books Worldwide, Inc., is a subsidiary of International Data Group, the world's largest publisher of business and computer-related information and the leading global provider of information services on information technology. IDG was founded more than 25 years ago and now employs more than 5,700 people worldwide. IDG publishes more than 200 computer publications in 63 countries (see listing below). Forty million people read one or more IDG publications each month.

Launched in 1990, IDG Books is today the fastest-growing publisher of computer and business books in the United States. We are proud to have received 3 awards from the Computer Press Association in recognition of editorial excellence, and our best-selling ...*For Dummies* series has more than 7 million copies in print with translations in more than 20 languages. IDG Books, through a recent joint venture with IDG's Hi-Tech Beijing, became the first U.S. publisher to publish a computer book in the People's Republic of China. In record time, IDG Books has become the first choice for millions of readers around the world who want to learn how to better manage their businesses.

Our mission is simple: Every IDG book is designed to bring extra value and skill-building instructions to the reader. Our books are written by experts who understand and care about our readers. The knowledge base of our editorial staff comes from years of experience in publishing, education, and journalism — experience which we use to produce books for the '90s. In short, we care about books, so we attract the best people. We devote special attention to details such as audience, interior design, use of icons, and illustrations. And because we use an efficient process of authoring, editing, and desktop publishing our books electronically, we can spend more time ensuring superior content and spend less time on the technicalities of making books.

You can count on our commitment to deliver high-quality books at competitive prices on topics customers want to read about. At IDG, we value quality, and we have been delivering quality for more than 25 years. You'll find no better book on a subject than an IDG book.

John J. Kilcullen

John Kilcullen
President and CEO
IDG Books Worldwide, Inc.

IDG Books Worldwide, Inc., is a subsidiary of International Data Group. The officers are Patrick J. McGovern, Founder and Board Chairman; Walter Boyd, President. International Data Group's publications include: **ARGENTINA'S** Computerworld Argentina, Infoworld Argentina; **AUSTRALIA'S** Computerworld Australia, Australian PC World, Australian Macworld, Network World, Mobile Business Australia, Reseller, IDG Sources; **AUSTRIA'S** Computerwelt Oesterreich, PC Test; **BRAZIL'S** Computerworld, Gamepro, Game Power, Mundo IBM, Mundo Unix, PC World, Super Game; **BELGIUM'S** Data News (CW) **BULGARIA'S** Computerworld Bulgaria, Ediworld, PC & Mac World Bulgaria, Network World Bulgaria; **CANADA'S** CIO Canada, Computerworld Canada, Graduate Computerworld, InfoCanada, Network World Canada; **CHILE'S** Computerworld Chile, Informatica; **COLOMBIA'S** Computerworld Colombia, PC World; **CZECH REPUBLIC'S** Computerworld, Elektronika, PC World; **DENMARK'S** Communications World, Computerworld Danmark, Macintosh Produktkatalog, Macworld Danmark, PC World Danmark, PC World Produktguide, Tech World, Windows World; **ECUADOR'S** PC World Ecuador; **EGYPT'S** Computerworld (CW) Middle East, PC World Middle East; **FINLAND'S** MikroPC, Tietoviikko, Tietoverkko; **FRANCE'S** Distributique, GOLDEN MAC, InfoPC, Languages & Systems, Le Guide du Monde Informatique, Le Monde Informatique, Telecoms & Reseaux; **GERMANY'S** Computerwoche, Computerwoche Focus, Computerwoche Extra, Computerwoche Karriere, Information Management, Macwelt, Netzwelt, PC Welt, PC Woche, Publish, Unit; **GREECE'S** Infoworld, PC Games; **HUNGARY'S** Computerworld SZT, PC World; **HONG KONG'S** Computerworld Hong Kong, PC World Hong Kong; **INDIA'S** Computers & Communications; **IRELAND'S** ComputerScope; **ISRAEL'S** Computerworld Israel, PC World Israel; **ITALY'S** Computerworld Italia, Lotus Magazine, Macworld Italia, Networking Italia, PC Shopping, PC World Italia; **JAPAN'S** Computerworld Today, Information Systems World, Macworld Japan, Nikkei Personal Computing, SunWorld Japan, Windows World; **KENYA'S** East African Computer News; **KOREA'S** Computerworld Korea, Macworld Korea, PC World Korea; **MEXICO'S** Compu Edicion, Compu Manufactura, Computacion/Punto de Venta, Computerworld Mexico, MacWorld, Mundo Unix, PC World, Windows; **THE NETHERLANDS'** Computer! Totaal, Computable (CW), LAN Magazine, MacWorld, Totaal "Windows"; **NEW ZEALAND'S** Computer Listings, Computerworld New Zealand, New Zealand PC World, Network World; **NIGERIA'S** PC World Africa; **NORWAY'S** Computerworld Norge, C/World, Lotusworld Norge, Macworld Norge, Networld, PC World Ekspress, PC World Norge, PC World's Produktguide, Publish& Multimedia World, Student Data, Unix World, Windowsworld; IDG Direct Response; **PAKISTAN'S** PC World Pakistan; **PANAMA'S** PC World Panama; **PERU'S** Computerworld Peru, PC World; **PEOPLE'S REPUBLIC OF CHINA'S** China Computerworld, China Infoworld, Electronics Today/Multimedia World, Electronics International, Electronic Product World, China Network World, PC and Communications Magazine, PC World China, Software World Magazine, Telecom Product World; IDG HIGH TECH BEIJING'S New Product World; IDG SHENZHEN'S Computer News Digest; **PHILIPPINES'** Computerworld Philippines, PC Digest (PCW); **POLAND'S** Computerworld Poland, PC World/Komputer; **PORTUGAL'S** Cerebro/PC World, Correio Informatico/Computerworld, Informatica & Comunicacoes Catalogo, MacIn, Nacional de Produtos; **ROMANIA'S** Computerworld, PC World; **RUSSIA'S** Computerworld-Moscow, Mir - PC, Sety; **SINGAPORE'S** Computerworld Southeast Asia, PC World Singapore; **SLOVENIA'S** Monitor Magazine; **SOUTH AFRICA'S** Computer Mail (CIO),Computing S.A.,Network World S.A., Software World; **SPAIN'S** Advanced Systems, Amiga World, Computerworld Espana, Communicaciones World, Macworld Espana, NeXTWORLD, Super Juegos Magazine (GamePro), PC World Espana, Publish; **SWEDEN'S** Attack, ComputerSweden, Corporate Computing, Natverk & Kommunikation, Macworld, Mikrodatorn, PC World, Publishing & Design (CAP), Datalngenjoren, Maxi Data,Windows World; **SWITZERLAND'S** Computerworld Schweiz, Macworld Schweiz, PC Tip; **TAIWAN'S** Computerworld Taiwan, PC World Taiwan; **THAILAND'S** Thai Computerworld; **TURKEY'S** Computerworld Monitor, Macworld Turkiye, PC World Turkiye; **UKRAINE'S** Computerworld; **UNITED KINGDOM'S** Computing /Computerworld, Connexion/Network World, Lotus Magazine, Macworld, Open Computing/Sunworld; **UNITED STATES'** Advanced Systems, AmigaWorld, Cable in the Classroom, CD Review, CIO, Computerworld, Digital Video, DOS Resource Guide, Electronic Entertainment Magazine, Federal Computer Week, Federal Integrator, GamePro, IDG Books, Infoworld, Infoworld Direct, Laser Event, Macworld, Multimedia World, Network World, PC Letter, PC World, PlayRight, Power PC World, Publish, SWATPro, Video Event; **VENEZUELA'S** Computerworld Venezuela, PC World; **VIETNAM'S** PC World Vietnam

Dedication

John would like to dedicate this book to Lydia, who knows why.

Margy would like to dedicate this book to Jordan, for many of the same reasons, to Meg (who thinks I'm writing *Access For Windows For Computers For Dummies*), and to my Dad, who puts up with a lot.

Acknowledgments

Lots of people helped us assemble the information for this book. Very helpful people include the folks at The Internet Access Company (in Bedford, Massachusetts), Delphi, The World (a service of Software Tool & Die), the Internet Pipeline, and Clarknet. We'd also like to thank James Mullen and Steve Emmerich for useful comments. We can't even begin to list the names of everyone who posed interesting questions and provided up-to-date answers on various newsgroups, not to mention those who distribute extraordinarily good freeware and shareware on the Internet.

Corbin Collins and Becky Whitney provided terrific editorial support, as usual. And as ever, Lexington Playcare Center provided the child-care without which this book would not have been possible (for one author, at least)!

Finally, thanks to all you smarties who have sent e-mail to us here at Internet For Dummies Central. If you have ideas, comments, or complaints about this book, e-mail us at `midummies@iecc.com`.

(The publisher would like to give special thanks to Patrick J. McGovern, without whom this book would not have been possible.)

Credits

Publisher
David Solomon

Managing Editor
Mary Bednarek

Acquisitions Editor
Janna Custer

Production Director
Beth Jenkins

Senior Editors
Sandra Blackthorn
Diane Graves Steele
Tracy L. Barr

Production Coordinator
Cindy L. Phipps

**Associate Acquisitions
Editor**
Megg Bonar

Assistant to Managing Editor
Jodi Thorn

Project Editor
Corbin Collins

Editor
Becky Whitney

Technical Reviewer
Samuel D. Faulkner

Production Staff
Tony Augsburger
Valery Bourke
Linda M. Boyer
Chris Collins
Sherry Gomoll
Steve Peake
Tricia Reynolds
Gina Scott
Robert Simon

Proofreaders
Alys Caviness-Brosius
Henry Lazarek

Indexer
Steve Rath

Contents at a Glance

Cartoons at a Glance

By Rich Tennant

page 5

page 234

page 127

page 41

page 102

page 126

page 220

page 289

page 154

page 275

Table of Contents

Part IV: 10,000 Interesting Things to Do on the Net *275*

Foreword

● ●

*W*elcome to John and Margy's *MORE Internet For Dummies,* their fourth brother-and-sister book together. It is, of course, exactly the right thing to follow John and Margy's excellent *UNIX For Dummies* and John's phenomenally successful *The Internet For Dummies* (written with Carol Baroudi).

John is mischievous and clever and seems to know everything, Margy is clever and gentle and wise. Both are frighteningly competent.

I'm terribly pleased to have the opportunity to write a foreword for them, because we've been friends for a very long time. I first met John and Margy in 1970, when they were members of the famous R.E.S.I.S.T.O.R.S. computer club of Princeton, New Jersey (Radically Emphatic Students Interested in Science, Technology, and Other Research Studies). The group was playful, zany, and smart. They ranged in age from 12 to 16 but were doing professional-level work in computer languages and programming.

The Levine home in Princeton was one of the warmest homes I have ever seen. Bob and Ginny Levine, the kind, trusting, and astute parents of John and Margy, made it a kind of clubhouse where everyone was welcome.

For me the Levine household became a home away from home. My excuse for hanging out in Princeton was that I was learning so much from the kids, but in fact it was also a place where my work was appreciated, as it was not yet appreciated in the Official Computer World.

John was the know-it-all patrician of the club, Margy was warm and clever and eager. Both of them seemed to understand everything, but John managed to turn his insights into a constant stream of wisecracks.

With his glasses and curly hair, John bears a curious and unplanned resemblance to the academic-looking cartoon figure of the . . . *For Dummies* books, although the character preceded him in the series. (I had forgotten John has a Ph.D. till I looked over the previous volume — most Ph.D.-encumbered friends don't let you forget it.)

John is a Class A wag, but his one-liners generally take a moment to understand. His dry delivery enfolds a pithy wisecrack like a fortune cookie. You can't laugh quickly because you have to unpack it.

He was always like that. When he was 16, I was driving a car full of R.E.S.I.S.T.O.R.S. around Princeton. Boisterously they called out contradictory driving instructions. "I demand triple redundancy in the directions!" I barked. It was John who replied laconically, "Right up ahead you turn right right away."

The coolest subject of our day

Now the Internet is today's cool subject. Everybody wants in on the Internet because they hear it's important, but most people don't know what it is.

However, as you insiders already know from the first book, *The Internet For Dummies,* the Internet is just a bunch of computers talking to each other, kind of. The Internet is not a Thing any more than the highway system is a Thing. You connect to the highway system by building a stretch of road from your house to any other piece of road that's *already* connected to the highway system; that makes the "highway system" include your piece of road as well. The Internet is like that.

And like the highway, the Internet is there for the taking, awaiting your particular use (except that the asphalt is a data-sending procedure that makes sure the messages get back and forth).

The hottest topics

Not only is the Internet a cool place, but all the hot topics are piling into it, like overheated people into a midsummer swimming pool.

Everybody wants to get into interactive multimedia — ahem, the *correct* term is *hypermedia,* which I coined 30 years ago — and everybody wants to produce interactive texts, movies, whatever, for the TV screen or computer screen (which will no longer be distinct from one another). The computer world is getting to be just like Hollywood, where everybody says he's a producer. As a matter of fact, the computer world isn't getting to be just *like* Hollywood, it's turning *into* Hollywood, and vice versa — Hollywood itself is now treating hypermedia as the new frontier.

But the hypermedia are no longer just on disks that people buy. Till recently, many people have thought electronic media meant CD-ROM disks — but CD-ROM publishing isn't electronic publishing, it's *plastic* publishing. CD-ROM forces a pre-Columbian view of the world: When you get to the edge, you fall off. The limited size of the CD-ROM — 600 megabytes — means that much of the editorial effort is concerned with deciding what's in and what's out. And it's not connectable: Every CD-ROM is absolutely separate from every other CD-ROM.

Whereas with *true* electronic publishing — that is, publishing *electrons, over networks* — there are no boundaries, there is no limit on size, nothing has to be left out. The publisher can keep filling up more disks up to any size, all available on-line; and you the reader/viewer can keep sending for the stuff indefinitely.

And this has begun. Notably, World Wide Web, which you use through Mosaic (see Chapter 14), is already a wildly successful network hypermedia publishing system. We will see many more network hypermedia systems that will make available media of every kind, across the world, under many different schemes of copyright and royalty. (Each of us seems to think that he, she, or it has the answer to copyright. We shall see what works.)

Another key issue now raging on the Internet is freedom of privacy. The American government is giving an awfully good imitation of a police state, claiming that it has a God-given right to spy on all communications and de- manding that something called the Clipper Chip be put in every electronic device so that users can *think* their communications are private — but the government can listen in at will. (Didn't a guy named Orwell talk about this quite a while ago?)

But the Clipper Chip is a fraud. First of all, no actual criminal will submit to it. Any high school kid can figure out a code that the government *can't* listen in on.

What, then, is the point of the Clipper Chip? What the advocates of the Clipper Chip *really* want is the laws that the chip was sneakily designed to impose on us — "enabling laws" that will make it illegal to aid and abet cryptography, enabling laws that will allow search and confiscation of computers, enabling laws that will allow search and confiscation of any private information and data by those suspected of actually trying to hide things in a way that the govern- ment cannot read. Welcome to the New Order.

But Americans are getting smart about such things. This book is intended to help make you smart.

Wasting time

People ask me: Do you surf the Internet?

Oh sure.

If your idea of fun is gossip columns, want ads, card catalogs, and graffiti, then the Internet is for you. A lot of Internet enthusiasts are people who apparently have nothing better to do than send and receive electronic chitchat and Hot News all day long.

But actually I'm talking sour grapes here. The problem really is that all that Internet stuff is *too* interesting. You can throw your every waking hour into it. Don't go near it unless you're good at Tearing Yourself Away.

So welcome back to the sequel

New kinds of moving data, winds of data, are sweeping across the world — eddies and gusts of data, hurricanes, cyclones of data.

Now, John and Margy guide you with their warmth and wit through this wild and windy world.

Ted Nelson
Sausalito, California
June 1994

Ted Nelson is best known for coining the terms hypertext *and* hypermedia *and for designing a worldwide network publishing system with automatic royalty in 1960, now called* Xanadu — *soon, we hope, to become a reality. He is the author of many works.*

Introduction

●●

*M*ore about the Internet? But we've written so much already! Are you sure you want to know?

Actually, so much has happened in the world of the Internet over the last year that we have lots of new, exciting things to report. The most exciting of all is the increased availability of direct connections to the Internet right from your PC or Macintosh at your house. Now you can use friendly software on your own computer at home to read your mail, peruse Usenet newsgroups, and explore all the other great Internet sources of information.

So welcome to *MORE Internet For Dummies!*

About This Book

This book covers tons of new stuff on the Internet, especially, as we already said, new ways for you to connect to it. If you are curious about the innards of the net, we suggest that you browse Part I, "Welcome Back." If you don't have an Internet connection yet, try reading Part II, "Public Internet Providers." And if you use Microsoft Windows, try Chapter 8, "Getting Your Windows Machine on the Net," and the rest of Part III, "Windows on the Internet," to decide how to proceed. And everyone should look through Part IV, "Ten Thousand Interesting Things to Do on the Net," for serious information as well as fun and games.

How to Read, or Not to Read, This Book

We think, of course, that this book is one of the finest books ever written in the English language, so the most appropriate way to read it is to

- ✔ Set aside several uninterrupted hours.
- ✔ Find a comfy chair and a suitable beverage such as (depending on your cultural background) a fine old Madeira, a double espresso, or a warm can of Diet Mr. Pibb.
- ✔ Savor each page of the book in turn.
- ✔ When you're finished, rush out and tell all your friends to buy the book and read it the same way you just did.

Unfortunately, in the hurly-burly of modern life, not everyone has the opportunity to read books that way. So you can also read the chapters of this book in any order you want because they are largely independent of each other. As with all books in the . . . *For Dummies* series, use this book as a reference. When you need to know something about the Internet, look it up in the Table of Contents or the Index, which refer you to the part of the book where we describe what to do.

Conventions

When you have to type something, it appears boldface in the text, like this: **something you type**.

Stuff on-screen — some of which you type, some of which just appears — looks like this:

```
Hello, Internet!
```

Type it in just as you see it. In many cases, you even must use the same capitalization that we do. We tend to use lowercase letters unless the program we are talking to insists on uppercase, because capital letters always sound like shouting to us.

If you have to follow a complicated, multistep procedure, we spell it out clearly in numbered steps with the main stuff you have to do highlighted in **boldface.** We also tell you what happens in response and what your options are. The numbered step sections are also marked with a Tootorial icon (see upcoming section "Icons Used in This Book").

Directory names, filenames, and Internet addresses are in `this special typeface`.

If you run into an unfamiliar term, don't panic — there's a full glossary of Internet terms in the back.

Who Are We Talking To?

As we wrote this book, we assumed that

✔ You use the Internet or are interested in doing so, but you don't want to turn into a nerd in the process.

✔ You have a copy of *The Internet For Dummies* around somewhere. *MORE Internet* builds on the first book and makes references to information that was fully covered there.

How This Book Is Organized

This book is split into five parts, each with its own theme. With few exceptions, each part stands on its own, so dip into the book as you see fit.

Here is what each part of the book contains:

Part I: Welcome Back

The part includes general information about the Internet, including technical information for those so inclined. Those who nod off at the thought of network innards can just skip right over the techy stuff. Chapter 1 contains a refresher course on the Internet, including a roundup of the services it offers.

Part II: Public Internet Providers

If you want to connect your PC, Macintosh, or other personal computer to the Internet, read Chapter 4, "The Internet from Your PC." It introduces you to the two major ways you can connect to the net and discusses how to choose between them. The rest of the chapters in this part describe how to connect to the Internet using some of the more popular Internet providers.

Part III: Windows on the Internet

Here you learn how to connect your Windows PC directly to the Internet — not as a measly, lowly terminal but as a full-fledged Internet host computer. Having done so, you learn how to download, install, and use some of the most popular Windows Internet software for reading your mail, browsing through Usenet newsgroups, grabbing files, chatting, searching on-line databases, and reading hypertext in the World Wide Web.

Part IV: Ten Thousand Interesting Things to Do on the Net

And now for the best part: Once you are up and running on the Internet, consult this part for lots of fascinating services that you can use on the Internet, including World Wide Web hypertext pages, Gopher menus, Usenet newsgroups, and more.

Icons Used in This Book

This icon warns you that nerdy, technoid information is on the loose nearby. Skip it if you don't like the looks of it.

This icon points out juicy information related to finding someone, something, or someplace on the net.

This icon appears when we describe a neat short cut, time-saving step, or other cool little item.

This icon introduces a step-by-step procedure you need to follow to get something done.

This icon points out something you *don't* want to do. Usually it's because you may lose a bunch of work or — every Internaut's worst nightmare — inadvertently send out a message to be seen by 150,000 people that makes you look foolish.

Talk to Us!

If you want to contact us with comments, questions, or complaints, send us e-mail at

    `midummies@iecc.com`

In fact, even if you just want to test that your e-mail program works, drop us a line — our computer will respond automagically.

Fuddy-duddies can send snail mail (you know, regular old paper mail) to the address on the reader response form in the back. Or you can write your comments on that form and send it in. For your trouble, you'll get an extremely attractive, full-color catalog of . . . *For Dummies* books. (Collect them all!)

Part I
Welcome Back

The 5th Wave   **By Rich Tennant**

"WELL'P — THERE GOES THE AMBIANCE."

In this part . . .

Hey, nice to see you! Haven't we met in cyberspace, maybe in a newsgroup or on a mailing list? You look awfully familiar...

Anyway, on with the book. In this part, we're going to delve into the technical mysteries of the Internet. Chapter 1 contains a useful overview of the Internet, to jog your memory, but after that this part gets into interesting but terminally technoid Internet lore. If you couldn't care less about hosts, addresses, protocols, and the like, just read Chapter 1 and then skip ahead to Part II.

Chapter 1

Something Old, Something New

● ●

In This Chapter

▶ What's new on the net?

▶ A short refresher course

● ●

What's New on the Net?

The Internet is crammed full of stuff that either is new since we wrote *The Internet For Dummies* or that we just couldn't fit in that book.

Naturally, you have read and memorized *The Internet For Dummies*, so let's get to work. Starting on page 31 in the discussion of V.32bis modems, we —

THWAAAP.

Ouch! What was that? It was the editor slapping our wrists, pointing out that this isn't one of those boring books for network weenies who enjoy memorizing TLAs (three-letter acronyms). This book is for people who have a life and want to get something done. Oh. Right. Sorry.

Anyway, since *The Internet For Dummies* came out nearly a year ago, there have been some significant changes on the net, including the following:

✔ Your typical Internet user used to be a student or technical employee with an expensive workstation who got net access from school or work. Now a large and growing group of people come to the net through independent providers and usually pay $10 to $20 per month for access. Accordingly, we have written a bunch of chapters about how to use the net through several popular providers: The World, America Online, and Delphi.

✔ For Microsoft Windows users, there's something called WinSock, a standard that lets people write cool Internet applications that run equally well no matter which brand of underlying Internet software you're using. As a result, lots of excellent new Windows Internet software is available, such as Mosaic, HGopher, Eudora, and Trumpet, and we spend several chapters looking at this software.

> ✒ The Internet has continued to grow faster than anyone expected, resulting in an explosion of new resources on the net. You can now find 600-page books that contain just Internet mailing lists. This isn't one of them. (The only thing more boring than reading a book full of mailing-list names is *writing* a book full of mailing-list names.) Still, you can be sure that we point out lots of swell new stuff worth looking at.

A Brief Refresher Course

We covered the basics of Internetology in *The Internet For Dummies,* and that's where you should look for the real introductory material. But in case you loaned your copy to a friend, this section provides a short course in Internet Basics.

What is the Internet?

The short answer to this question is that it's a bunch of computer networks all connected together. Several million computers all over the world are connected to those networks, and if you have access to one of them, you have access to all the others. (In reality, the number of computers that will let you connect to them and then do anything interesting after you're connected is much smaller, but a small fraction of a million computers is still a lot of computers.)

The Internet is a *peer-to-peer* network, which means that every computer on the net, from a tiny laptop to a behemoth supercomputer, is, in principle, equal and that any computer can connect to any other computer. Any computer attached to the net, therefore, can offer services to anyone else, and many do. When you use an Internet service, the computer on the other end providing that service can be anything from a PC to a CM-5 supercomputer.

Deep down, the only thing the Internet does is deliver data from one place to another. What makes that process interesting is that programs running on all the computers on the net use that data delivery to provide useful (considering that computers are involved) services such as electronic mail, remote file retrieval, and real-time networked versions of Dungeons and Dragons. What we talk about in this book are the cool services that use the Internet. (For the extremely cool people who read ... *For Dummies* books, only the coolest in computing will do.)

Too many abbreviations

Computer systems always have a number of obscure abbreviations, and networks have even more abbreviations than regular computers do. Table 1-1 lists a quick rundown of the ones you can't get away from on the Internet. (For a longer list, see the Glossary at the back of this book.)

Table 1-1	Some Abbreviations
Abbreviation	*What It Stands For*
IP	Internet Protocol, the scheme that gets a packet of data from one computer to another
TCP	Transmission Control Protocol, the scheme that keeps track of IP messages in case some of them get lost
TCP/IP	TCP and IP used together, the most common way programs communicate on the Internet
DNS	Domain Name System, a huge worldwide database that keeps track of the names of all the computers on the Internet
SLIP	Serial Line IP, which is IP data sent over a regular modem
PPP	Point to Point Protocol, a similar idea to SLIP, but with different details
CSLIP	Compressed SLIP, another mutant version of SLIP

Names and numbers

Computers on the Internet, known as *hosts* (which we suppose makes us users *parasites*), are identified by names and by numbers. The numbers are written in four parts separated by periods (pronounced *dots*) — something like this:

```
140.186.81.2
```

And the names are written in two or more parts, like this:

```
xuxa.iecc.com
```

Every machine on the net has a number. Machines that are connected to more than one network (which is relatively common for large systems) have a number for each network to which they're connected, although it doesn't matter which of those numbers you use.

Most machines on the net have a name, which is easier to remember than a number — unless you are blessed with a most unusual memory. The connection between names and numbers is flexible, so a single host can have several names, and a single name can refer to several hosts — which is useful for a service with multiple machines where it doesn't matter which of the machines you use. (Much can be said about the structure of the names, but because you don't need to know any of it to use the Internet, we say it in Chapter 2, where you can ignore it.)

Serve that client

In business computer circles, *client/server computing* is considered to be really cool and totally advanced. On the Internet, we've been doing client-server computing for 25 years, only at first we didn't know that that's what it would be called. Whoop-de-doodle. (Students of European literature may be reminded of a scene from Molière in which a character, newly apprised of literary styles such as poetry and prose, is astounded to discover that he's been speaking prose all his life.)

In fact, the idea of client/server computing is simple: One computer (the server) has some resource available, like, say, a database. Another computer (the client) wants to use that resource, most likely because a human being wants to. Some sort of network connects the two computers. The client sends a request to the server and asks it to do something, and the server sends back the response. (If the user is a human, the client generally presents the response to the user, perhaps after spiffing it up a little to make it look nice.) This dialogue repeats until the client is finished.

On the Internet, all the swell stuff you can do is provided by servers — remote login by remote login servers, file transfer by file transfer servers, and so forth. The program that you run is considered the client, but it contacts the server automatically, so in nearly all cases this client-server business is either obvious (if you're logged into some other machine, that machine is the server), or irrelevant. The primary case in which the cli-

ent-server distinction is notably evident is when the client machine is working, but the server isn't. In that case, you tend to get not-very-helpful messages from the client program — along the lines of `No Route to Host` —when it finds that it cannot contact the server.

On some low-rent kinds of networks (if we were naming names, *Novell* is one of the names we would name), some computers are permanently anointed as servers and the rest are clients. On the Internet, which is resolutely egalitarian, any computer can take either or both roles. If it runs server programs, it's a server; if it runs client programs, it's a client; if it runs both, as most do, it can be both.

In two cases, the clienthood and serverdom are a little (to put it mildly) obscure: electronic mail and the X Window system used on workstations to display stuff on-screen. In the case of e-mail, when you send a message, the recipient's machine is considered to be the server, the sender's machine is the client, and the service is that the server graciously agrees to accept mail from the client (sender). If you think about it for a while, this setup makes sense — think of the server as a mailbox into which you can drop letters. In the case of X Windows, the machine with the screen on which X is displaying its windows is considered to be the server, and the program doing the work and telling it what to display is the client. If this setup seems backward, that's because it is, but it's too late to do anything about it.

The most popular Internet service is electronic mail, and many mail systems not directly attached to the Internet have indirect connections, using an intermediate system on the net to pass messages back and forth. Originally, to send mail to these indirectly connected mail systems, you had to use strange and ugly mail addresses that involved lots of illegible and incomprehensible punctuation, but eventually the Internet powers-that-be arranged a special feature to handle all this mail: They added special *mail exchange,* or *MX,* host names. For the purposes of sending e-mail, an MX name works just like any other name does, but for any service *other* than e-mail, the host simply doesn't exist. MCI Mail has a mail connection to the Internet, for example, so you can send mail to users at `mcimail.com`. But because that's an MX address, you cannot use telnet, FTP, finger, or any of the other Internet services to contact `mcimail.com`.

Incidentally, upper- and lowercase don't matter in host names, so `xuxa.iecc.com`, `XUXA.IECC.COM`, and `XuXa.IeCc.CoM` all are valid forms of the same name.

Basic services

Here's a roundup of the basic services most Internet hosts support. We discussed them all in *The Internet For Dummies,* so we don't describe them in much detail here.

Electronic mail and mailing lists

Electronic mail remains the number one service people use on the Internet. All mail is sent to mail addresses that look something like `midummies@iecc.com` (that's us, by the way — drop us a line and tell us how you like the book). Each address has a name part that identifies the recipient, an @ (at sign), and a host part that identifies the host computer to which the message should be sent. Most addresses correspond to actual people, but many refer to other things, such as

- **Mailing lists:** Send a message to a whole slew of people
- **Mail-server robots:** Automatically send back a response of some sort
- **Gateways to other kinds of services:** Usenet, for example, which is discussed later in this book

Thousands of special-interest mailing lists are active on the Internet, and you can join them to exchange messages with people who have interests like yours. The topics of lists can be quite specific — for example, there is one list for dairy cattle and a separate list for beef cattle.

When you get on a number of mailing lists, you can easily get between 50 and 100 messages a day. In Chapters 10, we discuss ways to deal with the flood of e-mail. For a very long list of mailing lists, send e-mail to `LISTSERV@bitnie.bitnet` with the line **list global**.

Remote login

The *telnet* and *rlogin* services enable you to connect to a remote host and then use that computer as though you were sitting at a plain character terminal — that is, no fancy graphics, just text — directly connected to the remote host.

File transfer

The *File Transfer Protocol,* universally called *FTP,* enables you to copy files between remote hosts and your own system. A common convention called *anonymous FTP* lets you use FTP to retrieve files from remote systems even though you don't have accounts on those systems.

Network news

Also called *Usenet* or *netnews,* network news resembles a global BBS (bulletin board system). Each item that someone *posts* to netnews is passed from system to system until it eventually goes to all the Usenet hosts in the world. The amount of news is enormous — 140 megabytes per day and growing. To make some sense of this flood, items are tagged with topics known as *newsgroups,* and users can look at only the newsgroups they're interested in and skip the rest. Even within a single group, there can be a great deal of traffic — enough so that it would be easy to spend every waking minute of your day reading news. In Chapters 9 and 14, we discuss at some length how to avoid dreaded news overload.

Really cool stuff

The coolest Internet services are the most recent ones, particularly *Gopher* and *WAIS* and the *World Wide Web.* They let you access a world of on-line information in ways so cool we won't even try to describe them here. Turn directly to Chapters 11, 12, and 13 to learn about them.

Odds and ends

A dozen other minor services are available on the net. Most of these services are useful only to computers and the weenies who love them . . . such things as a service to get two computers' time-of-day clocks in sync and another that lets various computers on an Ethernet network check their network addresses.

A few minor services are useful to humans:

- ✔ **Finger:** Lets you check the status of a person or system. See Chapter 9 in *The Internet For Dummies* for more on finger.

- ✔ **Whois:** Looks up people in the official Internet directory. This would be a swell service except that the only people listed are the ones who run the various networks that comprise the Internet. If you happen to be looking for one of those people — for example, a certain author who takes care of the computers and who is listed as JL7 — then it's quite handy. But for the other 99.7 percent of the people on the net, whois is pretty useless.

- ✔ **Ping:** Just checks to see whether a remote system is alive. See Chapter 23 in *The Internet For Dummies.*

TIP

Netting in England

So far, the net in England hasn't reached the gigantic user levels that were anticipated a few years ago. There are only two service providers for Internet access at the time of going to press, and one of them, CompuServe, currently allows only e-mail access to Internet. But before you go and turn over the page, life isn't as bad as it sounds. Many users in England are using the net via college and university computers, which means that there are around 30 FTP sites from which you can FTP more or less interesting stuff. These sites represent around 40 percent of the UK users of the Internet, with the rest of them using the only commerical service provider available: Demon Internet UK.

Demon is a small company that runs three nodes on the UK mainland, providing around 350 lines into the Internet. Nodes are placed in London, Scotland, and the south coast of England, served from Reading. For a small registration charge of £12.50 and a flat monthly rate of £10, you receive full access, without the bother of all those on-line hourly charges. Demon can be contacted on 081 343 3881. Demon provides its own software for you to use when you register, and versions are available for the IBM PC and compatibles, Apple Macs, and Amiga machines. Subscribers can avoid the £7.50 disk charge by downloading these software packages with ordinary modem programs from Demon's guest account. CompuServe provides a mail-only access system to the Internet, and you also have to pay the privilege of 15¢ for every piece of mail that you send or receive. CompuServe is very big in the UK at the moment, but many people are switching over to Internet simply because of the lack of on-line charges.

The current estimate for English Internet users is hovering around the 10,000 mark, but this is growing every day. A good place to find some English people to chat with is on the #english-UK IRC conference. (See Chapter 15 for more details on IRC.) As many of the English users are studying in school, all you are likely to get out of them is a lot of technophobic drivel, but the occasional star shines through (such as the author of this section). Several UK computer magazines run monthly Internet columns and invite mail from all Internet users in the UK. *Personal Computer World* is a big supporter of the Internet, as is *PC Power* and *MPC* and *CD-ROM User* magazines. Sadly though, the UK scene is nowhere *near* the size of the American user base, so you're going to have to spend most of your time talking to Americans. But don't worry — they're much more interesting than we are!

Thanks to Dino Boni for contributing this note. His e-mail address is Dino@Dino-b.demon.co.uk.

Chapter 2

A Peek Inside the Internet

Chapters 2 and 3 of *The Internet For Dummies* had some fairly detailed descriptions of how computers communicate on the Internet. We figured that the information should be in that book but we thought nobody would read it. One reviewer even complained that those chapters were a waste of paper that otherwise would still have been healthy, living trees.

You Made Us Do This

Well, we were wrong. "More! More!" people demanded in their e-mail messages. Okay, your wish is our command. In this chapter, we look under the hood at some of the lower-level operations of the net.

 See that little guy with the glasses there? You see him often in this chapter — it's the most technical icon in the book. If you're not sure you want to read all this, check the first sidebar called "An executive summary of this chapter," and then you will *know* you don't want to read it.

An executive summary of this chapter

A lot of detailed glop goes on at the lower levels of the Internet. Big deal.

Feel *especially* free to skip this chapter unless you have a morbid need to know what's going on in the bowels of the Internet — or perhaps if you have a particularly stubborn case of insomnia.

On the Level

For those few readers who haven't committed *The Internet For Dummies* to memory, in this chapter we reprise the basics of how the Internet works.

The Internet, stripped down to its skivvies, is two things:

- ✔ A way to move data from one computer to another
- ✔ A bunch of conventions, known in network-ese as *protocols,* about how programs use the capability to communicate with each other

When you send electronic mail to someone over the Internet, for example, your mail program and the mail program at the other end communicate by using a convention called *SMTP* (the optimistically named *Simple Mail Transfer Protocol*) to transfer the message from your computer to the recipient's. SMTP in turn uses other protocols (TCP and IP, in particular, which we discuss in gruesome detail later in this chapter) to handle some of the details of message transfer.

Divvying things up

The workings of the Internet are complicated enough that nobody, not even the world-class network geeks who designed it, can keep the whole business in mind all at once. To make things understandable (at least by geek standards), it's traditional to divide up the design into *levels*. (Sometimes, just to keep us all confused, levels are also called *layers*.) At each level, you sort of take all the lower levels for granted and worry only about what happens at your own level.

To take a somewhat strained example, imagine that you're making a tuna salad sandwich. The recipe says that you take bread, tuna salad, and mayo and make a sandwich out of them. At that level — the Sandwich Construction level — you assume that you have the ingredients on hand. But at the next level down — the Sandwich Makings level — there's a recipe for making bread, a recipe for creating tuna salad, and a recipe for making mayonnaise. More likely you would buy the bread and the mayo, but at the Sandwich Construction level, that's a detail you can ignore. Enough of this — we're getting hungry.

What level, please?

Exactly what the levels are in the Internet is a religious issue among network types, but here's a typical list from highest to lowest:

- ✔ **Application level:** On this level, two useful programs talk to each other. The mail client program talks to the mail server program, for example. Typical message: "Deliver mail item to `midummies@iecc.com`." Each different kind of program (mail, file transfer, remote login, and so on) has its own protocol. This situation assumes that the next level down takes care of passing the messages reliably between the programs.

- ✔ **Transport level:** On this level, a program on one computer is connected to another program on another computer, carefully making sure that everything the first program sends is received by the second program and vice versa. Typical message: "We just received 14,576 characters of data from your program number 42. Urrp." The usual transport-level protocol used on the Internet is called *Transport Control Protocol,* or *TCP.* (Pretty creative naming, eh?) This protocol assumes that the next level down takes care of moving chunks of data from one computer to the other.

- ✔ **Internet level:** On this level, one computer sends a chunk (known as a *packet*) of data to another computer, which may or may not be on the same network. Typical message: "Send this packet to computer number 140.186.81.3 by way of computer number 127.45.22.81, which is on the same network I am." The usual Internet-level protocol is called (now this is really, really creative naming) *Internet Protocol,* or *IP.* This protocol assumes that the next level down takes care of moving packets on the local network.

- ✔ **Link level:** This level transfers data between two computers physically located on the same network. It might be an Ethernet link for computers connected in an office or a phone line for computers connected across town. Typical message: "Send this packet to computer number 127.45.22.81, which I can see across the hall."

Some people put another level below the link level to deal with the different physical ways in which two computers can be connected, but enough is enough.

One way to think of the flow of information is that it begins at the highest level, percolates down to the lowest level on the sending computer and across the actual network wires to the receiving computer, and then percolates back up from the lowest level to the highest.

Now we take a quick look (probably not quick enough) at the levels the Internet uses, from the bottom to the top. (Remember: You can bail out of this chapter at any time. There is no quiz at the end.)

What's a Packet?

The fundamental item the Internet slings around is called a *packet*. A packet of what? A packet of, er, stuff. One of the few notably consistent aspects of the Internet is that all data sent through the Internet is sent as packets. If you're logged into a remote computer, and you press the Z key, that Z is packed up in a packet and shipped from your computer to the remote system. The remote computer's response is also packed into a packet (or several packets if it's real long — a single packet is limited to about 1,000 characters) and shipped back to your computer, where it's displayed for you.

A single packet contains these items:

- Header bookkeeping stuff
- Even more header bookkeeping stuff
- Some actual data (because of network megalomania, the actual data is optional)

Each network level adds its own header information to keep track of what's happening at its level. With the encrustation of headers, a packet can easily end up with more header than actual data, which isn't great (it takes up space in memory and takes time to transmit over network links), but it's the price we pay for all the Internet's flexibility.

Down in the Links

Let's start here in the basement of the Internet, at the link level (which, as you recall, passes a packet from one computer to another on the same network). At the link level are two kinds of networks: the kind with only two computers and the kind with more than two computers. The kind with two computers is usually some kind of phone line with a computer at each end (including some rather exotic phone lines such as high-speed, fiber-optic connections that send 45 million bits a second). The kind with more than two computers is usually a local network, such as an Ethernet. The reason for the difference is simple: When your computer ships out a packet, if there's only one other computer on the network, there's no need to worry about specifying who the recipient is. But if there are several other computers, the link level has to make sure that the packet goes to the right one.

Getting to the point

For phone-line-style links (usually called *point-to-point* links, an amazingly normal term for network types to use), you might think that to send a packet from one end to the other all you have to do is ship it down the wire. Heck, how is it going to get lost between one end of a phone call and the other? Well, it won't get lost, but there are plenty of complications on the way. Some of them are shown in the following list:

- ✔ **Framing:** This 25-cent word merely means that because you can't automatically tell where one packet ends and the next begins, you need some way to mark the boundary between them.

- ✔ **Error detection:** If a bird is sitting on the phone line or something, it would be nice to know when a message is corrupted.

- ✔ **Multi-protocol support:** Suppose that you have an expensive, high-speed phone line connecting two branches of your company, and you have some modern, efficient, TCP/IP networks and some other kinds of grungy, obsolete networks — such as Novell NetWare and Digital's DECnet. It would be nice if all the various kinds of networks (or, in network-ese, *network protocols*) could share the expensive phone line.

- ✔ **Authorization:** If the connection involves one machine dialing up another by using a modem and a regular phone line, and you have the slightest interest in security (which admittedly many Internet sites don't), you want to require some passwords or something before you begin shipping data to whoever just dialed in.

How we SLIP-ed up

The least complicated approach to handling point-to-point Internet communication is known as *SLIP* (*Serial Line Internet Protocol*), declared in its defining document to be an official "nonstandard." It deals with most of the issues just listed by ignoring them. Errors in transmission? Tough. Multi-protocol support? Forget it. Authorization? Not our problem. (If this discussion gives you the impression that SLIP was designed in about two minutes on the back of a matchbook, you're getting the right idea.) SLIP *does* at least handle framing — by defining a special character to put between packets so that you can tell where one ends and the other begins.

Despite its, er, technical shortcomings, SLIP has become quite popular, partly because for a long time there wasn't any other widely accepted way to connect computers to the Internet by using a regular phone line. It actually works pretty well. Transmission errors aren't usually a problem because these days most modems do error correction automatically so that SLIP doesn't have to. Most systems with SLIP handle authentication somehow — usually your computer must send a login name and a password, and only then does SLIP start. But SLIP suffers from many slightly different versions, a topic we address up close and personal in Chapter 9.

As the bits flow by, a packet of data as sent by SLIP generally looks like this:

```
C0 hexadecimal (that is, a character containing binary 1100
          0000)
packet data, however long it is
C0 again
```

That is, the packet data is sandwiched between two special C0 characters.

But what if a C0 is in the packet? No problem — in that case, we send two characters, DB and DC. But what if there's a DB in the packet? Still no problem — in that case, you send a DB followed by a DD. But what if there's a DD? Stop bothering us! (In fact, those two substitutions turn out to be all that SLIP needs.)

One major mutant version of SLIP is called *CSLIP* (*Compressed SLIP*). A smart guy named Van Jacobson was looking at the data sent over a typical SLIP line and noticed that the header data in one packet was usually nearly the same as the header information in the preceding packet. So if he sent just the header differences rather than the entire header every time, it would speed up the link by sending less data overall. This scheme, give or take a few details that aren't worth going into, is now known as CSLIP. CSLIP uses the same C0 framing as SLIP.

If you have a choice, CSLIP is always preferable to SLIP because it sends less data and therefore is faster.

Getting to the point (for real this time)

After a while, system managers and a few users began to get tired of dealing with SLIP's flakiness. So the Internet Powers That Be, formally known as the *IETF* (for *Internet Engineering Task Force*), came up with a swell, new, industrial-strength, all-singing, all-dancing replacement called the *Point-to-Point Protocol,* or *PPP.* In fairness, PPP also solves some other problems with high-speed lines (see the sidebar called "On the backbone").

PPP is a much more complicated protocol than SLIP. The definition of SLIP is only six pages, four of which contain only descriptive examples. The PPP definition runs to 66 pages, not counting the descriptions of all the network-management information, which takes another 60 pages. PPP is built on top of a widely used low-level link-handling scheme known as *HDLC* (*Hierarchical Data Link Control,* for what it's worth), which is what most fast modems used already.

A typical packet sent by way of PPP looks like this:

```
7E (hex) Here comes a packet
FF (hex) Required by HDLC
03 (hex) Also required by HDLC
00 21 (hex) This is an Internet packet
   Actual data at last!
xx xx Frame Check Sequence (see below)
7E (hex) There went the packet.
```

The first three characters (7E FF 03) say that this is an HDLC message destined for whoever is at the other end of the link. Computers are fairly stupid, so they don't find that to be obvious. The 00 21 says that this is Internet data — not Novell, AppleTalk, DECnet, Hairnet, or anything else. Then there's the actual data, followed by a *Frame Check Sequence* (*FCS*) and a final end-of-packet flag. The FCS, which is used to see whether the packet was received correctly, is calculated by the sender by (this is a gross oversimplification, but the actual details would fill ten pages even more boring than this one) adding together the binary values of all the bytes in the packet. The receiver makes the same calculation and should come up with the same FCS. If not, the packet got messed up on the way, so the receiver throws it away to avoid using corrupted data.

PPP has all sorts of configuration facilities so that when a PPP link first starts up, the two ends can have a nice chat and introduce each other and nail down some last-minute details about the link, such as what is the largest packet it is willing to receive from the other. PPP includes optional compression, much like CSLIP compresses packets. During their initial chat, the two ends can agree on whether they want to use it.

Even though PPP is more complex than SLIP, it solves many more problems and works much better in the case of errors (phone-line glitches, garbled packets, and the like) than does SLIP.

Given a choice among SLIP, CSLIP, and PPP, choose PPP.

Through the Ether

Compared to sending your packets over a point-to-point link, sending them over an Ethernet is a breeze. Framing and error detection, the first two problems that provoked people to write PPP, are handled automatically by Ethernet hardware. (Sounds too good to be true, doesn't it?) Multi-protocol support is pretty much automatic as well.

On the backbone

As we've already mentioned about 400 times, the Internet is a collection of computer networks. Some of the networks are fast, long-distance ones (across the continent or across the Atlantic Ocean, for example) that have to be managed a little more carefully than does your typical dial-up phone line.

For one thing, it turns out that building a modem that works at a million bits per second is tougher than building one that works at 14,000 bits per second. Also, when you have a network link that runs that fast, many people will depend on it, and those people will get really annoyed at you if you're in charge of the link and it fails. So you need network-management tools in order to tell, for example, how often a message sent from one end of the link arrives garbled. (Links often go slightly flaky in preparation for dying completely — it's like the cough that might develop into pneumonia.)

Furthermore, these fast links are often set up in groups, so that if one fails, its traffic can be shifted to the others. And being long-haul links, they tend to be located all over the country. Because you can have dozens or more of these links all over the place, it would be a mite inconvenient to have technicians running to each end of each link to check whether it's okay.

So PPP supports *remote network monitoring*, which is one of those obvious ideas that took about 20 years to think up. It uses the network itself to transmit network-management information to a central site where a single set of technicians can manage the entire network. Because large networks take management seriously and have people monitoring them 24 hours a day, seven days a week, central management has the important benefit that the network needs only *one*

set of expensive, all-night network managers.

PPP has an extremely complete set of network-monitoring facilities, the details of which we spare you because the descriptions read like this:

"If true(2), then the local node attempts to perform Magic Number negotiation with the remote node. If false(1), then this negotiation is not performed. In any event, the local node complies with any Magic Number negotiations attempted by the remote node, per the PPP specification. Changing this object has effect when the link is next restarted."

(*Magic Number negotiation* is a way for a system to check whether a link was wired wrong and whether the system ends up talking to itself. See, we told you that you didn't care about this stuff.)

Another problem PPP solves for fast networks is that until PPP came along, there *was* no standard for fast Internet links. If a link was faster than SLIP could handle, or if the link was too important to put up with SLIP's cruddiness, manufacturers invented their own link protocols. If you had a Brand X router (a specialized computer that moves packets from one network to another) at one end of a link and a Brand Y router at the other end, you had to be sure that they could talk to each other. As you might expect, each router manufacturer would cheerfully point out that the easiest way to avoid such compatibility problems was to buy all your routers from it, and each network did indeed tend to have all the same kinds of routers.

PPP provides a standard link protocol that everyone is supposed to support, so eventually you should be able to plug in any kind of computer to any network link. We can only hope, but we're not holding our breath.

The only fly in this otherwise perfect ointment is *addressing*. Your typical Ethernet has 100 computers attached to it, so you need some way to tell for which of the 100 computers a packet is intended. An obvious solution is to put the Internet address of the destination computer at the front of the packet. Then as each packet flies by, only the computer with the correct address receives it, and the rest ignore it.

This is indeed almost what they do, except for the minor problem that Ethernet has its own rules for addressing, and they're not the same as the Internet's. Unlike Internet addresses, Ethernet addresses are much longer (48 bits rather than 32), and they are assigned almost entirely at random. (Not quite random — rules make sure that no two computers get the same Ethernet address, but other than that they might as well be random.) So before your computer can ship a packet out over the network, the minor issue of figuring out which Ethernet address corresponds to the desired Internet address must be addressed. If you're smart, you'll take our word for it when we say that there's a plan to handle that. Or if you insist, read the sidebar called "ARP, ARP, RARP!" (What about rap?)

ARP, ARP, RARP!

ARP is the *Address Resolution Protocol* for Ethernet that figures out the hardware Ethernet address that corresponds to a software Internet address. It's amazingly simple, considering that a network is involved—the computer that needs to know the address shouts "Hey, what's the address for 127.45.32.11?" and the computer with that address shouts back "I'm 374cdf9e32 on the Ethernet."

This system works because on an Ethernet you can *broadcast* a message, which means that the message is received by all the computers on that network rather than by just one of them. In this case, the one with the right address broadcasts an answer to the message, and the rest ignore it.

To add the inevitable confusion to this pristine situation, we have *Proxy ARP* and *Reverse ARP*, or *RARP*. In Proxy ARP, a computer answers an ARP request with a message saying "Send messages for that host to me, and I'll take care of it." It's there mostly to help out hosts that are so dumb they can't handle ARP themselves. Reverse ARP is for the benefit of diskless workstations. When one of them starts up, because it has no hard disk or floppy disk to load from, it has no software loaded and no idea of what its Internet address is. It loads itself up over the net by using something called BOOTP, the details of which we spare you. Then it sends a RARP message saying "My Ethernet address is 373db49c7e12—who am I?" A better informed computer, which presumably does have a disk, looks up the newly hatched machine in a list and sends back an ARP response telling it who it is.

(continued)

(continued)

This scheme makes it easy to have a network of a few dozen diskless computers on a network (all of which are physically identical except for their hardware Ethernet addresses), load them up with identical software (BOOTP handles that), and then use RARP to give them the separate Internet numbers that they need in order to work with the rest of the Internet.

Fortunately, ARP and RARP work largely automatically. If you're feeling inquisitive, on a UNIX system there may be a command called `arp` or `/etc/arp` that shows you the table of Ethernet and Internet addresses. On a PC or a Mac attached to an Ethernet, you can probably find the ARP table in the Status menu of your network software.

On the Internet Level

Enough of that link-level stuff already. Now step up one more level to the Internet level. The link level handles the details of getting a packet from one computer to another on the same network. What happens when you want to send a packet of data to a host on *another* network? That's where the Internet level comes in.

The process of passing a packet from network to network until it gets to its final destination is known as *routing*. It's quite common for a packet to pass through 20 or even 30 hosts on its way from your computer to a computer on a far-flung network.

Suppose that we have telnetted from a computer here at Internet For Dummies Central to one of the systems at Delphi, a widely used Internet provider (see Chapter 5). The packet leaves our computer, passes through three small routers (two of which are old 286 PCs, quite adequate for use as low-performance routers) to our local network provider, through another two routers to SprintLink (the long-haul network we use), through about five routers taking the packet from Boston to New York to Washington, where there's a connection to ANS (another long-haul network), through another five routers or so taking the packet to the connection to NEARnet (a regional network), through about three more routers to the connection at Delphi, through a router that connects all of Delphi's computers, and finally to the host computer at Delphi. The total distance the packet travels is about one thousand miles, and the trip takes about a fifth of a second. It just so happens that Delphi is physically about a mile away from us (we walk to a grocery store downstairs from Delphi, in fact), but the network is fast enough that the extra detour doesn't really matter.

Take this packet and . . .

Every time a host in the Internet receives an IP packet, it asks "Is this one for me?" If so, great — it passes the packet to the next higher level of software (usually TCP, which we get to in Chapter 3). If not, it has to route it. For your typical Internet host, it's attached to only one network, and there's only one *gateway* machine on that network that attaches it to the outside world, so it sends all packets for other networks to the gateway. For a host connected to more than one network, the routing is a little (or maybe a lot) more complicated. Indeed, it's complicated enough that in the network backbones (the high-speed links that connect the fastest networks), routing is done by dedicated routers, specialized computers that do nothing but fling packets from one network to another.

How Many Networks Would a Network Network?

Back when the Internet was young, and dinosaurs roamed the earth, routing seemed like a pretty simple problem. Only a dozen or so networks were in the Internet, so each computer could keep a little table that listed each network along with the best route to that network. When a packet arrived, it could look up the network number of the destination (remember from Chapter 1 that the network number is the first few digits of a host's address) and send the packet on its way.

That method worked fine for a while, but now the Internet has become a victim of its own success. For one thing, the communication links have gotten *much* faster, and for another, about 13,000 *networks* — who knows how many *computers* — are on the Internet, and more join every day. Both these things make routing much more difficult. In the dinosaur days, the fastest network link ran at 56,000 bits per second, which seems fast to people but is a snail's pace for a computer.

These days, your typical network link runs at a million bits per second (known in telephone-ese as T1), and the backbone links are trading as many as 45 million bits per second. (That's "T3." Nobody seems to know what happened to T2.) Because a typical Internet packet is about 1,000 bits long, in the old days a link could handle only about 50 packets per second, but T1 can handle 1,000 packets per second, and T3 has no trouble with 45,000 packets per second. We turn those numbers inside out in the following table to see how long the receiving machine has to handle a packet, measured in milliseconds (one one-thousandths of a second).

Line Speed	Packets per Second	Time per Packet
56,000	50	20 ms (milliseconds)
T1	1,000	1 ms
T3	45,000	.02 ms

(A note to the arithmetically inclined: Yes, we've rounded these numbers.)

The problem is that in 1 millisecond a typical modern computer just barely has time to look up a network number in a 13,000-entry table. In .02 millisecond, it barely has time to notice that a packet has arrived, much less do anything with it. For the hosts in the network backbones, which really *have* to know where all the networks are and can't punt most messages to a gateway, expensive special hardware that can look up routes and send packets on their way is now necessary.

TECHNICAL STUFF

Where does routing come from, and where does routing go?

The astute reader may have noticed that we haven't said anything about where tables of routes come from. If there were only a handful of networks, skilled network managers could load the routes into the routers and update the routes on the rare occasions when new network links were added. But as we say in the computer biz, *that doesn't scale well.* Now that the Internet comprises 13,000 networks, there are probably 40,000 routers, and there's no way an army of administrators of any size could keep them up to date. So instead the routes are updated automatically.

Even when the Internet was tiny, in fact, the routes were updated automatically. One of the major goals of the projects leading to the Internet was to create networks that would continue to work if some of the links and some of the routers failed. (The military, which funded the work, was worried about enemy attack, but the same techniques are just as useful when an errant construction crew cuts a buried cable, known puckishly as *backhoe fade.*)

Every few seconds, each router on the net sends messages to each of its neighbor routers — that is, other routers on the networks to which it is directly connected. By comparing notes, the routers can figure out who's connected to which network and which way to send packets to each of the thousands of networks. Originally, routers just tried to minimize the number of hops a packet would have to take to get to its destination. That made sense when all network links were about the same speed, but now it's much quicker to take four hops on T3 links (the superfast 45-million-bits-per-second kind) than one hop on an old 56,000 link. Political issues also exist because some networks allow general traffic, but others allow only research traffic, and you can't route from one general network to another through a research network no matter how fast the links are. So lots of Ph.D. theses are being written about schemes to come up with the best routes.

Cough, Cough, We Seem to Have Congestion

As though routing weren't a severe enough problem (and it's pretty bad), there's the related problem of *congestion.* If you think of network links as roads, imagine a pair of two-lane roads funneling into a third two-lane road. If both the incoming roads are full of traffic, there just isn't room for all those cars on the outgoing road, and traffic backs up. The standard solution to network congestion may surprise you: Throw the extra packets away. The IP level is officially "unreliable," which only means that if there's a problem delivering a packet, the heck with it. That may seem awfully antisocial, but it turns out to be the best solution, mostly because all the schemes to make the network reliable at this level are more trouble than they're worth. (There *are* ways to be sure your data gets delivered — we get to them in Chapter 3.)

When someone's packets get thrown away, the node that does the throwing away is supposed to send a special *source quench* message back to the sender, which tells it to talk more slowly. This message helps somewhat. But there's no question — at peak hours, the net can get awfully congested and slow — that the only solution is more and faster (and more-expensive) network links.

A Peek inside a Packet

Every packet handled by IP has a *header,* which is a bunch of information stuck on the front of the packet that IP uses to keep track of the packet's progress through the network.

This list shows what's in a packet header:

- **IP version number:** Always 4 (evidently versions 1, 2, and 3 didn't make the grade)
- **Header length:** The size of the IP information, as distinct from the actual data IP is supposed to be sending
- **Type of Service:** A hint that this packet should be sent faster or more reliably than normal
- **Total length:** The total size of the packet, including both the IP stuff and the contents
- **Identification:** A sequence number to help tell this packet apart from other packets of similar appearance
- **Fragment info:** See the sidebar "Aargh! I've been fragmented."

- ✔ **TTL:** *Time to live*, a freshness date saying how much longer this packet can be passed around before it gets stale and should be thrown away

- ✔ **Protocol:** The higher-level protocol (TCP, most likely) that uses this packet

- ✔ **Checksum:** Checks for scrambled or corrupted header info

- ✔ **Source addr:** IP address of the original sender

- ✔ **Dest addr:** IP address of the ultimate recipient

- ✔ **Options:** Every general's favorite features; such things as *top secret* and *priority flash override*

What Next?

Your eyes have probably glazed over, so here's a quick summary:

- ✔ The workings of the Internet are best explained as a series of levels.

- ✔ The lowest *link* level handles passing a packet of data from one host (computer) to another over one network. Far too many ways to do that.

- ✔ The next *Internet* level (IP) handles passing a packet of data from one host to another, even though they are on different networks. Figuring out how to route packets from network to network is darned complicated.

- ✔ The Internet level is "unreliable," and although it tries to get each packet to its destination, sometimes it can't.

We present more mind-numbingly technical information in Chapter 3.

TECHNICAL STUFF

Aargh! I've been fragmented.

You may occasionally hear network propellerheads complaining about *packet fragmentation*. Each network in the Internet has a largest-allowed packet size, known as the *maximum transmission unit*, or *MTU*. The MTU on an Ethernet is about 1,500 characters, and the limit on a dial-up link may be only 500 characters. So what happens when a 1,500-character packet has to be sent over a 500-MTU link? It gets broken up into pieces called *fragments*.

Fragmentation is, from the point of view of network implementors, a pain in the neck. If a sender breaks a packet into three fragments, the receiver must wait for all three fragments to arrive before it can reassemble the packet and send it along to the next network. And what if the fragments arrive out of order (which can happen)? Or what if one of the fragments gets lost? How long should it wait before it gives up and considers the whole packet to be lost? There's no good answer.

Tip: If you use network software that lets you set your own system's MTU (Trumpet WinSock is one — see Chapter 9), be sure to set it fairly low, like 500 or less, to avoid dreaded fragmentation.

Chapter 3

Yet More of a Peek
Inside the Internet

· ·

In This Chapter

▶ Even more technoid details about the innards of the net

▶ Deep, dark secrets about TCP, and other unspeakable acronyms

▶ How e-mail really gets delivered

· ·

You Made Us Do This, Too

You read Chapter 2 and you're still reading this? Are you nuts? There's no accounting for taste, evidently.

In the last chapter, we established that the Internet, by using the creatively named Internet Protocol (IP), is able to send packets of data from one computer to another, even when the two computers are on different networks in different parts of the world. But a single packet is rarely enough to say anything useful. (It's like saying "Hi" to someone, but not waiting around to hear if there's an answer.) In this chapter, we look at the way that the Internet uses packets — lots and lots of packets — to create conversations between two computers. (That's called the *transport* level of the net.) Finally, to show that it is actually possible to make all this nonsense do something useful, we show how to use the transport level to deliver an e-mail message.

Executive summary of this chapter

There's even more detailed glop going on at the lower levels of the Internet than we discussed in the last chapter. Big deal.

You don't have to read any of this chapter to follow the rest of the book or to use the Internet. In the unlikely event that you've read Chapter 2 and you're still interested in this stuff and/or your insomnia is still a problem, read on.

Controlling Those Transmissions

When you have a network connection between two computers, the most convenient kind of connection to have is known as a *circuit*. The most familiar example of a circuit connection is a telephone call. If we call you, once the connection is made, everything we say is transmitted to you, and everything you say is transmitted to us. (If this seems obvious, that's because it is.) A circuit connection between two computers works the same way — everything one computer sends is received by the other and vice versa. When you dial in over the phone to a BBS or a UNIX provider, you have a circuit connection to the BBS or UNIX provider.

The Internet, on the other hand, doesn't have circuits. It has packets. So what's a circuit lover to do? You fake it, that's what you do. You take the stream of data that you'd like to send over a circuit to another computer, slice it into packets, number them, and send them to the other computer using IP, and the other computer puts them back together in numbered order. This isn't a real circuit, but it's close enough that we can pretend it is — it's called a *virtual circuit*. The scheme that creates these virtual circuits is known as *Transport Control Protocol,* or TCP. Because it depends on IP to do the actual packet delivery, the two together are usually known as *TCP/IP*.

The good thing about a circuit is that it allows two computers to establish an ongoing connection for as long as it takes to deliver some e-mail, or transfer a file, or allow a human being to log onto and use a computer. Continuity is the key here.

If circuits are so swell, why not use them directly?

In olden days, people did. IBM has its own network scheme grandly named *Systems Network Architecture* (SNA) that, when you make a connection, establishes a circuit through the network for the duration of the connection. But it turned out that the TCP/IP approach, with virtual circuits created atop a sea of packets, worked a lot better.

The reason is that a network connection involves not just the two computers at the ends, but also all of the computers in between that route the data from one network (or piece of a network) to another. In an SNA-like scheme, all of the routers in the middle need to know about all of the circuits that pass through them. (We oversimplify here, somewhat. Don't worry about it.) This greatly complicates a router's job compared to the TCP/IP approach, in which a router merely moves packets from one network to another without regard to which virtual circuit each packet may be part of. In our network, for example, an ancient 1984-vintage 286 PC is quite adequate to route data from one network to another, even though there could be hundreds of virtual circuits active at any time. If it had to track each circuit, it probably wouldn't be up to the task.

The TCP/IP approach is also much more robust in the face of enemy attack (see *backhoe fade* in "How Many Networks Would a Network Network" in Chapter 2.) If a TCP/IP network link fails, but there are alternate links that can get packets to the same place as the failed link did, a router need only send packets via the alternate links. The computers on the end won't even notice. When a lot of alternate links are available, it's quite common to send different packets in the same virtual circuit via different links, depending on which is busier at the moment each packet arrives. Even if one of the routers fails, taking down all of its links, the network will still operate so long as there are alternate routes around it.

In a network system with real circuits, on the other hand, each circuit that used a failing link needs to be identified and rerouted individually. This is a slow, error-prone, administrative nightmare.

The future of virtual circuits

By the way, for over a century, telephone calls have all been circuit-switched, with the facilities for each call set up when the call is established, and dedicated to that call until you hang up. In recent years, even staid phone companies are climbing aboard the packet-switching bandwagon, turning your phone calls into lots of little packets of data, whipping them through the network at high speed, and turning them back into voice at the other end. The current telephone buzzword is *ATM* (an unhelpful acronym for *Asynchronous Transfer Mode*), which is actually high-speed packet switching for both voice and computer data.

TCP Takes Control

We've established (still awake? just checking.) that the job of TCP is to deliver data from one computer to another. Its job can be broken down into several parts.

✔ **Reliability:** Everything sent has to be received. This means that we have to be prepared to send everything over and over again until the receiving end confirms that it got there.

Living in duplex

A connection between two computers can be one-way, two-way, or sometimes both. (Strange but true.) In the interest of avoiding excess clarity, these possibilities are referred to as *simplex, full duplex*, and *half duplex*.

Say you're using FTP to retrieve a file from another computer. After you type your *get* command (or the equivalent click if you're using a spiffy full-screen FTP program), FTP makes a connection for the file's data, the data comes streaming across from the remote computer to your computer, and when it's done, that connection is closed. That's a simplex connection, because the data flows only one way.

On the other hand, say you're using telnet to connect to a remote computer. Everything you type is immediately sent to the other computer, and everything it says is immediately sent back to you, with no particular synchronization between the two directions. You can, for example, type ahead of what the remote computer is reading, and it will catch up with your typing when it gets around to it. That's a full duplex connection.

On the third hand (this lecture is evidently being given by a Hindu deity), in some cases the data flows in one direction for a while, then in the other direction for a while, flip-flopping back and forth. The classic example is talking to someone — actually talking, no computers here — via a radio phone. One person talks, says "over," the other person talks, says "over," and so forth. (Inciden-

tally, the terms simplex and duplex originally come from radiotelephony, the first place where the issue of one-versus two-way conversation arose, probably in the 1920s.)

When computers are talking to each other without pesky humans directly involved, for example when they are transferring news or e-mail, half duplex connections are the norm because they're easier for computers to keep straight than are full duplex. Simplex isn't usually adequate, since there needs to be some way to get errors and acknowledgments back in response to a message. (If you're wondering about FTP, it uses two connections, a half-duplex one for commands and messages, the ones you see when you type commands to FTP, and a separate simplex one for file data.)

For an excellent example of half-duplex communication, we recommend the old British WW II romantic comedy *I Know Where I'm Going* in which Wendy Hiller plays a gold-digging young Englishwoman who's heading for a remote Scottish isle to marry a rich old industrialist. But while waiting for a storm to clear so she can take a boat to the island, she instead falls in love with a impoverished but raffishly charming local nobleman. There are several scenes featuring Wendy at the post office, talking via the half duplex radio telephone to her industrialist, "I miss you, darling, over," and so forth. The non-half-duplex parts of the movie aren't bad, either.

✔ **Sequencing:** Everything sent has to be received in the correct order. The sending computer's TCP slices the data into packets, and it's possible that by the time the packets are routed through the network, they may arrive out of order. (One might run into a traffic jam.) The receiver has to put them back into the correct order to avoid having the message this like received be. TCP assigns a sequence number for each data byte sent, and each packet identifies the sequence numbers of the data in that packet.

✔ **Flow control:** A fast computer sending to a slow computer can easily send data faster than the receiver can process it. To avoid network congestion (known in the extreme case as network constipation — ouch!), the receiver sets a *receive window* that limits how fast the sender can send.

ACK! Marching in sequence

The operation of TCP is, in principle, actually pretty simple. (In practice, it's utterly baroque, but most of the barocity comes from being prepared to handle errors and exceptional conditions.) Each byte of data sent over a connection has a sequence number. Let's say, for the moment, that the sequence number of the last data handled was 1,000, and we're sending 100 data bytes per packet. So we send a packet that contains data 1,001–1,100. When the receiver gets that packet, it sends back an acknowledgment (ACK for short) saying "I've received up through 1,100, now send starting at 1,101" so the sender then can send 1,101-1,200.

If we waited for an ACK after each and every packet, we'd spend more time waiting than sending, so we're allowed to send several packets ahead of what's been ACKed. The number of data bytes we're allowed to get ahead is the *window*, and yes, people really do say "ACKed." If the window were 300 bytes wide, then we'd actually send 1,001-1,100, 1,101-1,200, and 1,201-1,300 before waiting for an acknowledgment. If we then receive an acknowledgment up through 1,200, we can now go 300 bytes beyond that, so we can now send 1,301-1,400 and 1,401-1,500. When the network is working smoothly (which, surprisingly, it does most of the time) the data and acknowledgment messages arrive at roughly the same rate so that the data keeps flowing at a constant speed.

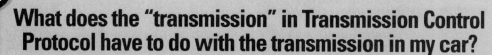

What does the "transmission" in Transmission Control Protocol have to do with the transmission in my car?

Nothing whatsoever. What did you expect?

ACK! Could you repeat that, please?

What happens if we send a data and we never get an ACK? Or, more commonly, we've sent up through 1,300, but we keep getting back ACKs only though 1,100? That means a packet has gotten lost. (Remember, IP is allowed to throw away packets in case of a transmission error or lack of network link capacity.) What do we do now? Simple: We resend the lost data. Since we have ACKs through 1,100, we resend 1,101-1,200 and 1,201-1,300. Eventually we'll get ACKs for the re-sent data (if not, we have to send it yet again until we do), and we can resume passing more data to the other end. An essential rule for TCP is that the sender has to hang on to a copy of everything sent until the receiver ACKs it, because it may have to be retransmitted.

ACK! Stereo networking

Adding a little more complication to this scenario (that's *little* as in when your dentist says "this may cause a little discomfort") is the full-duplex-itude of a TCP connection. If we have a connection between Boston and Geneva, data can be flowing both eastbound and westbound at the same time. So there is a separate set of sequence numbers for each direction, and a separate window for each direction. In the interest of packet economy, each TCP packet can include both data and a sequence number for one direction, and an acknowledgment and window for the other direction, so a packet might say "here's bytes 5,001-5,100 of my data, I'm ACK-ing up through byte 97,000 of your data, and my window is 600 bytes." Even though the packets are shared, each direction is logically separate, so you can think of them separately, sharing packets only to save network overhead.

ACK! I feel congested, could you close the window?

To keep the network working well, it's important that each receiver sets a reasonable window. If windows are too large, senders may send packets so fast that the network becomes overloaded. But if windows are too small, senders will spend most of their time waiting for ACKs, needlessly slowing down communication.

The traditional rule of thumb is that the window for a connection should be the amount of data that can be sent in the time it takes to make a round-trip on the network. For example, assume that you have a fast network that can transmit 100,000 bytes per second, and that the time to send a packet to a distant host is ¼ second. (These are fairly typical numbers.) So the round trip time is twice ¼ second, or ½ second. In ½ second we can send 50,000 bytes, so a reasonable window would be 50,000 bytes.

Now the black magic begins. If the network isn't congested at all, and no packets are ever lost to errors, this is the perfect window size. But in real life, the network's always congested when you want to use it, and errors do happen. It's fairly easy to detect network congestion — the sender may receive *source quench* packets from a router that had to throw packets away, and the receiver may notice packets arriving less often than they would if the network were flowing freely. So we should shrink the window to slow down the sender and alleviate the congestion. How much should we shrink the window? Well, er, some. There are lots of theories, but no accepted rules of thumb, so there are no doubt lots of Ph.D. theses yet to be written on congestion control.

A related question is how long after you send a packet do you wait for an ACK before you conclude that you have to send it again? If the time is too short, you'll be needlessly transmitting data twice, wasting network capacity. (The recipient can tell from the sequence numbers that the second copy of the data is redundant, so the situation is handled correctly, but it's still a waste.) If the time is too long, you can end up waiting a long time until the sender finally gets around to retransmitting a lost packet. The traditional rule of thumb is that you should wait about twice the round trip time, but there are lots of theories and upcoming Ph.D. theses here, too.

Socket to Me

So far we've considered how to handle one TCP connection (or virtual circuit) at a time. But on a real networked computer, you won't just have one, you'll have a whole bunch — potentially thousands on a large server system. TCP keeps them separate using *ports*.

If you think of a computer's Internet address as a phone number, the port is like an extension number. Any particular TCP connection runs from a particular port on one host to a particular port on the other host. A single port on a particular host can have multiple connections active so long as they connect to separate ports on other hosts.

By convention, standard server programs use agreed-on low-numbered ports. For telnet, you connect to port 23, for FTP to port 21, for gopher port 80, and so forth. On a UNIX system, the list of port numbers is in a file called /etc/services, and on PCs it's usually in a file called services or services.txt in your network software directory.

When a client program (that is, a program that wants to send mail or login using telnet or grab files using FTP) wants to establish a network connection, it asks its system for an unused port, usually in the 1200 range, and then connects to the low-numbered port on the server computer for the service it wants. When the connection is done, it gives its high-numbered port back to the system for later use.

Isn't there an awful lot of header glop on each and every packet?

You bet. TCP is what's known as a *heavyweight* protocol. A typical packet will have 40 bytes of TCP header and 20 or more bytes of IP header, which seems a wee bit top-heavy for a packet that may contain a single data byte representing a keystroke you've typed on a telnet connection.

The design of TCP/IP is cast in stone (two million computers would need to have their software updated if it were changed), but there are some gross hacks, er, advanced techniques, that can cut down the header bloat. The most notable is Compressed SLIP or CSLIP, which takes advantage of the fact that the headers in one packet tend to be very much like the headers in the packet that preceded it, so CSLIP usually just sends a single byte with a code for "same as last time." The original bloated headers are reconstructed by the recipient, so this saves time over slow links (by not sending the bloat) while remaining compatible with the rest of the TCP/IP world. PPP, the industrial strength successor to SLIP, offers similar header compression.

By the way, when we said that TCP/IP is cast in stone, we were lying. The Internet is running out of IP addresses, partly due to profligate handing out of addresses in the early 1980s to people who didn't end up using them, and partly due to the net growing a lot more than anyone expected. Some time in 1995 or 1996, everyone expects a new version of IP to be introduced that has much bigger addresses, 64 rather than 32 bits, enough addresses to assign a separate one to every electron in the universe, which we presume will be enough. Fortunately, whatever the new addressing scheme is (at this point there are several competing proposals), the old and new address schemes will be able to coexist for several years as everyone's host software is upgraded. But this will make the header bloat problems even worse, since the IP header will grow from a minimum of 20 bytes to more like 30 or 40 bytes. We presume that yet more header compression will allow people on slow links to avoid having all of their packets become larger and take longer to send, but the details of that aren't even under discussion yet.

Grotty Packet Details

For the masochists among you, here are the details of the header info that TCP puts on each and every packet it sends. Remember that TCP packets are sent inside IP packets, so the sender and receiver host addresses are already handled by IP.

- ✔ **Source Port:** the port number on the sender's machine.
- ✔ **Destination Port:** the port number on the recipient's machine.
- ✔ **Sequence Number:** the sequence number of the first data byte in this packet.

- ✔ **Acknowledgment Number:** (optional) the sequence number of the next data byte this sender is expecting to receive.

- ✔ **Data Offset:** the size of the TCP header, so the recipient can figure out where the actual data starts.

- ✔ **Control Flags:** special indicators like "reset this connection," "ACK number is present," and "end of data."

- ✔ **Window:** the size of the receive window, in bytes.

- ✔ **Checksum:** a control total of all of the data in the header, to be recalculated and compared by the recipient to detect scrambled packets.

- ✔ **Urgent Pointer:** Packets can contain *urgent* data that is delivered immediately to the recipient's program. (In a telnet session, Ctrl+C might be considered an urgent message.)

- ✔ **Options:** miscellaneous junk, which can include a hint to the recipient about a good maximum number of data bytes to send per packet.

An opposing view: Keep it simple

For some purposes, TCP is severe overkill. For example, a simple time service lets a sender send a request asking "What time is it?" and the recipient sends back a response with the time and date. Each of those can fit in a single packet, so it seems silly to use TCP, which needs a minimum of five packets to start and stop a connection, to send one packet each way.

For those lean, mean, network applications, there's an alternative to TCP, called *UDP*, the *User Datagram Protocol*. It has ports like TCP to handle multiple programs on a single host and an optional checksum for error detection, but other than that, it doesn't do you any favors. If a program sends a UDP message, that turns into one packet. This means that UDP can be a lot faster than TCP because it sends fewer packets and the packets it does send are smaller.

UDP is used both for very simple applications, like checking the time of day, and also for applications that do their own error-checking and so don't need TCP to do it for them. The most important of these is *NFS*, the *Network File System*. Each NFS operation involves a client program sending a request and the server program sending back a response. It doesn't matter whether the responses arrive in the same order the requests were sent (they often don't — some NFS operations take a lot longer than others) because NFS takes care of matching up a response with the corresponding pending request. NFS performance is extremely important (for many workstations, most or all of their disk operations are handled over the net via NFS), so small fast UDP is just the ticket.

Let's Play Postman

For the grand denouement of this chapter, we look at the operation of an actual Internet application, the euphemistically named Simple Mail Transfer Protocol, and watch as it delivers an e-mail message.

In an SMTP operation, the receiving machine is considered to be the server, and the sending machine the client. To deliver a piece of mail, the sending machine opens a TCP connection to the receiving machine on port 25, where the receiving machine's SMTP server should be waiting to receive something. The communication between the two machines uses plain old lines of text, just like telnet. (In fact, we see in Chapter 4 that you can use telnet to talk to a remote mail server to check for valid mail addresses.)

The sender sends a sequence of commands, each of which is a four-letter word (usually spelled wrong unless the word actually has four letters) perhaps followed by some parameters. The recipient sends back status messages. Each message starts with a three-digit number identifying the message, so that dumb computers can use the numbers to figure out what's going on without having to try to read the text that follows.

Note: In the examples that follow, we'll use S: and R: to identify lines from the sender and from the recipient. It's historically conventional for commands and responses to be in uppercase, although it doesn't matter whether they're upper, lower, or mixed.

Let's say that we're sending a message from aaron@aardvark.com to zeppo@zebra.org. The sender, aardvark.com, makes a connection to the recipient's server at zebra.org. The first computer to speak after the connection is made is the recipient:

```
R: 220 ZEBRA.ORG Mail server version 123.4A ready
```

Then the sender sends a HELO (we said these weren't spelled very well) to identify itself, and the recipient acknowledges it:

```
S: HELO AARDVARK.COM
R: 250 Hi, AARDVARK.COM, pleased to meet you
```

(Mail programmers have a sense of humor, too, sort of.) Then the sender announces that a piece of mail is coming and who it's from, followed by a recipient (spelled RCPT) line, identifying whom the mail is for:

```
S: MAIL FROM:<aaron@aardvark.com>
```

```
R: 250 OK
S: RCPT TO:<zeppo@zebra.org>
R: 250 OK
```

If there were more than one recipient, it could use more than one RCPT command. Here's what happens if mail is addressed to an invalid address:

```
S: RCPT TO:<elvis@zebra.org>
R: 550 No such user here
```

The recipients having been named, the sender prepares to send the text of the message:

```
S: DATA
R: 354 Start mail input; end with <CRLF>.<CRLF>
```

Then the sender sends the literal text of the message, ending with a line consisting of a single dot:

```
S: From: aaron@aardvark.com
S: To: zeppo@zebra.org
S: Subject: lunch
S: Date: 14 Sep 1994 11:30:00 EDT
S:
S: How about lunch at Elsie's?
S: .
R: 250 OK
```

The OK response means the message has been accepted. That's it — a QUIT command wraps up the session.

```
S: QUIT
R: 221 Sayonara
```

You can actually send mail this way by telnetting to a host and typing very carefully. (There's no provision for correcting typing errors, since SMTP is intended for computers, not for humans.) It's worth noting that this is, as is common in computer-to-computer communications, a half-duplex conversation. One side talks, then the other side, then the first, alternately until they're done.

Had Enough?

That wraps up our tour of the bowels of the Internet. Please remember to leave your hard hats at the exit and to wipe your feet on the way out.

If you're a glutton for punishment, the documents that define all of these protocols and many, many others, are available on-line. They are, as computer standards documents go, fairly readable, meaning they sort of make sense if you stare at them for a long time. The Internet documents are known, for some ancient reason, as Request For Comment documents or RFCs. (You can comment all you want about TCP, IP, UDP, and SMTP, but it's about 12 years too late now.) Some RFCs define standards, some comment on problems with standards or propose changes, and many propose possible standards that never went anywhere. You can find them by FTP or Gopher at the InterNIC, on a file server named `internic.net`. Each RFC is numbered, and there are now well over a thousand of them.

Table 3-1 lists a few you might, maybe, want to look at.

Table 3-1	Arcane Technical Documents about the Internet
RFC Number	*Subject*
rfc768	User Datagram Protocol (UDP)
rfc791	Internet Protocol (IP)
rfc792	Internet Control Message Protocol (source quench and all that)
rfc793	Transport Control Protocol (TCP)
rfc821	Simple Mail Transfer Protocol (SMTP)
rfc822	Format of Mail Messages

There should also be files available called `rfc-index.txt`, an index of all available RFCs, and `std-index.txt`, an index of the RFCs that define standards used on the net.

Part II
Public Internet Providers

The 5th Wave — By Rich Tennant

"IT HAPPENED AROUND THE TIME WE SUBSCRIBED TO AN ON-LINE SERVICE."

In this part . . .

*I*f you have a PC, how do you get on the Internet? A number of public Internet providers would love for you to open an account so that you can pay by the month or the hour to use the net. There are two types of Internet providers: so-called "shell" providers you log into by using a terminal and "SLIP" providers that put your lowly PC on the net. We talk about SLIP in Part III of this book, "Windows on the Internet." Here in Part II, we explain how to use the shell Internet providers.

Chapter 4

The Internet from Your PC

. . . .

In This Chapter

▶ Types of Internet providers

▶ What you need to hook up to the net

▶ Using communications programs

▶ Computing by committee

▶ Which files are where

. . . .

*T*his chapter explains the overall concepts behind calling an Internet provider from your PC.

Getting Connected

If you have a PC or other personal computer, you can connect to the Internet over the telephone. You need a modem connected to your computer and to a phone line, and you need an account on a service that provides Internet access. A number of services do this, ranging from national services such as Delphi, America Online, and Netcom, to local and regional providers such as ClarkNet, The World, and TIAC (The Internet Access Company), which provide service in only one city or region (that is, Maryland, Massachusetts, and Massachusetts, respectively).

Virtually all providers fall into two categories (see Figure 4-1):

✔ Shell systems

✔ SLIP systems

Shell systems

With a shell system, you use your PC as a terminal. Your PC isn't really "on the Internet" — instead, you use it to communicate with the provider's computer, which is on the net. Delphi, America Online, and the World provide this type of access. The provider's system runs Internet applications such as telnet and FTP. On your computer, you run a terminal emulator communications program such as Procomm, Crosstalk, or everyone's third choice, Windows Terminal (it isn't very good, but it's free with Windows.) We tell you how to set up your communications program later in this chapter.

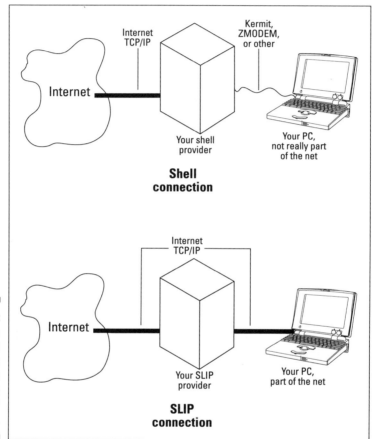

Figure 4-1: The difference between a shell connection and a SLIP connection.

Which provider should I choose?

A list of public Internet access providers, with their locations and phone numbers, exists right on the Internet. To get it, send e-mail containing the phrase **Send PDIAL** to `info-deli-server@netcom.com`. Or read the news.answers newsgroup — the list is posted regularly. Or FTP to `ftp.netcom.com`, and look in the `/pub/info-deli/public-access` directory for the file `pdial`.

SLIP systems

With SLIP, your PC actually becomes part of the Internet. TIAC and many other providers can give you SLIP access. With SLIP, while you're dialed up to your provider, your computer *is* part of the Internet, with its own host name and everything. Network applications such as telnet and FTP run on your own computer. Someone could FTP to *your* computer, in fact, if you allow it!

Other kinds of access, called CSLIP and PPP, do basically the same thing as SLIP, so to avoid saying *SLIP or CSLIP or PPP* a thousand times, we call them all *SLIP access* here.

In case you were wondering, SLIP is the Serial Line Internet Protocol (where a *serial line* is what network types call a phone line-type hookup.) CSLIP is Compressed SLIP, which uses some tricky techniques to send less data over the phone, which improves performance. PPP is the Point-to-Point Protocol, a full-featured, all-singing, all-dancing successor to SLIP. If you want more details (and if you're smart, you don't), consult Chapter 2.

For enhanced confusion, many providers such as Netcom provide both kinds of access. You may find this to be the best of both worlds: using one kind of access sometimes and the other kind at other times.

Neither fish nor fowl

A few systems, most notably America Online and Pipeline, have a hybrid system in which your PC runs a special program (always featuring flashy graphics and lots of putatively user-friendly glop) that communicates with the provider's system on your behalf. Despite having the programs that run on your PC, we categorize these systems as more like shell systems because the actual Internet *connection* is to the provider's system. Using America Online is covered in Chapter 7.

Your Basic Network Hookup

If you want details for SLIP, you can skip to Chapter 8 where we talk about setting up a SLIP connection.

This section shows your basic shopping list for using an Internet provider from your PC, regardless of whether you're using shell or SLIP access:

> ✔ **A modem connected to your computer (or installed inside it):** A *modem* is a gizmo that lets your computer talk to other computers by using a telephone line.

How the heck should I know whether I want shell or SLIP?

Here's some allegedly helpful advice:

Advantages of shell systems

It's easier to get started because there's much less to set up on your system.

All the network applications are set up by the provider.

They usually cost slightly less per hour.

The provider's system is connected to the net all the time, so you can arrange for files and documents to be available to the public.

Some shell systems provide lots of other services in addition to access to the Internet. Delphi provides lots of business and recreational information, for example, and the World provides a complete UNIX programming environment.

Disadvantages of shell systems

You can use only the applications your provider has set up.

Applications use plain old text — no fancy graphics. (Take a look at the screen pictures in Chapter 5, if you want to see the problem.)

File transfer is more complicated (see the section "Where Are Your Files?" later in this chapter).

You can run only one application at a time.

You must stay on-line all the time you are doing Internet-related work (it's not easy to set your system up so that you can compose your e-mail and read newsgroups off-line, for example).

Advantages of SLIP systems

Applications can and usually do use graphics, mice, icons, and other groovy Windows stuff. Rather than use some yucky UNIX editor like emacs or vi to write e-mail messages, you can use a nice Windows-based editor or your own word processor. Check out the screen pictures in Chapters 10 and 11 (Eudora and Trumpet) to see how nice these programs look.

You can run any network application you want, including cool free ones you can get from the net.

Multiple applications can run at the same time in different windows.

File transfer runs directly to and from the disk on your computer.

Disadvantages of SLIP systems

It's harder to set up.

Because it's a part-time Internet connection, it is impractical to provide files and services to other people.

The Windows applications are not always as powerful as their UNIX equivalents. The UNIX-based newsreading programs you use on a shell system, for example, are more powerful (though harder to figure out) than the Windows ones, especially when it comes to skipping articles you don't want to read.

Here at Internet For Dummies Central, we have both kinds of systems, naturally. If we had to choose one or the other, we definitely would choose the SLIP kind because the programs you can run are so much more fun.

✔ **A phone line:** You can use your regular phone line if you don't mind tying it up while you are using the Internet. (If you become a serious Nethead, you probably will want a separate computer line, particularly if you live with someone who is not amused by the phone being busy for four hours at a time.) You need a phone wire from the modem into a phone jack, too.

✔ **A communications program, such as Crosstalk, Procomm, or SmartComm:** The communications program mediates between you, the computer, and the modem, controlling when to dial the phone or send out information over the phone line and displaying the information that comes back over the phone. You need a communication program that can pretend to be a particular type of terminal. Crosstalk, Procomm, and SmartComm all can do this.

✔ **An account on an Internet shell provider:** The rest of the chapters in this part of the book talk about some popular providers, including how to get an account. When you get an account, the provider tells you the phone number (or numbers) to use. For more information about PC communications, consult *Modems For Dummies* by Tina Rathbone (IDG Books).

Here are some random tips that you may find very useful:

✔ If your phone line has call waiting, which beeps if another call comes in, it confuses your computer and your provider's system to no end. Therefore, you should turn off call waiting. To turn off call waiting for the duration of one outgoing call, dial *70 on your touchtone phone and wait for a confirming tone. To use this feature when you make calls from your computer, include *70, before the phone number (include the comma, too). This technique tells the modem to dial *70 and then wait a few seconds before dialing the number. (If you don't have touchtone, dial 1170 instead.)

✔ When — notice that we don't say *if* — you get a separate line for the modem, be sure to *not* get call waiting on that line.

✔ If you have a PC with Windows, you can use the Terminal program that comes with Windows. It's not wonderful, but at the price (free), it's hard to beat. As a cheap middle road, you may want to consider a shareware program such as MicroLink.

Setting Up Your Communications Software

Before you can place the first call to your Internet provider, you must tell your communications program how to call it. Whichever program you use, tell it the following information:

✔ **The phone number:** Enter the one your provider told you to use. (In Windows Terminal, choose Settings⇨Phone Number to enter the number.)

✓ **Baud rate (communications speed):** If your provider doesn't suggest otherwise, choose the highest speed at which your modem can communicate, up to 14400, for the communications speed. (In Windows Terminal, choose Settings⇨Communications to choose the baud rate as well as to enter the other communications parameters, which are described next.)

✓ **Communications parameters:** How your computer and the provider's computer send characters over the phone line. If your provider doesn't suggest other parameters, use *N81,* which means *no parity, eight data bits, and one stop bit.* Don't worry about what this means — as long as the computers understand this stuff, you don't have to.

✓ **Terminal emulation:** When a PC communicates over the phone, it always pretends to be some standard type of old-fashioned terminal. The type that most Internet providers expect is DEC VT-100 (ANSI) or VT-102. (In Windows Terminal, choose Settings⇨Terminal Emulation to enter this information.)

If your program allows you to save this information, do so. The next time you want to call your Internet provider, you can just use the same parameters rather than enter them all again. (In Terminal, choose File⇨Save As to save the parameters in a file. The next time you run Terminal, choose File⇨Open to retrieve parameters you saved.)

Who Talks to Whom

Before you make the call, let's review the players in this little game. Whenever you have two or more computers talking together, things get confusing. When you use an Internet provider (Delphi, for example), you call the provider by using your communications program. Your PC pretends to be a terminal, and all the Internet action is really on Delphi's computer. If you telnet to another computer — that is, you log into another computer on the Internet (see Chapter 15 in *The Internet For Dummies*) — your computer is still pretending to be a terminal, and Delphi's computer is just passing messages along to the other computer. It's a game of Whisper Down the Lane, computer style.

Where Are Your Files?

If you use a shell provider and an Internet service such as FTP to get files from another computer, FTP transfers the file from the other computer to Delphi's computer (or whatever shell provider you use). To use the file, then, you still have to transfer the file from Delphi's computer to your own PC. Transferring the file to your PC is called *downloading* the file.

Conversely, if you want to FTP a file from your PC to another computer on the net, you first have to *upload* the file to Delphi. (Of course, if you use a SLIP provider, FTP brings the files right to your own computer so that you never have to think about this extra step!)

TECHNICAL STUFF

Truth in bauds

One of the authors (the one with the Ph.D.) just can't stand it when people refer to a *14,400-baud modem* because it's incredibly wrong, even though everyone does it. So here he explains why it's wrong. Probably only 14 people in the world really care about this subject. Who knows — if you read this sidebar, maybe there will be 15.

There's a perfectly good technical definition of a *baud,* which is that it's a signal sent down a phone line. (The real definition uses a lot of long words, but that's close enough.) Back in the Bronze Age of computing, around 1970, there were 300-baud modems. As the computer sent its binary language of ones and zeroes to the modem, the modem sent them one at a time over the phone line. You can think of the modem saying "one one zero one . . ." over the phone, and the modem at the other end of the connection listening and sending ones and zeroes out to the computer on the other end. The computer sent 300 *bits* (that's what we call the ones and zeroes, short for *binary digits*) per second to the modem, the modem turned them into 300 signals on the phone, and they turned back into 300 bits at the other end. Everything was clear, simple, and by current standards, incredibly slow.

The next step up, in computing's Iron Age, was to send 1,200 bits per second (bps) over the phone. You might, and many people did, call this a 1200-baud modem. But that would be wrong. The reason is that the faster the modem sends signals down the phone line, the harder it is for the modem at the other end to understand them correctly. So some smart engineer at AT&T, which back in the Iron Age was still the largest maker of modems, figured out that if you sent the bits in

pairs, you could send signals at half the rate and they would be easier to decode. It's as though the modems agreed on a code: Rather than say "zero zero," they would say "pig," "zero one" would be "cow," "one zero" would be "horse," and "one one" would be "duck." So if the computer sent 010011, rather than send "zero one zero zero one one," the modem would send "cow pig duck." (In case it's not obvious, we're being a *wee* bit metaphorical here.) But because the modems had to send only three "words" rather than six, although they were sending 1,200 *bits per second,* they were sending only 600 *baud* because the words correspond to baud.

This coding scheme worked so well that when the modem biz went to 9,600 bits per second, it sent the bits in groups of four, so the modem was really sending only 9600 divided by 4, or 2400 baud. The latest 14,400 bps modems are still 2400 baud, sending 6 bits for each baud, and the 28,800 modems send 12 bits for each baud, again really running at 2400 baud. It turns out that for technical reasons, you can't reliably send more than 2400 baud over a phone line, so all the action in recent years has been in figuring out how to squeeze more and more bits into each baud.

If someone says that she has a 9600-baud modem, you know that she really has a 9,600-bit-per-second, 2400-baud modem. Your pedantic author understands that correcting this sort of misunderstanding is not a great way to make friends, so he'll excuse you if you let it pass when other people confuse your bauds. But you at least can strike a blow for accuracy and say "9,600 bits per second."

Thanks, I feel better now — *John.*

Files on the move

When you transfer a file between your computer and your provider's computer, you use something called a *file-transfer protocol.* Scary words, but it's no big deal — it's a way for the two computers to transfer a file while making sure that it is received correctly despite possible noise on the phone line.

Any method that computers use to transfer files is called a *file-transfer protocol.* Then there's the most famous one of all, called *File Transfer Protocol,* or *FTP,* which is a method that computers use to exchange files through the Internet. Chapter 16 in *The Internet for Dummies* explains how to use FTP on the Internet.

The most commonly used PC and Macintosh file-transfer protocols are shown in the following list:

- ✔ XMODEM (the slowest)
- ✔ YMODEM (faster)
- ✔ ZMODEM (even faster)
- ✔ Kermit (the most reliable on a lousy phone line)

Before you can transfer files, you have to find out which file-transfer protocols your communications program can handle and which ones your Internet provider can use.

Windows Terminal can handle XMODEM and Kermit. You select which one to use by choosing Settings➪Binary Transfer from the menu.

Let's keep it!

If you see something interesting on the screen (some text that Delphi has just displayed, for example), you can use your communications program to grab the information and store it in a file on your PC. In Windows Terminal, for example, you can use your mouse to highlight information in the Terminal window and choose Edit➪Copy from the menu to copy it to the Windows Clipboard. Then you can paste the text into your word processor or edit and save it.

If you expect interesting information to be displayed soon, you can tell your communications program to start *logging* your conversation with your Internet provider, which means that it stores it in a file on your PC. In Windows Terminal, you choose Transfers➪Receive Text File and specify the filename. Everything you type or that the Internet provider displays is stored in a file (you see it on-screen too, as usual). When the interesting stuff has gone by, you choose Transfers➪Stop. At that point, the good stuff is in the file, which you are free to edit, display, or print at your leisure.

Chapter 5
Using the Internet via Delphi

*I*f you want to use a PC, Macintosh, or other personal computer with a modem to connect to the Internet, one of the best ways is to use Delphi. Delphi is an on-line service based in Cambridge, Massachusetts that provides the usual mail, news, weather, shopping, and chatting services in addition to a complete connection to the Internet. By using Delphi, you can use telnet, FTP, Gopher, WAIS, the World Wide Web, and all those other cool Internet services right from your own lowly personal computer.

Signing Up for Delphi

To use Delphi, you need an account and some money. Delphi charges hourly and bills you monthly. When you open your account, Delphi tells you the Delphi local access phone numbers nearest you, your username, and your password.

 Because Delphi is still relatively new, the Delphi folks give you five free hours when you sign up. Just tell your computer to dial 1-800-365-4636, using the communications instructions in the next section. When you are asked for your username, type **JOINDELPHI**. For the password, type **DUMMIES**. If that doesn't work, try **INTERNETSIG** as the password. If you want to see just current prices and information rather than sign up, use the password **INFO**.

Dialing for Delphi

Before you can place your first call to Delphi, you must set up your terminal program to do so. Follow the instructions in Chapter 4 to enter the phone number and other information about how your computer should place the call.

You should use the terminal settings in 5-1:

Table 5-1	Delphi Terminal Settings
Set This	*To This*
Data Bits	8
Parity	None
Duplex	Full Duplex
Stop Bits	1
Auto-Line Feed	No
Carriage Return Line Feed	No
XON/XOFF (Flow Control)	Enabled (On)
Local Echo	Off
Terminal Emulation	VT100 or VT102

Now you are ready to try making the call:

1. **Tell your communications program to dial the phone, by using the information you just entered.**

   (In Windows Terminal, choose Phone Dial.) The program may have to dial a few times because the line may be busy. If the Delphi people gave you more than one phone number, you can try a different one.

   Sooner or later, your communications program should tell you that you are connected.

2. **Press Enter once or twice so that Delphi knows that you are there.**

   You should see this line:

   ```
   Username:
   ```

   If you connect with Delphi but the characters look like they are in Greek, try hanging up and changing the terminal-emulation parameter. If you used VT-100 last time, try VT-102 (or vice versa).

3. **Enter your username and press Enter.**

   Then you see this line:

   ```
   Password:
   ```

4. **Enter your password and press Enter.**

   Your password doesn't appear on-screen (in case some malefactor is looking over your shoulder).

5. **Delphi displays some welcoming text, like the stuff shown in Figure 5-1.**

   This figure shows Delphi's MAIN menu, with its list of commands you can give. You are ready to roll!

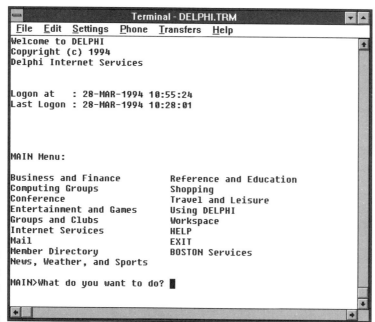

Figure 5-1:
Delphi says
hello!

Typing Commands

Delphi always displays a menu to tell you which commands you can give. You see different menus, depending on what you are doing.

Some tips for giving commands

Delphi doesn't care whether you use capital or small letters when you type commands.

After typing a command, press Enter or Return.

You can abbreviate all commands to the first four letters. In fact, you have to type only enough letters for Delphi to guess which command you want. For example, if only one command on the menu begins with D, just pressing D followed by Enter chooses that command.

When in doubt, type **help**.

To return to the preceding menu, type **exit** or press Ctrl+Z.

If you don't type anything for about ten minutes, Delphi hangs up on you. This may be annoying, but it does save you connect-time charges if you forget to hang up when you are finished. If this is a real problem, type **using** at the MAIN menu and then **set** at the Using-DELPHI menu to change the amount of time Delphi waits before hanging up.

When you are reading information that Delphi displays, you can press the following keys to slow it down or cancel uninteresting stuff:

- ✔ To freeze Delphi in its tracks so that you can read the information on the screen, press Ctrl+S (stop).
- ✔ To unfreeze Delphi after pressing Ctrl+S, press Ctrl+Q (quit stopping).
- ✔ To cancel the rest of the message Delphi is sending, press Ctrl+O (off). Even better, if you can tell your communications program to send a Break character, do that.
- ✔ To cancel whatever is going on and return to the last Delphi prompt, press Ctrl+C (cancel).

If you are typing information and make a mistake, use these keys:

- ✔ To cancel whatever you have typed on this line, press Ctrl+U (up one line).
- ✔ To display the line you are typing, press Ctrl+R. This keystroke is useful if you have edited the line a great deal and you are not sure whether you are seeing the text you typed.

Type **bye** at any time to log off. Another way to log off is to return to the MAIN menu by typing **exit** or pressing Ctrl+Z and then typing **exit** one more time.

Delphi's MAIN Menu

Here are the choices on Delphi's MAIN menu:

- **Business and Finance:** Displays a menu of business-oriented databases to choose from, including the UPI Business News, Donoghue's Money Fund Report, The Dow Jones News, Financial and Commodity News, Futures Focus, stock and commodity quotes, a mortgage calculator, and SOS Stock and Options Advisor.

- **Computing Groups:** Lets you joins groups of users of various types of computers for exchanging messages and sharing programs (shareware only, of course).

- **Conference:** Lets you use the interactive conversation system, which means that you can type messages to other Delphi users who are logged in right now. Although this system can be fun, it can also eat up lots of connect time, so watch out!

- **Entertainment and Games:** Displays a menu of games you can play by yourself or with other users, in addition to entertainment information, such as movie reviews. The games include adventure games, logic games, board games, and collaborative novels. Again — these games are fun, but they can be costly if you end up staying logged in for hours.

- **Groups and Clubs:** Lets you chat with other Delphi users about aviation, golf, hobbies, music, photography, radio, religion, yachting, and lots of other topics.

- **Internet Services:** Lets you use FTP, Gopher, telnet, and most other Internet facilities. (The details are described later in this chapter.)

- **Mail:** Lets you send e-mail to other Delphi users or to anyone on the Internet. You can also send faxes or telexes.

- **Member Directory:** Lets you enter information about yourself and find out information about other people, based on their usernames.

- **News, Weather, and Sports:** Lets you read news reports from UPI and weather reports from Accu-Weather.

- **Reference and Education:** Lets you consult several on-line encyclopedias and other reference works or participate in an on-line radio show.

- **Shopping:** You can shop on-line, if you like that sort of thing. There are also product-support services for specific software packages, computer systems, or software developers (choose Vendor and Product Support Services from the Shopping Menu).

- **Travel and Leisure:** Lets you find out about low-cost airfares, car rental, and other travel information. You can also use EAASY SABRE, American Airlines' on-line reservation system, to make reservations on most U.S. airlines.

- ✔ **Using DELPHI:** Displays a menu with lots of helpful topics about Delphi, including how to find phone numbers for Delphi, billing plans, and information about your own Delphi bills. This is also the place where you can change the settings that Delphi stores about you and your computer, such as how long to wait before logging you out automatically and how many lines you can see in your communication program's window (choose Settings from the Using Delphi Menu).

- ✔ **Workspace:** Lets you store files on Delphi's computer. You can upload and download files from your personal computer and store files you have retrieved by using FTP.

- ✔ **HELP:** Displays information about what you can do at the current menu. Then it usually says `Topic?`, which means that it wonders whether there is a topic you want more information about. If so, enter a topic, such as a command you want more information about. If not, press Ctrl+Z to stop getting help. The Using DELPHI command on the MAIN menu displays lots of helpful information too.

- ✔ **EXIT:** Displays whatever was the preceding menu. If you are looking at the MAIN menu, this option logs you out, and Delphi hangs up.

- ✔ **BOSTON Services:** Displays a menu that includes information about the Boston area, where Delphi happens to be physically located.

Signing Up to Use the Internet

If you plan to use Delphi's connection to the Internet (and if you aren't, why are you reading this chapter?), you must tell Delphi about your plans — that is, you must *register* to use the Internet. We're not quite sure why, but it seems to have to do with making you agree to some terms and conditions. The terms looked reasonable to us (it is not acceptable, for example, to use it for illegal purposes). Registering for Internet use also costs an extra few dollars a month.

To register to use the Internet connection, follow these steps:

1. **Type** `using` **at the MAIN menu so that you see the Using DELPHI menu.**

2. **Type** `int` **to see the Internet Registration menu:**

   ```
   Internet>Terms, Register, or Cancel>
   ```

3. **Type** `terms` **to read the terms you are agreeing to.**

   After a long list of demands, you see the Internet Registration menu again.

4. **Type** `reg` **to register.**

You see this line:

```
Have you read the Terms of Use, and do you agree to them?
```

5. **Type** yes.

You see this line:

```
You are now registered to use Internet services.
```

6. **Press Ctrl+Z to return to the MAIN menu.**

To check that you are registered, use the STATUS command from the Internet Registration menu.

Sending and Receiving Mail

Delphi has its own e-mail system that lets you send messages to any other Delphi user. You can also send messages to anyone on the Internet or EasyLink or to anyone with a fax or telex machine.

Anyone on the Internet can send you e-mail messages at this address:

```
username@delphi.com
```

Replace *username* with your own username. If your username is JLEVINE, for example (you can probably guess who that is), your address would be

```
jlevine@delphi.com
```

Getting into the MAIL menu

Before you can send or read mail, you go to Delphi's Mail menu, like this:

1. **At the MAIN menu, type** mail.

You see the MAIL menu, like this:

```
FAX Service  Easylink
Mail (Electronic)   Translation Services
Scan for New Messages     Workspace
SetMail HELP
Telex      EXIT
```

```
DMAIL>(Mail, FAX, Telex, Trans):
```

2. **To send e-mail (rather than faxes and so on), type** mail **again.**

   You see the MAIL prompt:

```
MAIL>
```

   The preceding line means that you are in the MAIL menu, ready to send or receive e-mail.

It's a little strange that you have to type **mail** twice to get into the real MAIL menu. Here's what makes it confusing: After you type MAIL the first time, you see a list of commands entitled "MAIL menu." Don't be fooled — it's not the real MAIL menu because the prompt at the bottom is DMAIL. Type **mail** again to see the MAIL menu with the MAIL prompt.

Sending e-mail messages

From the MAIL menu, these steps show you how to send e-mail:

1. **Type** send **to send a message.**

   Delphi asks for the address to which to send the message.

2. **If you are sending a message to another Delphi user, type the username, as shown in this example:**

```
jlevine
```

   To send a message to an Internet address, type it like this:

```
Internet"dummies@iecc.com"
```

   or

```
IN%"dummies@iecc.com"
```

   Just insert between the quotes the Internet address you want. Be sure *not* to type a space between *Internet* or *IN%* and the quote — there are no spaces in addresses.

3. **Delphi asks for the subject of the message — enter a one-line summary.**

   Delphi tells you to type the message.

4. **Begin typing, and be sure to press Enter as you get to the end of each line.**

(Delphi doesn't perform word wrap, as many other e-mail systems do.) If you spot a typo on the line you are typing, you can press the Backspace key to back up and fix it.

5. **When you finish typing the message, press Ctrl+Z.**

Delphi sends the message.

If you see an error on a previous line, you are out of luck. There is no easy way to fix it. If the error is really embarrassing, you can cancel the entire message and begin again, by pressing Ctrl+C.

Sending mail to Delphi Central

If you want to send a message to the folks who run Delphi, either to ask a question or make a comment, type **go using service** from any menu. This command takes you to the SERVICE area of the Using-DELPHI Menu. There, you can send e-mail to the username SERVICE to reach the Delphic oracle itself. The service people are happy to answer any sort of question about using Delphi, even though it is their job to do so.

Mailing to foreign climes

This sidebar shows you how to address e-mail to people on other on-line services from Delphi (in all these examples, you can replace *Internet* with *IN%* if you prefer):

America Online: If the person's AOL username is abc, use the address Internet"abc@aol.com".

AppleLink: If the person's AppleLink username is abc, use the address Internet"abc@applelink. apple.com".

AT&T Mail: If the person's AT&T Mail username is abc, use the address Internet"abc@attmail.com".

Bitnet: If the person's Bitnet address is abc@def, use the address Internet"abc@def.bitnet".

CompuServe: If the person's CompuServe ID is 7654,321, for example, use the address Internet"7654.321@compuserve.com". **Note:** Be sure to use a period rather than a comma in the middle of the CompuServe ID number.

Fidonet: If the person's name is Joe Blow and his Fidonet address is 1:23/456.7, use the address Internet"Joe.Blow@p7.f456.n23.z1.fidonet.org".

The four numbers are the zone (z), the net (n), the node (f), and the point (p). Be sure to type the person's name separated by periods (rather than spaces) followed by @ (at sign). Then press p and the last of the four numbers, f and the preceding number, n and the number before that, and z and the first number. If this system is too complicated, get the person to send you a message, and use the REPLY command to send a message back.

GEnie: If the person's GEnie mailname is t.edison, use the address Internet"t.edison@genie.geis.com".

MCI Mail: If the person's MCI Mail name is abc, use the address Internet"abc@mci.com".

If the MCI mail number is 123-4567, you can also use the address Internet"1234567@mci.com".

Prodigy: If the person's Prodigy ID is X1Y2Z3, use the address Internet"X1Y2Z3@prodigy.com".

Making your mail more personal

To enter your name so that it appears right after your Delphi username in mail you send to other people, follow these steps:

1. In the MAIL menu, type this line:

```
SET PERS "your name"
```

and replace *your name* with your actual name.

(In the preceding command, *PERS* is short for *PERSONAL_NAME.*)

2. To make sure that it looks right, type this line:

```
SHOW PERS
```

If you ever want to stop providing your real name in your mail, you can always type **set nopers** to cancel it. You can also type **show all** to see all the options you can use with the set command, and how they are currently set.

Sending longer messages

For sending messages of more than a sentence or two, it is much more convenient to use an editor to create the message first. Delphi lets you create messages in your workspace before sending them as e-mail. Your *workspace* is your private storage area, usable for files you have uploaded for your personal computer, files you plan to download to your PC, files you have FTP'd from the Internet, and any other files you might want to work with.

The catch is that files on Delphi don't last forever. Delphi deletes your oldest files when its disks begin to fill up. So be a good citizen and delete your files when you're finished with them so that the useful files can stay around.

When you transfer a file from your computer to Delphi or from Delphi to your computer, you must use something called a *file-transfer protocol.* Scary words, but it's no big deal — it's a way for the two computers to transfer a file while making sure that it is received correctly. The most commonly used file-transfer protocols are the following:

- ✔ XMODEM (the slowest)
- ✔ YMODEM (faster)
- ✔ ZMODEM (even faster)
- ✔ Kermit (usable from a wide range of computers, but slow)

Delphi can handle all the preceding protocols. However, you have to find out which file-transfer protocols your communications program can handle before transferring any files. The Windows Terminal program, for example, can handle XMODEM and Kermit. Tell it which you plan to use by choosing Settings⇨Binary Transfer from its menu.

To create a message on your own computer and upload it to your Delphi workspace, follow these steps:

1. **Compose the message by using your favorite word-processing program or editor on your PC, Mac, or whatever your own computer is.**

   You can compose the message, in fact, before you even log in to Delphi. Save the message as an ASCII text file with no formatting.

2. **On Delphi, if you are at the MAIL menu, press Ctrl+Z to return to the DMAIL prompt and then type** workspace **(or just** work — **remember, you never have to type more than the first four letters of a command).**

   This command switches you to the workspace prompt.

3. **To upload the file, type** upload menu **(or just** upl menu**).**

   This command tells Delphi that you want to transfer a file from your computer and that you want to see a menu of file-transfer protocols.

4. **Choose a file-transfer protocol your communications program can handle.**

   To use ZMODEM, for example, type **zmodem** (or just **zm**). If your communications program doesn't do ZMODEM, type **xmodem** or **ymodem** or **kermit**.

   For some protocols, Delphi asks for the name of the file you want to upload. For other protocols, it doesn't ask — it just uses the same name the file has on your personal computer.

   Delphi asks this question:

   ```
   What kind of files are you uploading?
         (TEXT,BINARY,MIXED,HELP)
   ```

5. **Type the type of file — for example, if you are uploading a plain ASCII file, type** text.

   Delphi tells you to get ready to send the file.

6. **Tell your communications program to begin sending the file.**

   In Windows Terminal, for example, choose Transfers⇨Send⇨Binary File. (Yes, we know that you are sending a text file, but you have to choose Send⇨Binary File to use a file-transfer protocol. Weird.) You must tell your communications program the directory and filename of the file you want to send.

7. **Delphi and your communications program chat as they send the file.**

   Your communications program may display something to tell you how long the transfer will take and how it is proceeding. When Delphi has received the file, you see the `WS>` prompt again.

8. **Now that you have uploaded the file that contains the message you want to send, type** `/mail` **to go to Delphi's MAIL menu.**

9. **To send the file, type** `filename` substitute the name of the file you created in your workspace. Delphi asks for the address to which to send the file.

10. **Enter the address.**

    Delphi asks for a subject line.

11. **Enter the subject of the message.**

    Delphi sends the mail.

12. **Now return to the workspace by pressing Ctrl+Z.**

    Poof! — you are in your workspace again! The /MAIL command you entered in Step 8 told Delphi that you wanted to come back later.

13. **Delete the file after you send it.**

    Type `delete filename` substituting the name of the file. (You can shorten this command to **del**, if you want.) Delphi asks you to confirm deleting the file.

14. **Press** `y`.

Here are some tips for uploading messages to your workspace and sending them as mail:

- ✔ If you want to send a regular, readable text message, be sure to save your message as straight ASCII text with no formatting codes. Almost every word-processing program can save as text.

- ✔ To see a list of the files in your workspace, type **dir**. You see a file called MAIL.MAI, which is your mail, along with any files you've created.

- ✔ To see what a file contains, type **list** followed by a space and then the filename. Delphi doesn't pause when the screen is full, so to pause the listing, press Ctrl+S. Press Ctrl+Q when you want it to continue.

- ✔ You can send large files by Delphi mail — the Delphi people say the size is unlimited. Internet mail is usually limited to about 200K, however.

- ✔ Delphi expects mail messages to contain a carriage return at the end of each line. You may have to tell your word processor or editor to do this when you are writing your message.

✔ You can edit a file in your workspace by using Delphi's EDT editor. Type this line:

```
EDIT filename
```

✔ For information about how to use EDT, type **help edit** at the Workspace menu. It's a fairly ugly editing program, so you're usually better off creating files on your PC and uploading them instead of editing them on-line.

Reading your messages

From the MAIL menu, here's how to read your mail:

1. **Type** `read/new` **to read incoming e-mail you haven't read yet, one at a time, or type read/all to read all your messages.**

   Note: Actually, all you have to do is press Enter, and Delphi guesses that you want to read something! Typing **read** usually does it, too.

2. **After reading each message, you can choose to delete them by typing** `delete` **(or just** `del`).

   Otherwise, the messages are kept. If you receive a new piece of mail while you are using Delphi, you see a message like this on your screen:

```
New mail on node BOS1D from BOS::JLEVINE
```

   Again, who cares which nodes Delphi is using? Whatever *nodes* are! But at least the message tells you the username of the person who sent the mail.

When you get mail from non-Delphi Internet addresses, you see lots of lines of garbage at the top, including all kinds of gobbledy-gook addresses indicating how the message was routed. Feel free to ignore that stuff. *We* certainly do.

Replying to a message

After you read a message, it is easy to reply to it:

1. **Type** `reply`.

   Delphi starts a new message, addressed to the person who sent you the last message you read, with the same subject (preceded by `RE:`).

   Delphi tells you to type your message.

2. **Type the message and press Enter at the end of each line.**

3. **Press Ctrl+Z when you are finished typing the message.**

   Delphi sends the message.

The great thing about *replying* to messages is that you avoid typing long, arcane, and downright confusing mail addresses.

Managing your mail

Delphi stores your message in three *folders:*

- ✔ **NEWMAIL:** Contains mail you haven't read yet.
- ✔ **MAIL:** Contains mail you have already read.
- ✔ **WASTEBASKET:** Contains mail you have deleted (until you leave the MAIL menu, at which point it really is deleted).

To choose which folder to work with, type **select** and the name of the folder, as shown in this example:

```
SELECT NEWMAIL
```

To see a list of the messages in the folder, type **dir**. The messages are numbered, and the first line tells you the name of the folder you are looking at.

To read a particular message, type its number after the READ command, like this:

```
READ 3
```

To delete a particular message, you can also specify it by number, like this:

```
DELETE 2
```

Downloading mail messages

If you read a message you want to keep, you can download it to your own computer as a text file. The following steps show you how, assuming that you are at the MAIL menu:

These steps work for text. but not for messages that are programs or other binary information. Luckily, all Internet mail is limited to text.

1. **Tell Delphi which messages you want to keep by using the SELECT command.**

   To select all your unread mail, type the following line:

   ```
   SELECT NEWMAIL
   ```

To select all the mail you have already read, type this line:

```
SELECT MAIL
```

2. Tell Delphi to *extract* it into a text file, like this:

```
EXTRACT/ALL  filename
```

Substitute a name for *filename,* as shown in the following example:

```
EXTRACT/ALL  JUNKMAIL
```

The messages are now stored in a file in your workspace. Now that these messages have been saved in a text file, you can delete them from your mailbox, unless you want to do something else with them, such as forward them or reply to them.

3. To delete the messages, type the following line:

```
DELETE/ALL
```

4. Leave the MAIL menu and go to your workspace by pressing Ctrl+Z to return to the DMAIL prompt and then typing workspace.

5. Download the file by typing the name of a protocol that both Delphi and your communications program can handle.

Use a file-transfer protocol that your communications program can handle (the protocols are d2escribed in the preceding section and in Chapter 4). Type **download menu** (or just **downl menu**). Delphi shows you a list of the file-transfer protocols it can handle.

6. Enter the name of the file you created in Step 2.

Your communications program may begin receiving the file automatically, or you may have to tell it to begin receiving a file.

7. After you have downloaded the file, you can delete it from your workspace and avoid storage costs by typing this line:

```
DELETE  filename
```

Rather than choose the file-transfer protocol from a menu, you can avoid typing one extra command. Rather than type **download menu**, use one of these commands:

- ✔ XDOWN *filename* (for XMODEM)
- ✔ YDOWN filename (for YMODEM)
- ✔ ZDOWN filename (for ZMODEM)
- ✔ KDOWN filename (for Kermit)

If you use Windows Terminal, choose Transfers⇨Receive Binary File after you tell Delphi to transmit the file.

Another way to download messages is to display them on-screen and tell your communications program to capture them as they fly by. To display messages on-screen, one after another without pausing, type this line:

```
EXTRACT/ALL TT
```

If you want to save only the mail message you just read, you can type **extract** (or just **ex**) and a filename at the MAIL menu. This command copies only the current message to a file. Then you can download it as explained in the preceding steps.

If you delete a message by mistake, you can get it back using the command **select/wastebasket.** This command selects the folder that contains all your deleted messages.

Forwarding your mail

If you use more than one on-line service, such as Delphi and CompuServe, it is annoying to get mail in both places. Why? Getting mail in two places means that you have to check both services to read all your mail. But you can solve this problem by forwarding your mail so that it all arrives at one place.

To forward all the mail that arrives in your Delphi mailbox to another address, follow these steps:

1. **To forward your mail to another Delphi account, at the MAIL menu type this line:**

```
SET FORWARD delphiusername
```

   To forward your mail to an Internet address, type this line:

```
SET FORWARD INTERNET"""address"""
```

   Yes, that's three (count 'em, three) double quotes before the address, and three more after the address. Only true Delphi wizards understand why this works. Make sure not to type a space before all those quotes, either. For example, to forward all your mail to the Dummies e-mail address (a bad idea that will not make you popular here at Dummies Central), you type this line:

```
SET FORWARD INTERNET"""dummies@iecc.com"""
```

2. **To check that your forwarding address looks right, type this line:**

```
SHOW FORWARD
```

   When Delphi displays Internet forwarding addresses, the extra double quotes have mysteriously vanished. You should see just one double quote before and after the Internet address.

3. **To cancel mail forwarding, type** set noforw.

A summary of MAIL commands

Table 5-2 shows a list of commands you can use at the MAIL prompt. (Remember that you have to type only the first four letters of commands):

Table 5-2	Delphi MAIL Commands
Command	*What It Does*
[Enter]	Reads the next message
BACK	Reads the preceding message
COPY	Copies the current message into another mail folder (not into a text file); if the folder doesn't exist, it creates it
CURRENT	Displays the current message again
DELETE	Deletes the current message or the message you specify
DELETE/ALL	Deletes all messages from the current folder
DIRECTORY	Displays a list of all messages in the current folder (to see all the messages in a different folder, type the folder's name after dir)
DIR/FOLDER	Displays a list of all folders
EDIT	Runs the EDT editor to enable you to edit the current message
EXTRACT	Creates a text file containing the current message
EXTRACT/APPEND	Adds the current message to the named file
FIRST	Displays the first message in the current folder
FORWARD	Forwards the current message
LAST	Displays the last message in the current folder
MAIL	Sends mail (just like SEND)
MOVE	Moves the current message into the folder you name; if the folder doesn't exist, it creates it
NEXT	Skips to the next message
READ	Reads the next message or the message you specify
REPLY	Lets you reply to the current message
SEARCH	Searches the current folder for a text string
SELECT	Selects which folder to use
SEND	Sends mail (just like MAIL)
SEND FILENAME	Sends the file you specify as a mail message
SET	Sets Mail options (type show all to see a list)
SHOW	Shows the current settings of Mail options

Getting on Mailing Lists

Getting on Internet mailing lists works the same from Delphi as it does from any other service at which you can receive mail. You send a message to the mailing list administrator, requesting to be added to the mailing list. Then you begin receiving all messages sent to the mailing list.

Look ahead to Chapter 16 in this book and/or see Chapter 10 of *The Internet For Dummies* for the story on mailing lists and interesting ones to try.

Chatting Live

If you are interested in chatting with other Internet users live rather than by way of the delayed-reaction mode of e-mail, you can use *IRC* (Internet Relay Chat). For lots of information about it, see Chapter 15.

Here are instructions for getting into IRC. Once you are in, skip to Chaper 15 to find out how to issue IRC commands to choose a channel and get talking. To get into Delphi's IRC area, follow these handy steps:

1. **Type** `IRC` **at the Internet SIG menu.**

2. **If you have never chatted on IRC, type** `ABOUT` **to get more information about how IRC works.**

3. **When you are ready to dive in, type** `IRC` **at the Internet Relay Chat Menu.**

    Delphi displays some helpful messages and then asks you for the nickname you want to use whenever you send a message. (IRC sticks your nickname on the front of any messages you type so that you can tell who's saying what.) It suggests using your Delphi username, but you can type a different nickname.

4. **Delphi then asks for your personal name — we're not sure what the system means by personal name, so we just type the same nickname.**

    Now you are ready to find out which channels are open and get started chatting. See Chapter 15 for how to give IRC commands, which are the same for most Internet providers. (Hint: Type **/list** to list the channels and **/join** to join a channel.)

5. **When you have had enough, type** `/QUIT`**.**

    You return to the Internet Relay Chat Menu.

6. **Press Ctrl+Z to return to the Internet SIG menu.**

Using Internet Services

What about all those *other* fun things you can do on the Internet, such as telnetting to other computers, using Gopher to search for information, and FTP-ing files from other systems? You can do all these things from Delphi.

From the MAIN menu, type **internet** (or just **int**). You see a cute Internet logo made of slashes, followed by some other pithy information and a menu.

This menu is the Internet **SIG menu** (SIG stands for *special interest group,* and no, we don't know why it's part of the name of this menu). When you are finished doing Internet-type stuff, press Ctrl+Z to return to the Delphi MAIN menu.

If you type **email** as the menu suggests, you see a message about how to address mail from Delphi to the Internet. Instead, just type **mail** to jump into the MAIL menu described earlier in this chapter. When you type the MAIL command from the Internet Menu, Delphi remembers where you came from so that when you press Ctrl+Z to exit from the Mail Menu, you return to Internet Land.

Reading Newsgroups

Delphi has its own SIGs, special interest group discussions that are similar to *newsgroups.* When you use the Computer Groups or Groups & Clubs commands in Delphi, in fact, some newsgroups are presented along with Delphi's own groups. However, to read any or all of the thousands of Internet newsgroups, you must use the Internet **SIG menu**.

Delphi provides two news-reading programs:

- ✔ Delphi's own Delphi Newsreader
- ✔ A UNIX-like newsreader named nn.

The Delphi Newsreader is easier, so start out with it.

By the way, if you want background information about newsgroups along with suggestions for some interesting ones to read, see Chapter 11 of *The Internet For Dummies.*

Getting into Usenet

The easiest way to read Usenet newsgroups is to use the Delphi newsreader. Its advantage is that it uses commands and menus just like the rest of Delphi.

To enter Usenet Land, follow these steps:

1. **At the Internet SIG menu, type** usenet **(or just** use**).**

   You see the Usenet menu.

2. **Type** usenet **or** use **again to run the Delphi Newsreader.**

   You see a huge, long menu.

   The long menu is the Usenet Discussion Groups Menu. Its exact content changes frequently as the sysops (*system operators*) add and update newsgroup names. The rightmost column tells you what kind of command it is: *Text* means that it just displays a message, *Menu* means that you will see another menu of commands, *Search* means that it's a command that lets you search for something, and *Usenet* means that it's an actual newsgroup.

3. **Use the** more **and** prev **commands to move among the pages, looking for newsgroups of interest.**

4. **If you see a newsgroup you want to read, type its number.**

Before you get started with newsgroups, however, it is a good idea to find out about the lore and legend surrounding them. Read on!

Getting started with newsgroups

Before you spend much time reading Usenet newsgroups and *certainly* before you post any articles, try out these hints for reading some interesting and vital information (experienced newsgroupers, skip this section):

1. **From the Usenet Discussion Groups Menu, press 5 to choose New User Topics and FAQs.**

   You see a menu of items interesting to new newsgroup readers.

2. **Press 1 to choose the Help File for the DELPHI Newsreader option.**

   It explains how the Delphi Newsreader works. Alternatively, read the next few sections of this chapter, which explain it all a little more clearly.

3. **Press 2 to choose READ BEFORE POSTING!!!**

   It explains the etiquette of posting articles to newsgroups. This message is not intended to intimidate you but to help you to avoid major, embarrassing gaffes. Trust us — you'll be glad that you read it.

4. **Press 5 to choose the FAQ — Frequently Asked Questions in Delphi Internet SIG — option.**

   You see a list of the most frequently asked questions. Press the number by a question to read the answer. To exit from this menu, press Ctrl+Z.

5. **When you are finished reading information on the New User Topics Menu, press Ctrl+Z to return to the Usenet Discussion Groups Menu.**

Finding a newsgroup

Thousands of Usenet newsgroups exist, far more than can fit on the Usenet Discussion Group Menu. The Delphi people have chosen the most popular newsgroups to get you started, but *you* have to ferret out the ones you are really interested in.

If the newsgroup you want to read appears on a page of the Usenet Discussion Groups Menu or if you know its exact name, skip to the next section.

Otherwise, to search for a newsgroup, follow these steps:

1. **From the Usenet Discussion Groups Menu, choose Search for Newsgroups and Mailing Lists.**

   (We don't tell you here which number to press because it may have changed.)

2. **Press 1 to choose Search for Specific Newsgroups.**

   You see something like this:

   ```
   "Search for Specific Newsgroups (excludes alt. groups)" is
           an indexed service.
   Please specify a word or words to search.
   Search for:
   ```

3. **Type a word or part of a word to search for.**

   To search for newsgroups about vegetarians, for example, you might just type **veg**.

4. **To read a newsgroup that Delphi lists, type its number.**

If you have no luck with Search for Specific Newsgroups, you can try one of the other options on the Search for Newsgroups and Mailing Lists Menu.

For a list of interesting newsgroups, see Chapter 12 in *The Internet For Dummies*.

Reading a newsgroup

The Delphi Newsreader works like the rest of Delphi — you can abbreviate commands, you can always press ? or type **help**, and pressing Ctrl+Z causes you to exit from what you're doing.

To read a newsgroup, follow these steps:

1. **Type the number of the newsgroup on the Usenet Discussion Groups Menu.**

   (If you can't find the group you want, see the preceding section.)

Alternatively, if you know the exact name of the newsgroup, press 2 at the Usenet Discussion Groups Menu for Access Any Newsgroup. Then enter the newsgroup name, carefully spelling it correctly.

To see a list of active newsgroups, choose Newsgroup Lists from the Usenet Discussion Groups Menu.

The Delphi newsreader tells you how many messages are available and how many you have already read. Choosing the `rec.puzzles` newsgroups, for example, results in something like this:

```
Puzzles (rec.puzzles)
349 messages have been posted in the last 14 days; You've
     read approximately 0.
Select which messages: Unread, All, Date or ?> [unread]
```

Now you can press Enter or u to see a list of the messages you haven't read, press a to see a list of all the messages including ones you have read, press ? for help, or press Ctrl+Z to skip this newsgroup.

3. **Press u or Enter to see a list of the messages you haven't read.**

   What appears is a list of *threads*, which are groups of messages on the same topic. There are usually too many threads to list on one screen, so you can type **more** or **mo** to see the next page of threads, **prev** or **pr** to see the preceding page, or **page** and the page number to jump directly to a particular page.

4. **To read the messages on an interesting-looking topic, press the number by the topic.**

5. **To read the next message in the thread, press Enter. To move on to the next thread in order, press n. To see the list of threads (topics) again, press Ctrl+Z.**

6. **When you are finished reading the newsgroup, press Ctrl+Z until you return to the Usenet Discussion Groups Menu.**

Saving your favorite newsgroups

If you are reading a newsgroup, and you decide that you will want to read it frequently, add it to your list of personal favorite newsgroups. While reading the newsgroup, type **save**. Delphi asks you to confirm adding the newsgroup to your personal-favorites list — press y or n.

Now when you want to read the newsgroup, choose 1 from the Usenet Discussion Groups Menu, PERSONAL FAVORITES. Delphi shows you a list of the newsgroups you have saved. Pick one.

If you have trouble getting the SAVE command to work, use it when you are looking at the list of threads for the newsgroup.

Other newsgroup commands

This section lists some other things you can do while reading newsgroups:

✔ To reply to an article publicly, type **reply**. This command posts a follow-up article in the same newsgroup. Before doing this, however, make sure that you are saying something new, interesting, nonredundant, and inoffensive.

✔ To reply to an article privately, type **mail reply**. This command sends an e-mail message to only the person who posted the article you are reading.

✔ To post a new article, starting a new thread, type **add**. Again, make sure that the subject hasn't been beaten to death within the last few weeks and that it isn't covered in the newsgroup's FAQs (lists of frequently asked questions).

✔ To post a new article that you have already written and stored in a file in your workspace, type **add** followed by the filename.

✔ To save the text of a message as a file in your workspace, type **file**. Delphi asks for a name to give the new file. After you have done this, you can save the message for posterity, mail it to people, or download it to your own computer.

✔ To mark all the messages in the newsgroup as having been read so that you don't see them again, type **mark**. After you have read all the threads that look interesting, use the MARK command so that you don't see the rest of the threads the next time you read the newsgroup.

✔ To see a list of other commands you can use, press ? or type **help**.

Telnetting out of Delphi

If your purpose in using Delphi is to be able to log into computers all over the world, then you want to *telnet*. The telnet program lets you log into any computer on the Internet that has been set up to receive this type of invasion and run commands on that computer.

For lots of information about telnetting, see Chapter 14 of *The Internet For Dummies*. Chapter 15 of that book contains a list of computers that are interesting to telnet to. You may also want to use telnet in connection with Gopher, Archie, WAIS, or WWW, which are described later in this chapter.

Some Delphi commands telnet automatically to other computers to provide you with the service you requested. If you want to do it yourself, though, the following steps show you how:

1. **At the Internet SIG menu, type** `telnet`.

    Delphi asks you which computer you want to log into (called the *host*).

2. **Type the name of the host you want to telnet to.**

    To telnet to our computer, for example, you type this line:

    ```
    iecc.com
    ```

3. **Make note of the escape character it suggests (in this case, ^\ or Ctrl+\), and then log in just as though you had called that host computer directly.**

    In the process of logging in, if the host computer asks what kind of terminal you are using, lie and tell it that you are using a VT-100 (this is a common terminal, and Delphi is good at pretending to be one).

4. **When you are finished using the other computer, log off.**

    Depending on what kind of computer it is, you might type **bye** or **exit** or **off** or **logout**.

5. **Telnet usually notices that you have logged off the host computer and exits.**

    If it doesn't, get its attention by pressing the escape character (the one you found out about in step 3) a few times and then type **quit**.

Some computers use full-screen menus, which may not display correctly on your screen. If this happens, all the computers involved (your computer, the Delphi computer, and the host computer) may be getting their signals crossed.

Here are some things to try when you have a problem:

✔ Be sure to set your line width to 80 columns by typing /**width=80**.

✔ Make sure that all the computers are emulating DEC VT-100 terminals. To tell Delphi to act like a VT-100, type /**term_type=VT100** and then type /**save**. Delphi remembers this setting forever.

✔ If you call Delphi by way of Sprintnet or Tymnet, type /**echo host** to Delphi every time you log on and before you telnet. This step tells Delphi to pass what you type on to the remote system as you type each character rather than wait for the end of each line.

✔ Some telnet host computers require a special setting to prevent extra line-feeds. If you see extra line-feeds while you're telnetting, use the command **telnet_nocrlf** rather than **telnet**.

✔ Sometimes your response time can get rather sluggish or jerky when you're telnetting, so just type slowly and be patient!

✔ To save time, you can enter the host computer name on the same line as the telnet command, like this:

```
TELNET locis.loc.gov
```

(This line connects you to the U.S. Library of Congress on-line catalog.)

FTP-ing

FTP (File Transfer Protocol) transfers files between computers on the Internet.

Delphi lets you FTP files to or from your Delphi workspace. For general information about FTP-ing, including the famous anonymous FTP, consult Chapter 16 in *The Internet For Dummies.* Chapter 18 in that book contains a list of interesting files you can get by way of FTP. Or use Archie to find files of interest (as described later in this chapter, and in Chapter 19 in *The Internet for Dummies*).

Grabbing files from the net

The following steps show you how to copy a file from another computer to your Delphi workspace by using anonymous FTP:

1. **At the Internet SIG menu, type** `ftp`.

   Delphi asks you for the destination Internet address.

2. **Type the name of the computer that has the file you want, as shown in this example:**

   ```
   iecc.com
   ```

   (**Note:** You can combine the first two steps by typing the host name on the same command line as the FTP command.) Delphi asks for your username.

3. **If you press Enter, it logs you in as** `anonymous`.

   Delphi asks you for the password.

4. **Enter your Internet address, which is your Delphi username followed by** `@delphi.com`.

   (Delphi suggests this, so all you have to do is press Enter.) You see messages from the computer from which you want to FTP and this prompt:

   ```
   FTP>
   ```

   The first thing to do is to look around and find the file you want. Through the magic of networks, you can use commands to see listings of files and move from directory to directory on the host computer.

5. **To see a directory of the files in the current directory, type** `dir`. **To move to another directory, type this line:**

   ```
   cd "dirname"
   ```

   Replace *dirname* with the name of the directory and capitalize it just as you see it in FTP's listings.

To move up one directory level, type this:

```
cdup
```

6. **When you see a file you want a copy of, determine (or guess) whether it contains text or binary information (if you are not sure, guess binary), and then type either** binary **or** ascii **(for text).**

Now you are ready to copy the file.

7. **Type the following line:**

```
get "filename" newfilename
```

Replace *filename* with the name the file has now and *newfilename* with the name you want the file to have when it arrives in your Delphi workspace. Be sure to include the quotation marks around the current filename and to capitalize the current filename just as you see in the directory listing. (Some systems, UNIX for one, care about case in filenames.)

8. **When you are finished copying files, type** exit **or press Ctrl+Z.**

You return to the Internet SIG menu.

Downloading FTP'd files

After you have copied a file to your Delphi workspace, type **work** to switch to your workspace. The **list** command is displayed on-screen. If you want to keep the file, download it to your own computer and then delete it on Delphi.

To download a file from your workspace to your computer, follow these steps:

1. **At the Workspace menu (your prompt looks like** WS> **), type** download menu **(or just** downl menu **).**

Delphi shows you a list of the file-transfer protocols it can handle.

2. **Type the name of a protocol that your communications program can handle too.**

Delphi asks for the name of the file in your workspace to download.

3. **Type the filename to download.**

4. **Your communications program may begin receiving the file automatically, or you may have to tell it to begin receiving a file.**

For example, to tell Windows Terminal to receive a file using the XMODEM protocol, you choose Transfers⇨Receive Binary File.

5. **After you download the file, type this to delete it from your workspace:**

```
DELETE filename
```

Handing out files

You can also copy files *to* other computers, although this procedure is not as commonly done. After you have used the FTP command to connect to the other computer, move to the directory in which you want to put the file. Rather than use the *get* command, type **put** followed by the name of the file in your Delphi workspace, followed by the name to give the copy of the file when it reaches the other computer.

Using Archie

Archie is a way-cool program that searches cyberspace for the file you want. The catch: You have to know the name of the file. After you find a computer that has the file, you can use FTP to get it.

Delphi doesn't run Archie per se; it connects you to a computer that runs it. After you are running Archie, you can use lots of commands. See Chapter 19 in *The Internet For Dummies* for the most useful commands.

The following steps show you how to run Archie:

1. From the Internet SIG menu, type gopher.

You see the Internet SIG Gopher menu. (We talk more about Gopher in the next section of this chapter. For now, let's stick with Archie.)

2. Choose INTERNET SEARCH UTILITIES AND INFORMATION.

You see another little menu. (Because this menu is updated frequently, we can't tell you what number it is on the menu.)

3. Press 1 to choose Internet Search Utilities.

You see the Internet Search Utilities Menu.

4. Press 1 to choose Archie.

You see a list of possible computers on which you can run the Archie program, like this:

```
Archie—Search for files at FTP Sites
Page 1 of 1


1 Archie at InterNIC        Telnet
2 Archie at ANS       Telnet
3 Archie at Rutgers Telnet
4 Archie Quick Instructions          Text
5 Archie Full Instructions Text


Enter Item Number, SAVE, ?, or BACK:
```

5. **This list of Archie server computers changes from time to time, so which computer you run Archie on doesn't really matter — pick one.**

Delphi connects to the computer running Archie, and it asks you to log in.

6. **Type** `archie`.

Note: Be sure to use lowercase letters. When you see the `archie>` prompt, you can use Archie commands to search for files.

7. **To search for files that contain *brazil* in their filenames, type**

```
prog brazil
```

To search for files that contain *brazil* in either their filename or their description, type

```
whatis brazil
```

You can control lots of things about the way Archie searches. Type **help** for more information.

8. **Now you can use FTP to get the files.**

(Using FTP from Delphi is described earlier in this chapter).

9. **Log off from the Archie server by typing** `exit`.

You return to the Archie Menu.

10. **Press Ctrl+Z to exit from the menus you see until you get back to the Internet SIG menu.**

If you have trouble getting through to a computer that runs Archie, press Ctrl+\ or Ctrl+C to cancel and choose a different Archie system in Step 4.

The list of files that Archie finds can be long. You might want to tell your communications program to begin capturing the information on-screen to a file so that you can review it later.

Using Gopher

Gopher is a great way to wander around the Internet, looking for interesting information. It is much more flexible than Archie because you *don't* have to know the name of the file you are looking for.

Wandering in Gopherspace

Chapter 20 of *The Internet For Dummies* describes how Gopherspace works. Also check out chapter 12 of this book.

Here's how to run Gopher from Delphi:

1. **From the Internet SIG menu, type** gopher.

   You see the Internet SIG Gopher menu.

   Gopher consists of nothing but lots of menus that look just like that one.

2. **Choose entries from the menus based on your interests.**

   If you decide that a menu looks boring, press Ctrl+Z or type **BACK** to leave it. The words to the right of each menu entry tell you what it does: *Menu* means that you see another menu, *Search* means that it lets you enter information to search for, *Telnet* means that Gopher automatically logs you into the computer that has the information, and *Text* means that it displays some text. If you see *File*, it means that you can ask Gopher to mail you a copy of the file.

3. **When you are finished using Gopher, press Ctrl+Z until you get back to the Internet SIG menu.**

As you choose items from Gopher menus, it automatically connects you with the computer that has the information for that menu choice. Occasionally, the computer with the information isn't available, and you get a message like Unable to connect. Just try it again later.

If you find an interesting-looking Gopher menu, you can type **SAVE** to add it to your list of personal favorites. You can always get to menus on this list quickly by choosing PERSONAL FAVORITES from the Internet SIG Gopher menu.

Veronica and Jughead

Gopherspace is a big place, and it can be hard to find what you want. Two search programs can be useful: *Veronica* and *Jughead.*

   ✔ Veronica searches every item in all Gopher menus for interesting words and shows you just the menus you may want to try.

   ✔ Jughead searches only Gopher menu names.

To run Veronica from Delphi, follow these steps:

1. **From the Internet SIG menu, type** gopher.

   You see the Internet SIG Gopher menu.

2. **Choose INTERNET SEARCH UTILITIES AND INFORMATION.**

   You see another little menu.

3. **Press 1 to choose Internet Search Utilities.**

   You see the Internet Search Utilities menu. (So far, it's just like running Archie.)

4. **Press 10 to choose Veronica.**

5. **As it suggests, press 1 to see yet another list of computers that run Veronica (Veronica servers).**

6. **Choose a computer on which to run Veronica.**

   For example, press 1 again. You see the following lines:

   ```
   "Search gopherspace by veronica at NYSERNet" is an indexed
           service.
   Please specify a word or words to search.
   Search for:
   ```

7. **Enter a word or words to search for.**

   If you enter two words, Veronica looks for Gopher entries that contain both words. You can also use the words *and, or,* and *not,* in addition to parentheses, to specify what to search for. The following line, for example:

   ```
   key lime pie
   ```

   finds you approximately one zillion copies of the Usenet Cookbook key lime pie recipe (which is pretty good, by the way).

8. **When you are finished using Veronica, press Ctrl+Z until you get back to the Internet SIG menu.**

If you get a message like `Too many connections — try again soon,` try a different Veronica server.

To run Jughead, which does the same kind of thing as Veronica, follow these steps:

1. **From the Internet SIG menu, type** `gopher.`

   You see the Internet SIG Gopher menu.

2. **Choose INTERNET SEARCH UTILITIES AND INFORMATION.**

   You see another little menu.

3. **Press 1 to choose Internet Search Utilities.**

   You see the Internet Search Utilities Menu.

4. **Press 5 to run Jughead.**

5. **Enter a word to search for — for example,** `tomato.`

   You see a list of the Gopher directory titles that Jughead found.

6. **Choosing an entry from the menu takes you directly to the Gopher menu item you found.**

7. **When you are finished using Jughead to find information in Gopherspace, press Ctrl+Z until you return to the Internet SIG menu.**

Using WAIS

WAIS is yet another way to search for information on the Internet. But unlike Archie, Veronica, Jughead, and the like, WAIS looks at what's *inside* files rather than mere filenames or Gopher menu entries.

Chapter 21 in *The Internet For Dummies* has lots of information about using WAIS, which can be confusing.

The following steps show you how to run WAIS from Delphi:

1. **From the Internet SIG menu, type** `gopher`.

   You see the Internet SIG Gopher menu.

2. **Choose INTERNET SEARCH UTILITIES AND INFORMATION.**

   You see another little menu.

3. **Press 1 to choose Internet Search Utilities.**

   You see the Internet Search Utilities menu.

4. **Press 11 to choose WAIS.**

5. **Press 2 to run WAIS at WAIS, Inc.**

   It telnets to the computer at WAIS, Inc. and prompts you to log in.

6. **Type** `wais` **as your login name.**

   You may have to wait a little while for the connection to get through.

7. **When you are asked for your user identifier, enter your Internet address, which is your Delphi username followed by** `@delphi.com`.

8. **When you are asked for your terminal type, enter** `vt100` **(or just press Enter).**

   You're now using the standard, user-hostile WAIS program. See Chapter 21 in *The Internet For Dummies* for details.

9. **When you are finished using WAIS, press q.**

   You return to the WAIS Menu.

10. **Press Ctrl+Z until you return to the Internet SIG menu.**

Using WWW

Finally, you can use the *World Wide Web* (WWW) to browse through hypertext systems. Chapter 14 in this book and Chapter 22 in *The Internet For Dummies* describe the WWW system in detail.

The following steps show you how to run WWW from Delphi:

1. **From the Internet SIG menu, type** `gopher`.

   You see the Internet SIG Gopher menu.

2. **Choose INTERNET SEARCH UTILITIES AND INFORMATION.**

   You see another little menu.

3. **Press 1 to choose Internet Search Utilities.**

   You see the Internet Search Utilities Menu.

4. **Press 12 to choose World Wide Web.**

   You see a list of WWW sites.

5. **Pick a site.**

   Different WWW sites use different browsing programs, but they all have access to the same information. Delphi telnets to the WWW site.

6. **For the login name, enter** `www` **or use the login name the system suggests.**

7. **Follow the directions on-screen to choose topics of interest.**

8. **When you are finished, follow the system's instructions to exit.**

   Pressing x or q usually does it.

9. **When you return to the World Wide Webs menu in Delphi, press Ctrl+Z until you get back to the Internet SIG menu.**

Finding Out More about Delphi

For more information about what Delphi can do, use the HELP command. You can also order a book about Delphi, called *DELPHI: The Official Guide*. To order it, type **USING** at the MAIN menu, then **MEM** to see the Member Services menu, and then **MAN** to see information about manuals and documentation.

How not to see "More?"

If you are capturing text to a file with your communications program, it can be annoying to see the More? prompt at the end of each screen. To tell Delphi to display text without pausing, type the following on a line by itself: **/LENGTH=0.**

To turn More? prompting back on, type **/ LENGTH=24** (or whatever your screen length is).

The /LENGTH command works only for your current session, unless you type **/SAVE** to save the setting forever.

Alternatively, when Delphi asks *More?*, you can type **all** to tell it to display the rest of the message without stopping.

Chapter 6

The Internet via Public UNIX Providers

● ●

In This Chapter

▶ Signing up for the World

▶ Calling the World

▶ Typing commands

▶ Sending e-mail

▶ Chatting live to the World

▶ Reading newsgroups

▶ Using telnet to use computers that are out of this World

▶ Using FTP to grab files

▶ Finding files with Archie

▶ Using Gopher, WAIS, and the World Wide Web

● ●

*M*any Internet providers provide access to a plain UNIX system, with more or less the classic UNIX Internet programs. In this chapter, we look at a typical UNIX provider: the World. We chose the World for two reasons:

✔ It's a good example of a well-run, UNIX-based system.

✔ It happens to be located about three miles from where we live.

Most major cities now have UNIX Internet providers. See the list of providers in the back of *The Internet For Dummies* for a list, or see the sidebar at the end of Chapter 4 about an up-to-date list of Internet providers.

An account on the World, a service of Software Tool and Die, gets you access to the Internet, just as Delphi and America Online do. Rather than show you lots of user-friendly menus, however, the World is a plain-vanilla UNIX system, and you must learn some UNIX commands to use it. For you UNIX aficionados, this is heaven, of course, but for the rest of us it's a mild pain in the neck. After you get used to it, though, you can navigate around on a UNIX system considerably faster than you can on a more user-friendly system with menus and prompts, and nobody will call you a sissy either.

For all kinds of useful information about using UNIX, get *UNIX For Dummies* (IDG Books Worldwide) by us, John Levine and Margaret Levine Young.

Signing Up for World

To get an account on World, you can call it up with your computer, enter **new** as your username, and leave your password blank. In the Boston area, the access number is 617-739-9753. After you are on, you can type **help** and then **Phone.Info** to get information about more-convenient access numbers.

Dialing for World

Before you can place your first call, you must set up your communications program. You can use the terminal program that came with your computer, if any, or you can use another communications program such as Crosstalk, Procomm, or SmartComm. Chapter 4 describes how to tell your communications program to call Internet providers, such as the World.

Now you are ready to try to make the call:

1. **Tell your communications program to dial the phone.**

   When your modem connects to the World's modem, you see a message like this:

   ```
   Login as 'new' if you don't have an account
   ```

2. **Enter your username.**

3. **When World asks for your password, enter it.**

   (If you are signing up for an account and have logged in as *new,* leave your password blank — that is, just press Enter.)

You see all kinds of friendly messages, like this:

```
Last login: Mon Apr  4 12:44:24 from CHICO.IECC.COM
OS/MP 4.1C Export(STD/arlie)#15: Fri Mar 18 17:25:40 1994
 Welcome to the World!  A 6 CPU Solbourne 6E/900.
 Public Access Unix — Home of the Online Book Initiative

 Type 'help' for help!  — Stuck? Try 'help HINTS'.

 Use 'exit' or 'logout' to leave the system.
 Still Stuck?  Send mail to 'staff'.

    * New Local Calling Numbers in Eastern Massachusetts
      *
    Type 'help world.info modem.numbers'

 -> When you see MORE, hit the SPACE BAR for the next
       page <-
 -> Hitting RETURN to the MORE prompt gets you one more
       line <-
```

The World asks for your terminal type and suggests VT-100.

4. Press Enter to accept its suggestion.

You see some more messages, like this:

```
Erase is Backspace
No new messages.
You'd better beat it.  You can leave in a taxi.  If you
      can't get a taxi, you can leave in a huff.  If
      that's too soon, you can leave in a minute and a
      huff.
  — Groucho Marx
world%
```

The first line tells you that to erase, you have to press Backspace when you are typing. The second line tells you whether you have e-mail. Following that is the pithy quote of the day. The last line is the World's prompt: world%.

5. Now you are ready to enter any UNIX command you know.

If you don't know any UNIX commands, read on!

Typing Commands

This section presents a list of rules for typing UNIX commands that you must follow when you're using the World, as well as how to stop using it when you are done.

Rules of the road

Every system has rules, and UNIX systems have lots of them. Here are some that you'll need to follow when you're typing commands:

- ✔ If you make a typing mistake, press Backspace (or try Delete).

- ✔ To cancel the entire command before you press Enter, press Ctrl+U. The command disappears.

- ✔ When you finish typing a command, press Enter (or Return).

- ✔ If you type a command that UNIX doesn't know, it displays a message saying that it couldn't find the command. What probably happened is that you mistyped the command.

- ✔ UNIX cares about capitalization. Enter commands exactly as they appear in this book or else UNIX doesn't recognize them. For example, UNIX considers **ls** and **LS** to be two totally different commands. Most UNIX commands are all lowercase. When you're typing filenames, uppercase and lowercase matter too: **FROG**, **Frog**, **FrOg**, and **frog** are four different names and can be four different files. (We didn't say that this would be easy.)

- ✔ Don't stick any extra spaces in the middle of commands. Do, however, press the spacebar after a command and before any other information you type on the command line.

- ✔ If you are stuck, type **help**. You can also try **help HINTS**.

- ✔ If you are really stuck, send a mail message to staff (or staff@world.std.com). If you are even stucker than that, you can call them (using your real voice — pretty retro, eh?) at 617-739-0202.

Hanging up

When you are ready to leave, type **exit**. The World logs you off and hangs up on you.

Sending and Receiving Mail

Anyone on the Internet can send you e-mail messages at this address:

```
username@world.std.com
```

Replace *username* with your own username, of course. If your username were `jlevine` (you can probably guess who that is), for example, your address would be

```
jlevine@world.std.com
```

std doesn't stand for *sexually transmitted diseases,* as we at first suspected. Nor does it stand for *standard.* It stands for the name of the company that runs the World: Software Tool and Die.

The World has several standard mail programs, including our favorites, *elm* and *pine.* For info on using them and *mail,* that crummy old mail program, see Chapter 7 of *The Internet For Dummies.*

Downloading mail messages

If you read a message you want to keep, you can download it to your own computer as a text file. The following steps show you how:

1. **In elm or pine, save the message (or messages) as text and then exit from the program.**

2. **If your communications program can handle ZMODEM file transfers, type the following line:**

```
sz filename
```

Replace *filename* with the name of the file in which you saved the message. If it's a file full of text (as opposed to a program, picture, compressed, or other nontext file), type the following line:

```
sz -a filename
```

If your communications program cannot do ZMODEM but can handle XMODEM, type the following line:

```
sx filename
```

Replace *filename* with the name of the file in which you saved the message. If it's a file full of text, type this line:

```
sx -a filename
```

If your communications program speaks Kermit, type

```
kermit
```

3. **When you see the C-Kermit> prompt, type**

```
send filename
```

Replace *filename* with the name of the file in which you saved the message.

4. **Tell your communications program to begin receiving the file.**

Your program may even begin receiving it automatically, particularly with ZMODEM.

Note: If you used Kermit to send the file, type **quit** when you see the C-Kermit> prompt again.

5. **When you are sure that the file has been received on your own computer, delete the file on the World to avoid getting charged for storage.**

Type this line:

```
rm filename
```

World asks you to confirm that you want to delete the file.

Forwarding your mail

If you use more than one on-line service, such as the World and CompuServe, it is annoying to get mail in both places. Getting mail in two places means that you have to check both services to read all your mail. You can solve this problem by forwarding your mail so that it all arrives at one place.

Assuming that you want to read all your Internet mail somewhere other than on the World, you can forward to another address all the mail that arrives in your World mailbox. To forward your mail, follow these steps:

1. **At the world% prompt, type the following line:**

```
pico .forward
```

The *pico* editor runs, editing a file named .forward. If the file already exists, you see it. Otherwise, you see nothing.

2. **Enter the Internet address to which you want your mail forwarded, as in the following example:**

```
midummies@iecc.com
```

This is our address here at Internet For Dummies Central, so it's probably not a good idea to forward all your personal mail to us, but you get the idea.

3. **Press Ctrl+X when you are finished.**

   The pico editor asks whether you want to save what you just typed.

4. **Press y.**

   The pico editor suggests the filename `.forward` again.

5. **Press Enter to accept the suggested filename.**

Getting on Mailing Lists

You can get on Internet mailing lists from the World the same way you can from any other service where you can receive mail: Send a message to the mailing list administrator requesting to be added to the mailing list. Soon after, you begin receiving all messages sent to the mailing list.

See Chapter 10 in *The Internet For Dummies* for the complete story on mailing lists and ideas about interesting ones to try out.

Chatting Live

To waste vast amounts of time chatting with other Internet users live rather than by way of the delayed-reaction mode of e-mail, you can use *IRC*, which stands for *Internet Relay Chat*. This list of steps gets you into IRC, but you'll have to skip ahead to Chapter 15 to find out what to do after you're in it.

To use the Internet Relay Chat, follow these steps:

1. **Type** `irc`.

   You see some messages like this:

```
*** Welcome to the Internet Relay Network jlevine
*** If you have not already done so, please read the new
       user information with
+/HELP NEWUSER
*** Your host is world.std.com, running version 2.8.16
*** There are 2907 users and 1540 invisible on 133 servers
*** There are 85 operators online
*** 1295 channels have been formed
*** This server has 4 clients and 3 servers connected
*** - world.std.com Message of the Day -
*** -
*** -    Welcome to World's IRC server
*** -
```

```
***  -   For additional details on IRC, check 'help irc' on
         World.
***  -   Topics include a guide to basic commands and a
         schedule
***  -   of special IRC discussions for World customers.
```

2. Now you are ready to find out which channels are open and get chatting — flip to Chapter 15 to learn how to chat.

3. When you have had enough, type /QUIT.

You return to the World prompt.

One point about IRC: Many of the channels appear to contain, ahh, prurient material, based on the channel names. So if you are easily offended by sexual stuff, we recommend staying away from the whole thing.

Reading Newsgroups

The World offers the full panoply of Usenet newsgroups. At least two newsreaders are available: *nn* and *trn*. See Chapter 11 in *The Internet For Dummies.*

Telnetting Out of This World

If your purpose in using the Internet is to be able to log in to computers all over the world, then you want to *telnet*. The telnet program lets you log in to any computer on the network that has been set up to receive this type of invasion and run commands on that computer.

For lots of information about telnetting, see Chapter 14 in *The Internet For Dummies.* Chapter 15 in that book contains a list of computers that are interesting to telnet to. You may also want to use telnet in connection with Gopher, Archie, WAIS, or WWW, which are described later in this chapter.

To telnet to another computer, follow these steps:

1. Type this line:

```
telnet host
```

Replace *host* with the name of the computer. To use the U.S. Library of Congress on-line catalog, for example, you type

```
telnet locis.loc.gov
```

You see something like this:

```
Trying 140.147.254.3,23 ...
Connected to locis.loc.gov
Escape character is "^\"

Welcome to the Library of Congress ...
```

2. **Make note of the escape character it suggests (in this case, ^\ or Ctrl+\) and then log in just as though you had called that host computer directly.**

3. **When you are finished using the other computer, log off.**

   Telnet usually notices that you have logged off the host computer, and it exits. If it doesn't, get its attention by pressing the escape character (the one you found out about in Step 2) a few times and then type **quit**.

FTP-ing

FTP (File Transfer Protocol) enables you to transfer files between computers on the Internet. For general information about FTP-ing, including the famous anonymous FTP, consult Chapter 16 in *The Internet For Dummies.* Chapter 18 of that book contains a list of interesting files you can get by way of FTP. Or use Archie to find files of interest.

Where do files live?

When you use FTP to copy files, you copy them to or from your directories on the World. You have a *home directory,* which is the directory you use all the time unless you tell it otherwise. You can create subdirectories (by using the *mkdir* command) and move from one directory to another (by using the *cd* command). In fact, UNIX directories work almost exactly like DOS directories do (not a coincidence because DOS ripped off the whole idea from UNIX — hi, Mark).

The key differences between UNIX and DOS directories are shown in this list:

- ✔ In UNIX, you type **mkdir** rather than **md** to make them.

- ✔ In UNIX, capitalization counts in directory names and filenames.

- ✔ In UNIX, when you're stringing names together into a pathname, you use regular slashes (/) rather than backslashes (\). If you make a subdirectory of the Games directory named kids, for example, it's called Games/kids.

For the full story on UNIX files and directories, see Chapters 4 and 5 in *UNIX For Dummies.*

Grabbing files from the net

This section shows you how to copy a file from another computer to World by using anonymous FTP:

1. **Type this line:**

```
ftp host
```

To FTP a file from the WUARCHIVE of programs, for example, at Washington University in Missouri, type this line:

```
ftp wuarchive.wustl.edu
```

You may have to wait a minute while the World establishes a connection. You see some messages from the computer from which you want to FTP, like this:

```
Connected to wuarchive.wustl.edu.
220 wuarchive.wustl.edu FTP server (Version wu-2.2(1) Mon
       Apr 4 20:55:15 CDT 199
4) ready.
Name (wuarchive.wustl.edu:jlevine):
```

2. **For your name, enter** `anonymous`.

3. **For your password, enter your complete e-mail address.**

   To use your World address, enter ***username*@world.std.com** and replace *username* with your username.

   You see a bunch more messages, probably welcoming you to the system.

4. **The first thing to do is to look around and find the file you want.**

   Through the magic of networks, you can use commands to see listings of files and move from directory to directory on the host computer. To see a directory of the files in the current directory, type **dir**.

5. **To move to another directory, type this line:**

```
cd dirname
```

   Replace *dirname* with the name of the directory and capitalize it just as you see it in FTP's listings. To move up one directory level, type

```
cdup
```

   When you see a file you want to copy, determine (or guess) whether it contains text or binary information. (If you're not sure, guess binary.)

6. **Type either** `binary` **or** `ascii` **(for text).**

   Now you are ready to copy the file.

7. **Type this line:**

```
get filename newfilename
```

Replace *filename* with the name the file has now and *newfilename* with the name you want the file to have when it arrives in your World account. Be sure to capitalize the current file just as you see it in the directory listing. If you want to keep the same name, you can omit *newfilename*.

You see a message like this:

```
200 PORT command successful.
150 Opening ASCII mode data connection for README (558
        bytes).
226 Transfer complete.
```

8. **When you are finished copying files, type** `quit`.

You return to the World prompt.

If the name of a file on a remote system contains spaces, type its name in double quotes. While you're at it, give your copy a name without spaces, as in

```
get "Profound Thoughts" blather.txt
```

Downloading FTP'd files

After you have copied a file to your World directory, you probably will want to download it to your own computer and delete it from your World directory. (This technique avoids World storage charges).

To download a file from your World directory, follow these handy steps:

1. **If your communications program can handle ZMODEM file transfers, type this line:**

```
sz filename
```

Replace *filename* with the name of the file in which you saved the message.

If your communications program cannot do ZMODEM but can handle XMODEM, type this line:

```
sx filename
```

Replace *filename* with the name of the file in which you saved the message.

Otherwise, if your communications program speaks Kermit, type

```
kermit
```

and when you see the C-Kermit> prompt, type both these lines, in this order:

```
set file type binary
send filename
```

Replace *filename* with the name of the file in which you saved the message.

2. **Tell your communications program to begin receiving the file.**

   Your program may even begin receiving it automatically.

   (If you used Kermit to send the file, type **quit** when you see the C-Kermit> prompt again.)

3. **When you are sure that the file has been received on your own computer, delete the file on the World to avoid getting charged for storage.**

   Type this line:

```
rm filename
```

   World asks you to confirm that you want to delete the file.

4. **Press y.**

Before you download a file by using ZMODEM or Kermit, make sure that the filename is acceptable to your PC. UNIX allows long filenames with funky characters in them but DOS doesn't, and ZMODEM and Kermit tell your communications program to use the same filename when you're creating the file on your PC.

If necessary, you can rename the file on the World by using the *mv* command so that it has a DOS-compatible type of name.

The mv command works like this:

```
mv currentname newname
```

Just replace *currentname* with the file's current name and *newname* with a new one.

Handing out files

You can copy files *to* other computers, though this is not commonly done. After you have used the ftp command to connect to the other computer, move to the directory in which you want to put the file. Rather than use the get command, type **put** followed by the name of the file in your World directory, followed by the name to give the copy of the file when it reaches the other computer.

Using Archie

Archie is a nifty program that searches cyberspace for the file you want —
assuming that you know the name of the file. After you find a computer that has
the file, you can use FTP to get it. It's described in more detail in Chapter 19 of
The Internet For Dummies.

To use Archie to find a file, follow these steps:

1. **Type this line:**

   ```
   archie -s text
   ```

   Replace *text* with the exact name of the file you are looking for.

   There is a long pause, during which the World says absolutely nothing.

2. **Sit tight because it is contacting a remote Archie server and asking the
   Archie server to look for the file you want.**

   Eventually you see something like this:

   ```
   Host etext.archive.umich.edu      (192.131.22.7)
   Last updated 04:39 30 Mar 1994
      Location: /pub/Politics/QRD/qrd/world
         DIRECTORY        drwxr-xr-x     512 bytes      20:11 28
            Nov 1993     brazil
      Location: /pub/Politics/QRD/world
         DIRECTORY        drwxr-xr-x     512 bytes      08:18 20
            Dec 1993     brazil
      Location: /pub/Politics/QRD/world/americas
         DIRECTORY        drwxr-xr-x     512 bytes      08:30 24
            Jan 1994     brazil

   Host nic.stolaf.edu(130.71.128.8)
   Last updated 21:13 3 Mar 1994
      Location: /pub/travel-advisories/advisories
         FILE    -rw-r-r—       16919 bytes   23:00 1 Jun 1993
            brazil
   ```

   With luck, this list shows FTP hosts that contain files with the names you
   are looking for.

3. **Now you can use FTP to get the files (using FTP from the World is
   described earlier in this chapter).**

Alternatively, you might get an error message such as `archie failed: Timed out (dirsend)`. If this happens, the Archie server is too busy to pay any attention to you. To find an Archie server that will work, type this line:

```
archie -L
```

This command displays a list of available Archie servers, like this:

```
Known archie servers:
  archie.ans.net (USA [NY])
  archie.rutgers.edu (USA [NJ])
  archie.sura.net (USA [MD])
  archie.unl.edu (USA [NE])
  archie.mcgill.ca (Canada)
  archie.funet.fi (Finland/Mainland Europe)
  archie.au (Australia)
  archie.doc.ic.ac.uk (Great Britain/Ireland)
  archie.wide.ad.jp (Japan)
  archie.ncu.edu.tw (Taiwan)
* archie.sura.net is the default Archie server.
* For the most up-to-date list, write to an Archie server
      and give it the command 'servers'.
```

The default Archie server (`archie.sura.net` in this case) is too busy to help you, so try another one by adding *-h servername* to the Archie command.

For example, to search for the `pkzip.exe` file by using the Archie server `archie.rutgers.edu`, type this line:

```
archie -s pkzip -h archie.rutgers.edu
```

Archie can take a *long* time — even hours — to get back to you. To cancel an Archie command, press Ctrl+C until you see the World prompt again.

To see a quick list of the ways you can use the Archie command, type **archie - -** (that's two hyphens). You can also perform Archie searches by e-mail. Mail your request to `archie@`*archiehost* where *archiehost* is one of the Archie servers listed by `archie -L`. The message should contain a line containing the word `prog` followed by the filename to search for, like this:

```
prog pkzip
```

You get the results back by return mail, eventually. In the meantime, though, you can do something else.

Using Gopher

Gopher is a great way to wander around the Internet looking for interesting information. It is much more flexible than Archie because you don't have to know the name of the file you are looking for.

Wandering in Gopherspace

Chapter 20 in *The Internet For Dummies* describes how Gopherspace works. The following steps show you how to run it from the World.

1. Type gopher **(all lowercase letters, remember).**

You see something like this:

```
Welcome to the wonderful world of Gopher!




Press RETURN to continue
```

2. Press Enter.

You see a menu like this:

```
Internet Gopher Information Client v1.13

        Root gopher server: gopher.std.com

 -> 1. Information About The World Public Access UNIX/
    2. The World's ClariNews AP OnLine & Reuters Newswire
       Index/
    3. OBI The Online Book Initiative/
    4. Internet and USENET Phone Books/
    5. Shops on The World/
    6. Commercial Services via the Internet/
    7. Book Sellers/
    8. Bulletin Boards via the Internet/
    9. Consultants/
    10. FTP/
```

```
   11. Government Information/
   12. Internet Information and Resources/
   13. Libraries/
   14. Membership and Professional Associations/
   15. News and Weather/
   16. Non-Profit Organizations/
   17. Other Gopher and Information Servers/
   18. Periodicals, Magazines, and Journals/

 Press ? for Help, q to Quit, u to go up a menu
        Page: 1/2
```

Gopher consists of nothing but lots of menus that look just like the preceding one. Choose entries from the menus based on your interests.

3. **To choose an entry, press the up and down arrows to highlight an interesting choice and then press Enter to see what it contains.**

   Or just type the number of the menu item.

4. **When Gopher displays an article, it displays this little menu at the end:**

```
 Press <RETURN> to continue, <m> to mail, <s> to save, or
        <p> to print:
```

You can mail a copy of the article to yourself or someone else or save it in a file for later downloading or printing. Don't bother to press p at this point because World doesn't let you print stuff on its printers. To print an article on your own printer, press s to save it in a file and then download it (see the section "Downloading FTP'd Files" earlier in this chapter).

If World doesn't ask you the filename, it isn't saving the article. Sometimes this happens. Try pressing s when you select the document from the menu rather than after reading it.

5. **If you decide that a menu looks boring, press u to leave it.**

   You can also press m to return to the main Gopher menu.

6. **When you are finished using Gopher, press q to quit.**

   You see the World prompt again.

As you choose items from Gopher menus, Gopher automatically connects you to the computer that has the information for that menu choice. There may be a delay, and you probably see a message such as `Retrieving directory`. Occasionally, the computer with the information isn't available, and you get a message such as `Unable to connect`. Just try it again later.

If you want to know the latest-breaking news, the World gives you access to both the AP and Reuters newswires. Just choose item 2 from the main Gopher menu.

Gopher commands

The following are commands you can use when you're in Gopherspace.

- ✔ Press the arrow keys to move up and down a list of items.

- ✔ Press Enter or the right-arrow key to choose an item.

- ✔ Press u or the left-arrow key to leave the current menu and return to the preceding one.

- ✔ For material that is more than one page long, press >, +, PgDn, or the space-bar to see the next page. To see the preceding page, press <, -, PgUp, or b.

- ✔ To see a specific item on a menu, type its number and press Enter.

- ✔ To return to the main menu, press m.

- ✔ To leave Gopherspace, press q.

- ✔ To save the current item to a file, press s.

- ✔ To search for a specific word (or part of a word or phrase) in this menu, press /. After you find one instance of the work, you can press n to find the next one.

- ✔ To change your Gopher options, press O (that's a *capital* O). You see a list of options and their current settings, which you can change. These options include which program to use to present long articles one page at a time, which program to use if you want to mail a copy of an article to someone, and so on.

Bookmarks

You can also create *bookmarks,* which are reminders to yourself of places you might want to return to. This list shows you commands for making and using bookmarks:

- ✔ To create a bookmark at the highlighted item, press a.

- ✔ To create a bookmark at the current directory (menu), press A.

- ✔ To see a list of your bookmarks, press v.

- ✔ To delete a bookmark from your list, press d.

See Chapter 16 for more advice about Gopher. Chapters 17 through 19 list lots of interesting Internet resources you might want to look at, some of which are Gopher menus.

Using WAIS

WAIS stands for *Wide Area Information Server*, and it is yet another way to search for information on the Internet. But unlike Archie, WAIS looks at what's *inside* files rather than just at filenames or Gopher menu entries. In Chapter 13 of this book, along with Chapter 21 of *The Internet For Dummies,* you'll find lots of information about using WAIS, which can be confusing.

Here's an important point for those who want to impress people in casual conversation: WAIS is pronounced "ways," not "wace." Saying "wace" is almost (but not quite) as tacky as pronouncing DOS as "dose."

These steps show you how to run WAIS from the World:

1. **Telnet to a WAIS host, most likely** `quake.think.com`.

   ```
   telnet quake.think.com
   ```

2. **When it asks you to log in, type** `wais`.

3. **When it asks for your user identifier, type your e-mail address.**

   That is, type ***username*@world.std.com** and replace *username* with your username.

4. **When it asks for your TERM (terminal type), press Enter to accept its suggestion of VT-100.**

   You see a welcoming message and the WAIS menu.

5. **Follow the directions in Chapter 21 of *The Internet For Dummies* for using WAIS.**

   That is, choose one or more databases from the list of sources. Then tell it what keywords to look for.

6. **When you are finished, press q to quit.**

   You see the World prompt.

Using WWW

Finally, you can use the World Wide Web (WWW) to browse through hypertext systems. Chapter 22 in *The Internet For Dummies* describes the WWW system in detail. Or see Chapter 14 in this book.

These steps show you how to run WWW from the World:

1. **Telnet to a WWW server, such as** `info.cern.ch` **(in Switzerland),** `www.njit.edu` **(in New Jersey), or** `hnsource.cc.ukans.edu` **(in Kansas).**

2. **When it asks you to log in, type** www.

   You see a hypertext-type screen with instructions for using the system. Follow the directions on-screen to choose topics of interest.

3. **When you are finished, follow the system's instructions to exit.**

   Pressing x or q usually does it. You see the World prompt again.

Sending Files to the World

If you want to upload a file from your computer to the World, perhaps so that you can include it in a mail message, try one of the following commands. The command you use depends on which file-transfer protocols your communications program can handle.

> ✔ If your communications program can handle ZMODEM file transfers, type this line:

```
rz filename
```

> Replace *filename* with the name of the file in which you saved the message. If it's a file full of text, type this line:

```
rz -a filename
```

> ✔ If your communications program cannot do ZMODEM but can handle XMODEM, type this line:

```
rx filename
```

> Replace *filename* with the name of the file in which you saved the message. If it's a file full of text, type this line:

```
rx -a filename
```

> ✔ Otherwise, if your communications program speaks Kermit, type

```
kermit
```

> When you see the C-Kermit> prompt, type

```
receive filename
```

> and replace *filename* with the name of the file in which you saved the message.

Then tell your communications program to begin sending the file.

If your communications program has ZMODEM built in, you can just tell it to upload a file, and it automatically types the *rz* command for you.

Other Cool Things

In addition to using Gopher and FTP to see information displayed by other organizations, you can create information that others can see. For instructions on how to create new Gopher pages with your own information and how to make files available for FTP-ing by everyone on the Internet, type **help world** and then choose `Vendor Archives`. To take a look at Gopher pages that other World users have created, choose `Shops on the World` from the main Gopher menu.

Because the World is a UNIX system, you can use it for more or less anything UNIX can do, including (if you are so inclined) writing and compiling C programs.

The World also sponsors something called the Online Book Initiative (OBI). The idea is to collect the text from a bunch of books, journals, reference materials, and conference proceedings and make them available to researchers and others. You can download the text, print it, and use it. For information, type **help obi**. Or you can send mail to `obi@world.std.com`.

Getting More Information

To learn more about how to use the World, you have to learn more about UNIX. We recommend, of course, that you buy and read *UNIX For Dummies* (IDG Books Worldwide) because we wrote it. Masochists can also use the *man* command to see the on-line manual page about a command. To find out more than you ever wanted to know about the *ls* command, for example, type **man ls**.

Chapter 7

The Internet via America Online

*A*merica Online (AOL to its friends) is a widely used information system that includes Internet access. It comes with a nifty Windows- or Macintosh-based access program, so you can do lots of pointing and clicking and not so much typing of arcane commands. This chapter describes its Internet-related abilities (and mentions the ones that the service's arch-rival CompuServe plans to add Real Soon Now).

Signing Up for America Online

No problem! Just call 1-800-827-6364 and ask for a trial membership. Specify that you want the Windows version of the software (unless you want the Mac version). These folks will send you an introductory package with instructions and a disk containing the program America Online for Windows. While you are at it, ask about pricing because after you use up your free introductory hours, you pay by the hour.

If you're using a Mac

Attention Mac users: In this chapter, we discuss the Windows version of AOL software. The Mac version is similar enough that you should be able to follow along and make a few adjustments for the Mac.

Installing the AOL software

To install the America Online for Windows software, follow these steps:

1. **Start Windows and stick the disk in the drive.**

2. **Choose File⇨Run from the Windows Program Manager's menu bar.**

3. **For the command line, type the following:**

   ```
   a:\install
   ```

   (If your disk is in drive B, substitute b for a.)

4. **Choose OK.**

   The installation program is very friendly and tells you what to do.

5. **Choose Continue when it asks.**

   When the program asks which directory you want to install the program into, it suggests a reasonable directory name.

6. **Change the directory name if you have another idea and then choose Continue.**

   It copies the program into the directory it has created and then tells you that the installation is complete.

7. **Click OK to make the message go away.**

The installation program creates a Program Manager program group named America Online that contains one icon: a cute, triangular item *also* named America Online. If you want to move the America Online icon to another program group, just drag it there. To copy the icon, hold down the Ctrl key while you drag it. If you put the icon in another program group, you then can delete the America Online program group — after all, it seems silly to have a whole program group containing just one icon. To delete the program group, select the title bar of the program group (which must be empty) and press Del.

Setting up your AOL account

The first time you use your trial package, you have to tell it which username you want to use and how you want AOL to bill you after you have used up your free hours.

Follow these steps to set up your account:

1. **Click on the America Online icon.**

2. **Follow the instructions on-screen.**

   First AOL calls up an 800 number to find out the closest local access number to you. You type your area code, AOL shows you the access phone numbers in your area, and then you choose the ones you want to use (in case you don't know, you should choose those that are local calls).

   If you received a *registration certificate* with your trial membership, you are prompted for it — it contains a long number with a couple of dashes.

3. **Type the number and the password that appears below the number on the certificate.**

   (We love it — ours was *SPECS-RICHES.* Who thinks these things up?)

4. **Pick a username (which they call a *screen name* — sounds glamorous) for yourself.**

   Your screen name can be as long as ten characters and can contain spaces. You can use a combination of capital and small letters, as in *MargyL* or *J Levine.* When AOL asks you to enter the username, it checks its list of existing usernames. If someone is already using that name (*John Smith,* for example), you have to invent another one.

5. **Pick a password.**

   AOL asks you to type your password twice to make sure you don't make a typo. The password doesn't appear on-screen — you just see asterisks.

   Yes, here's the part that you knew was coming. AOL asks how you want to pay after you use up your ten free hours.

6. ***Cha-ching.* Enter a credit-card number and expiration date.**

   Bummer. The good news is that the time you spend doing this registration doesn't count as part of your ten free hours. When you are finished, you see the Welcome! window in the America Online window (see Figure 7-1). You are ready to boogie!

The America Online window always displays the menu bar and, below it, the *Flashbar* (a row of cute little icons).

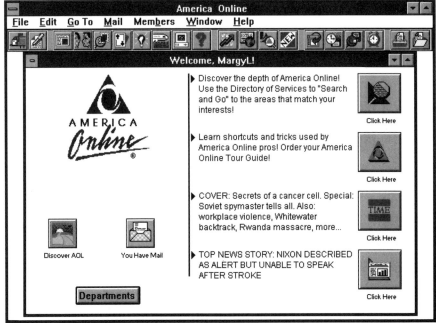

Figure 7-1:
The
Welcome!
window
shows you
lots of
friendly
icons.

Signing Off

With all the friendly little pictures on the screen, you would think that one of them would show a door or an EXIT sign or something. But no. To get the heck out of AOL (and stop using connect time), choose File⇨Exit from the menu bar or press Alt+F4. AOL asks whether you really, truly want to leave. Choose Yes to sign off from AOL but remain in the America Online for Windows program (unlikely) or Exit Application to end everything.

We can't help but feel that this is a sleazy maneuver on the part of AOL to keep us on-line (and paying) for as long as possible. Tacky, no?

Calling America Again

After you have gone through the registration process, it's a much quicker process when you call AOL again:

1. Click the AOL icon.

You see the Sign-On Window (see Figure 7-2).

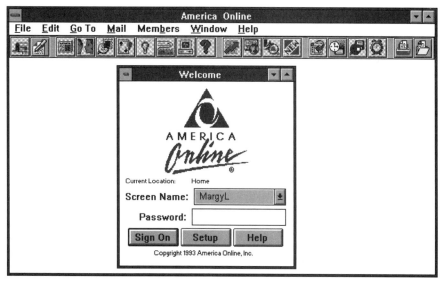

Figure 7-2:
Before you
can use
America
Online, you
have to sign
on.

2. **Enter your America Online username, the one you chose when you registered your trial membership.**

   In fact, your username probably already appears in the box.

3. **Press Tab to move to the password box and then enter your password.**

4. **Click the Sign On button or just press Enter.**

   Poof! You see some messages about how it is initializing your modem and making the call. You are ready to surf the net when you see the Welcome! window (see Figure 7-1).

If your PC has a sound board, or if you are using a Mac, don't be surprised if your computer suddenly says "Welcome!" when you log onto AOL.

Lost in America

AOL has tons of *departments* — that is, things you can do. The little icons just below the menu bar correspond to some of them, and your trial-membership booklet lists what they do.

In addition, though, a bunch more departments *don't* have little pictures. Instead, you use *keywords* to find them. This concept is important because using Internet services requires a keyword — there's no little picture for the Internet.

Finding a department

If you know a department's keyword, to go there follow these steps:

1. **Choose Go To⇨Keyword from the menu bar or press Ctrl+K or click the icon on the Flashbar for the Keyword Window (it's the picture of a red arrow pointing at a window, or maybe at a TV).**

   You see the Go To Keyword dialog box.

2. **Enter the keyword, such as** BILLING **for billing information.**

3. **Press Enter or click OK.**

If your Welcome! window goes away, choose Window from the menu bar and you will see it listed at the bottom of the Window menu.

Other tips

Here are some other tips for using the America Online for Windows program:

✔ To get the heck out of the department you are finished with, double-click the little box in the upper left-hand corner of the window — you know, the one with the little horizontal line in a gray box, just to the left of the title bar in the window.

✔ You can be in several departments at a time, and you can have several windows open at a time. You can minimize them to get them out of the way without closing them — just click the downward-pointing *minimize* button in the upper right-hand corner of the window.

Sending and Receiving Mail

America Online has a mail system by which AOL members can send messages to each other as well as to the rest of the Internet.

Departments you may need

Here are some departments you may need to use:

To change your billing information or your password, go to the BILLING department.

To cancel your account, go to BILLING.

To ask a question, go to SUPPORT or CSLIVE.

For a complete list of keywords, choose Go To⇨Keyword and click the Keyword List button.

Your Internet address is your username (omitting any spaces) plus *@aol.com*. If your username is *John Smith,* for example, your Internet address is JohnSmith@aol.com.

Do I have mail?

When you sign on to AOL, it tells you whether you have any mail. On the left side of the Welcome! window, you see either the message No New Mail or the message You Have Mail. Another way to tell whether mail is waiting for you is to look at the List Unread Mail icon on the Flashbar — it's the first one, a picture of a little mailbox. If the little red flag is up, you have mail.

Reading your mail

You probably *do* have mail, in fact, because every new member gets a nice note from the president of AOL. To read your unread mail, follow these steps:

1. **Click the leftmost icon on the Flashbar, just below the world** *File.*

   This is the List Unread Mail icon. Alternatively, you can choose Mail⇨Read New Mail from the menu or press Ctrl+R.

   You see the New Mail dialog box. Each line on the list describes one incoming mail message with the date it was sent, the sender's e-mail address, and the subject.

2. **To read a message, highlight it on the list and click Read or press Enter.**

   You see the text of your message in another cute little dialog box.

3. **To reply to the message or forward it, see the following sections.**

4. **To see the next message, click the Next button.**

5. **When you are finished, double-click the little box in the upper left corner of each window you are finished with.**

From the Welcome! window, you can click the You Have Mail icon to see your new mail.

Seeing messages you've read before

It's not always a good idea to respond to messages right away. You might have to get some information or you may have to cool off after reading the brainless message some jerk sent you. Either way, you can reread messages you have already read by choosing Mail from the menu and then choosing Check Mail You've Read.

Sending a reply

To reply to a message you have received, display it as described in the preceding two topics. Then follow these steps:

1. **Click the Reply button.**

   You see a dialog box. The To address is already filled in with the address from which the original message came, and AOL suggests a subject line.

2. **Type the text of your message in the box in the lower part of the dialog box.**

3. **To send the message, click the Send icon.**

Composing a new message

You don't have to reply to other messages — you can start an exchange of messages, assuming that you know the e-mail address of the person you want to write to.

1. **Click the second icon from the left on the Flashbar, the picture of a pen at an angle.**

   Alternatively, you can choose Mail from the menu and then choose Compose Mail. Or just press Ctrl+M. You see the Compose Mail dialog box.

2. **Enter the recipient's address in the To box.**

   For AOL members, just enter the username. For others on the net, type the entire Internet address.

3. **In the CC box, enter the addresses of anyone you want to send a copy to.**

   You don't have to send a copy to yourself — AOL keeps copies of mail you have sent.

4. **Enter a brief subject line in the Subject box.**

5. **In the box with no name, type the text of your message.**

   Don't use the Tab key because it moves your cursor from one box to the next in the dialog box. Press Enter to begin a new paragraph.

6. **When you like what you see, click the Send button.**

   AOL confirms that the mail is winging on its way.

7. **Click OK to make the message go away.**

Sending a file from your PC

If you want to send a file from your PC to someone as an e-mail message, AOL makes this process easy. When you are writing the message, click the Attach button. A dialog box appears that lets you choose any file from your PC.

This technique works great, except that AOL refuses to send a message with an attached file out over the Internet — this feature only works for sending files to other AOL members.

The following steps show you a way around the files-to-other-AOL-members-only limitation by utilizing the Windows Clipboard:

1. **Run Windows Notepad, your word processor, or any other program that can display the text you want to send.**

2. **Using that program, copy the text to the Windows Clipboard.**

   In most programs, you copy by highlighting the text and choosing Edit⇨Copy from the menu. Most Windows programs also let you copy highlighted text by pressing Ctrl+Ins or Ctrl+C.

3. **In America Online, begin a new message by replying to a message or by composing a new message (see preceding few sections).**

4. **Put your cursor in the text box where you type the text of the message.**

5. **Choose Edit⇨Paste (or press Ctrl+V or Shift+Ins).**

   The text appears.

6. **Send your message as usual.**

There *is* a limit to how much text you can copy at a time into the Windows Clipboard, but it's big. If you have trouble, copy the text a piece at a time. Also, this method works only for text, not for pictures or data files.

Saving a message on your PC

If you get a message on AOL that you want to download to your PC, display it on the screen as described in the section "Reading Your Mail," earlier in this chapter. Then choose File⇨Save As from the menu bar. AOL lets you choose the directory and filename in which to save the file on your computer. When you click OK, it saves the e-mail message as a text file. Nice and easy!

Other mail tricks

AOL lets you make an address book of the e-mail addresses of your friends and coworkers, forward messages, and other nice things. They have nothing to do with the Internet, however, and they are easy to figure out. If you run into trouble, choose Help from the menu bar.

Chatting Live

To waste vast amounts of time (and, unfortunately, money) chatting with other people live rather than by way of delayed-reaction mode (e-mail), you can use AOL's People Connection department. **Note:** AOL doesn't provide access to the Internet's own Internet Relay Chat (IRC). (They may eventually.)

To use People Connection, click the People Connection icon on the Flashbar (the picture of the woman whispering into a man's ear — hmm . . .). You get dropped into a conversation on one of the active *rooms,* as shown in Figure 7-3. You can move to other rooms, participate in the conversation, and leave when you get bored (double-click in the upper left-hand corner of the window).

Remember that conversations in the People Connection, like those in the Internet Relay Chat, are *in no way private.* Anyone with an AOL account might be listening, including your mother or your kid's English teacher. Keep that in mind before revealing anything too personal or saying anything nasty about anyone. (If you want privacy, you can create a private room for the conversation — click on the List Rooms icon and then the Private room icon.)

AOL mail shorthand

AOL lets you abbreviate the Internet addresses of people on some other services:

Messages to MCI Mail users can be addressed to *name*@mci rather than the complete address, *name*@mcimail.com. (You can replace *name* with the person's MCI Mail name *or* number.)

Messages to CompuServe users can be addressed to *7654.321*@cis rather than the complete address, *7654.321*@compuserve.com.

(Use the person's actual CompuServe ID rather than *7654.321* and be sure to type a period in the middle of the number, *not* a comma.)

Messages to AT&T Mail users can be addressed to *name*@att rather than the complete address, *name*@attmail.com.

Messages to AppleLink users can be addressed to *name*@apple rather than the complete address, *name*@applelink.apple.com.

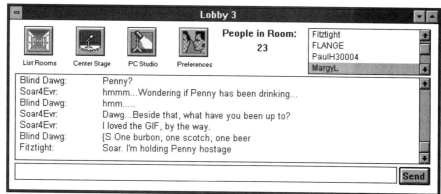

Figure 7-3:
Conversations
can be just
as
scintillating
on-line as in
real life.

Time flies when you're having fun, and chatting is definitely fun. One of our 14-year-old nieces found that her AOL bill for one month was $85 — almost all of it chat time. That's right: *Uh-oh.* You may want to set a kitchen timer to avoid Information Superhighway Hypnosis. (AOL has also added a Parental Control button to many windows, to allow parents to shut kids out of certain services.)

Getting to the Internet

At the time we're going to press, AOL is just getting its Internet connection organized. What they've finished so far is very nicely done and easy to use. To get at AOL's Internet services, choose Go To⇨Keyword from the menu (or press Ctrl+K) and enter the keyword **internet**. You see the Internet Center window, shown in Figure 7-4.

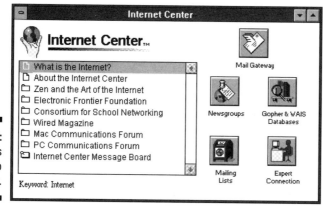

Figure 7-4:
AOL's
gateway to
the Internet.

The Internet Center has the following icons you can use:

- ✔ **Mail Gateway:** Send and receive mail from the Internet. You can use the Mail Gateway icon to send mail to people on the Internet, but it works exactly as though you used the regular Compose Mail icon on the Flashbar. Either way, you can enter complete Internet addresses in the To box when you're addressing a message.

- ✔ **Newsgroups:** Read Usenet newsgroups.

- ✔ **Gopher and WAIS Databases:** Search the Internet for the information you want.

- ✔ **Mailing Lists:** Choose mailing lists to join (described later in this chapter).

- ✔ **Expert Connection:** Shows which Internet services AOL is planning to add later.

When you are finished using the Internet Center, double-click the little box in the upper left-hand corner of its window to close the window.

Getting on Mailing Lists

Mailing lists work the same no matter how you connect to the Internet. To get on one, send a message to the mailing-list administrator requesting to be added to the mailing list. Soon you'll start receiving all messages sent to the mailing list. For the complete story on mailing lists and ideas about interesting ones to try out, see Chapter 10 in *The Internet For Dummies*.

However, AOL has created a nice way for you to find and join mailing lists that might interest you: Click the Mailing Lists button on the Internet Center window. You see the Internet Mailing Lists dialog box.

When this book went to press, AOL's list of available mailing lists was skimpy at best, and searching didn't work very well. But by the time you read this, the AOL folks probably will have beefed it up.

Searching for interesting lists

To search for a list you might want to join, follow these steps:

1. **Click the Search Mailing Lists icon.**

   You see the Internet Mailing List dialog box.

2. **Type a word in the upper box.**

   You can also look for both of two words or either of two words — for example, type **Brazil OR Brasil** or type **kids AND software**.

3. Click List Articles or press Enter.

Why is this button called List Articles rather than List Mailing Lists? Maybe by the time you read this, they'll have renamed it. At any rate, AOL searches the mailing-list description for the words you typed. In many cases, you have to try various different words — be sure to try entering just the first few letters of a word (such as **expat** rather than **expatriate**) in case the description contains an abbreviation.

In the lower box, a list of matching mailing-list names appears.

4. To find out more about the mailing list, including how to subscribe and unsubscribe, double-click the name.

For example, the following is the description of the `bras-net` mailing list (no, it's not about women's underwear).

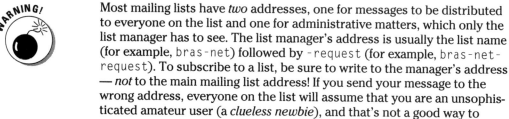

```
brasil

Contact: bras-net-request@cs.ucla.edu (B. R. Araujo Neto)

Purpose: Mailing list for general discussion and informa-
         tion. To join, send name, e-mail, phone number,
         address, and topics of interest.  Portuguese is
         the main language of discussion.
```

If you want to join the list, you have to send a mail message to the appropriate address, as explained in the description of the list.

5. Keep the window with the instructions visible and click the Compose Mail icon on the Flashbar (or choose Mail⇨Compose Mail).

The Compose Mail window appears.

Most mailing lists have *two* addresses, one for messages to be distributed to everyone on the list and one for administrative matters, which only the list manager has to see. The list manager's address is usually the list name (for example, `bras-net`) followed by `-request` (for example, `bras-net-request`). To subscribe to a list, be sure to write to the manager's address — *not* to the main mailing list address! If you send your message to the wrong address, everyone on the list will assume that you are an unsophisticated amateur user (a *clueless newbie*), and that's not a good way to introduce yourself. Don't let this happen to you.

6. By clicking and dragging the title bars of the Compose Mail window and the window with the instructions about the mailing list, you should be able to see both of them.

You can even copy the address of the list from one window to another by highlighting it with the mouse, pressing Ctrl+C to copy it to the Windows Clipboard, moving the cursor to the To box in the Compose Mail window, and pressing Ctrl+V to retrieve it from the Clipboard.

7. **Finish writing the message asking to subscribe and send it as usual.**

8. **When you are finished, double-click the little box in the upper left-hand corner of each window you are finished with.**

Beware mailbox clutter

Don't let your mailbox fill up! Some mailing lists can generate a staggering amount of mail. AOL lets your mailbox hold as many as 550 messages. That sounds like a lot, sure. But if your mailbox fills up, AOL starts deleting your mail, beginning with mail you've read and continuing on to unread mail. This includes your personal e-mail, not just mailing-list messages. So be sure to delete or move your mail regularly to prevent it from piling up. One of us (John) is on roughly a dozen mailing lists, which produce nearly 100 messages a day.

Unsubscribing to a mailing list

Joining a mailing list isn't irrevocable. You can always *unsubscribe.* To unsubscribe, send a message to the mailing-list manager (whose address is usually the list name plus `-request`) asking to have your name removed. Compose and send it the same way you did when you sent the message to get on the mailing list in the first place. And for your own good, please go back and read the warning two sections ago about clueless newbies before sending the unsubscribe message.

Reading Newsgroups

Mailing lists arc interesting, but to our minds, newsgroups are where most of the action is. Chapters 11 and 12 in *The Internet For Dummies* describe how newsgroups work — in a nutshell, they are a large collection of bulletin boards, each on a particular topic. Topics range from recipe swaps (*rec.food.cooking*) to arguments about abortion issues (*talk.abortion*) to technical discussions of multimedia computing (*comp.multimedia*).

To use newsgroups from AOL, click the Newsgroups button on the Internet Center window. You see the Newsgroups window, shown in Figure 7-5.

There are thousands of newsgroups, so you aren't going to read all of them. The idea is to find the ones which discuss subjects that interest you. After you've selected one or more newsgroups, you still have to sift through the messages (also known as *postings*) to find the ones you want to read — some newsgroups get hundreds of postings a day.

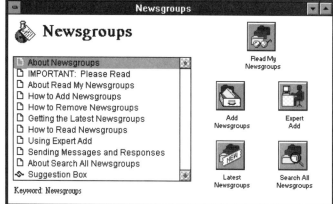

Figure 7-5:
Getting
ready to
dive into
some
newsgroups.

Reading newsgroup messages

AOL remembers which newsgroups you are interested in. To get you started, those nice AOL folks even suggest a few. When you click the Read My Newsgroups icon on the Newsgroups window, you see the list of "your" newsgroups.

If you aren't interested in the newsgroups AOL has suggested, don't worry. You can delete them from your list of newsgroups.

For each newsgroup on your list, you can see the total number of messages in addition to the number you haven't read yet. Yikes!

For some mysterious reason, AOL uses *slightly* different newsgroup names from the rest of the Internet. For example, it replaces the dots in newsgroup names with dashes. Who knows whose bright idea this was — just sounds confusing to us. Anyway, if you want to see the actual Internet name of a newsgroup on AOL's list, click the Internet Names icon in the Read My Newsgroups window.

To read the messages in a newsgroup, follow these steps:

1. **Select the newsgroup from the list in the Read My Newsgroups window.**

   (If the newsgroup isn't on that list, see the section "Finding a Newsgroup" later in this chapter.)

2. **Click the List Unread Subjects button to see a list of the subjects of all the messages in that newsgroup you haven't read yet.**

   There may be several messages on the same topic (an exchange of messages on the same topic is called a *thread*), and the number of messages is shown for each subject.

3. **Choose a subject that looks interesting.**

4. **Click the Read Messages button.**

   The message appears in its own little window. You can use the Next and Previous buttons to read the other messages on this subject, if there are any.

5. **When you have read the messages, double-click in the upper left-hand corner of the window to make it go away.**

In the window that lists the subjects of the messages in the newsgroup, after you have read the messages that interest you, you can "dismiss" the rest of them. Click the Update All As Read button to mark all the messages in this newsgroup as having been read by you. The next time you read this newsgroup, those moldy old messages don't appear.

Removing boring newsgroups

You can't get rid of a newsgroup (what would those people do who *like* it?), but you can delete it from your list of newsgroups. Out of sight, out of mind.

To delete a newsgroup from your list, choose it and click the Remove button. AOL asks you to confirm. The newsgroups don't disappear from the list immediately (who knows why not), but the next time you choose the Read My Newsgroups button from the Newsgroups window, they don't appear.

Mouthing off

Always read a newsgroup for at least a week before you send anything to it. AOL users have a reputation (well-earned, unfortunately) of barging into newsgroups and having no idea of what the group is about or what people on it are discussing. So *please* restrain your creative impulses for a few days before contributing to a group. The rest of Usenet will thank you.

After you have read a message, you can send a response. Make sure, however, that you read all the existing responses first! Someone may already have made the excellent point you want to make. You see a Post Response dialog box, which lets you enter the text of your message. If you are changing the subject, be sure to change the Subject of the posting also.

In addition to making sure that you are not repeating what someone may have already said, be sure to write clearly, proofread your message, stay calm rather than get emotional (emotional responses don't work well in newsgroups), be polite (net surfers are people too), and keep it brief. After all, tens of thousands of people are likely to read your posting, so don't waste their time!

If you begin to compose a reply and then think better of it, you can cancel sending the reply. Double-click in the upper left-hand corner of the Post Response dialog box rather than click the Send button.

Finding a newsgroup

AOL's kindly suggestions about newsgroups are certainly helpful, but you will want to choose your own. After all, what's the point of Internet access if you can't read the newsgroup devoted to, say, your favorite musical group?

To find a newsgroup and add it to the list of newsgroups you read, follow these steps:

1. **In the Newsgroups window, click the Add Newsgroups button.**

   You see the Add Newsgroups - Categories window.

2. **Browse down through the list for the type of newsgroup you want.**

   The list is so long that AOL sends it to you a section at a time. When you get to the end of the list, click the More button for the next section. You've really seen all of them when the More button is gray.

   For suggestions about which categories to try, see the sidebar titled "The usual suspects."

3. **Double-click a likely-looking category.**

   AOL displays — no, you're not finished yet! — the list of *topics* within that category (see Figure 7-6). To the right of each topic is the number of newsgroups on that topic.

4. **Double-click a topic that interests you.**

   You see a list of the newsgroups about that topic (see Figure 7-7).

   Now you can see the subjects of the messages in each newsgroup and read the messages, just as we described in the section "Reading Newsgroup Messages," earlier in this chapter.

Figure 7-6:
Categories
contain
topics, and
some topics
contain
more than
one
newsgroup

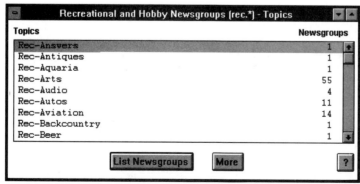

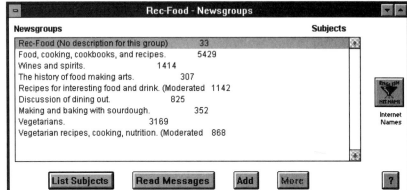

5. If you plan to read the newsgroup regularly, click the Add button to add it to your list of newsgroups.

Then it appears on the list of newsgroups you get when you click the Read My Newsgroups button on the Newsgroups window.

6. When you are finished, double-click the little box in the upper left-hand corner of each window you are finished with.

To see the actual Internet names for the newsgroups listed, click the Internet Names button.

Finding a newsgroup if you know its name

Finding a newsgroup by using the procedure described in the preceding section can take all day, though it's nice to browse around and see what's there.

If you already know the name of the newsgroup you want to read, however, there is a faster way:

1. Click the Expert Add button in the Newsgroups window.

AOL asks you for the Internet name of the newsgroup (that's the newsgroup name with dots between the words, usually all in small letters).

2. Enter the newsgroup name.

3. Click the Add button. When AOL asks you to confirm adding the newsgroup, do so.

4. When you are finished, double-click the little box in the upper left-hand corner of the window.

The usual suspects

This sidebar lists the most popular categories of newsgroups:

Alternative (*alt.**): Newsgroups that have been set up informally, avoiding the usual procedures. These are frequently temporary groups that are used until an "official" group is set up, or groups that discuss subjects so nasty that the regular newsgroups won't touch them.

Computers and Computer Science *(comp.*)*: Newsgroups that discuss computer hardware and software.

K-12 (School): Newsgroups for elementary and high-school students and teachers.

Mailing Lists Echoed to Usenet (*list.**): Newsgroups that are mailing lists. You may find it more convenient to read mailing-list messages as though they come from a newsgroup rather than have them clutter up your mailbox. (These aren't real newsgroups available anywhere except on AOL — they're a convenience provided by AOL for its users.)

Miscellaneous, Uncategorized (*misc.**): Newsgroups on miscellaneous topics, but as miscellaneous as alternative newsgroups.

Usenet News and Information (*news.**): Newsgroups about organizing, reading, and posting to newsgroups. It's a good idea to read *news.announce.newusers* (which AOL calls News-Announce-Newusers).

Recreational and Hobby (*rec.**): Newsgroups about sports, music, gardening, cooking, travel — you name it. If it's fun, there's a group for it.

Science and Research (*sci.**): Newsgroups about pure and applied science, including medical topics.

Social Issues and Socializing (*soc.**): Newsgroups about relationships, religion, culture, and that kind of thing.

Talk/Debate and Issues (*talk.**): Newsgroups about contentious topics (such as abortion and New Age religion), rumors, or general gossip.

In addition to these categories, try the regional category for your area (if you live in Colorado, for example, several categories of newsgroups concentrate on Colorado-oriented topics). For more ideas about choosing a newsgroup, see Chapter 12 in *The Internet For Dummies*.

AOL offers every newsgroup in the known universe, even the notably uncensored ones, such as *alt.sex.spanking*. If you know the name of the group you want, you can add it to your list, even if it's not present in the list that AOL displays. Complete lists of newsgroups are posted in the group *news.lists* (or in AOL-ese, *news-lists*) on the first day of each month under the titles List of Active Newsgroups and Alternative Newsgroup Hierarchies. Some of them can get pretty raunchy, so if you or your family members who use AOL are young, impressionable, or easily offended, don't say that we didn't warn you. If you stick to the groups in AOL's lists, the worst thing you will find, other than some incredibly bad spelling, is an occasional rude word uttered (typed, actually) in frustration.

Searching for a newsgroup

If you don't know the name of the newsgroup you want to read, another way to find it is to click the Search All Newsgroups button in the Newsgroups window. You can then enter a word, and AOL shows you the newsgroup names that contain that word.

Using Gopher and WAIS

As we write this book, AOL is setting up a way to use both Gopher and WAIS to search for information on the Internet. Gopher is a system (see Chapter12) that enables you to use lots of menus to search for what you want — there are so many different menus that the whole collection is known as *Gopherspace*. WAIS (Wide Area Information Servers) lets you enter a word or set of words you are interested in and searches on-line libraries for those keywords.

To use either Gopher or WAIS, click the Gopher and WAIS Databases button in the Internet Center window. You see the Gopher and WAIS window shown in Figure 7-8. (AOL may well change the windows in the Gopher and WAIS section as it works the kinks out of the system.)

Searching for stuff

To search for some information, follow these steps:

1. **Choose a category from the Main Categories list.**

   Because there are so many categories, you have to click the More button to see the bottom part of the list.

2. **Double-click the category from which you want information.**

   You see a window with a list of topics in that category. Not only does the list of topics vary, the buttons available also vary, depending on the category.

3. **The Editor's Choices list shows the Gopher menus and WAIS databases that AOL thought were the most interesting.**

   Gopher menus show up with a little folder icon, and WAIS databases appear with a little picture of an open book. For other Gopher menus and WAIS databases in the same category, click the More *category* Resources button (if the category is Weather, for example, the button is called More Weather Resources).

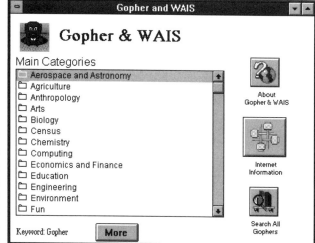

Figure 7-8:
Choosing a
category to
search in
Gopher and
WAIS.

4. To see the Gopher menus for a topic with a little folder icon to its left, double-click on the topic.

You see another window with more choices. Congratulations! You're in Gopherspace, which consists of lots of menus. Just keep choosing items (by double-clicking them) until you find the information you want. To backtrack and make a window go away, double-click in its upper left-hand corner.

If a menu is very long, you may have to click the More button to see the bottom of it.

5. To search a WAIS database for a topic with a little open book to its left, double-click on the topic.

You see a WAIS server window like the one in Figure 7-9.

6. In the top box, enter a word to search for.

You can enter several words, using *AND* and *OR* to indicate whether you want either one or only entries with both. Then click the Search button. In the lower box, WAIS lists the items it finds. To read the text of an item, just double-click it. When you are finished searching the WAIS database, double-click in the upper left corner of the window to make it go away.

Click the Help & Info button in the WAIS server window for more information about that particular WAIS database. You will find out the best way to enter search words for that database, or where the information comes from.

7. When you are finished searching Gopher menus about a particular category, close the windows by double-clicking on upper left-hand corners.

You can dismiss the Gopher & WAIS window in the same way.

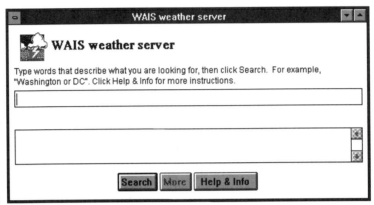

WAIS weather server

WAIS weather server

Type words that describe what you are looking for, then click Search. For example, "Washington or DC". Click Help & Info for more instructions.

Search | More | Help & Info

Figure 7-9: Searching for something interesting about the weather.

All these menus can clutter your screen with windows. To move a window out of the way temporarily, click the downward-pointing triangle in its upper right-hand corner. (This step *minimizes* the window, so it appears as an icon at the bottom of the AOL window. You can get the window back by double-clicking the icon.)

If *The Internet For Dummies* and this book aren't enough Internet information for you, click the Internet Information button on the Gophers and WAIS window and then click the More Internet and Network button on the Internet and Network Information window. You see an item by Adam Gaffin. (Check it out! — hint: it's no relation.)

Saving stuff on your PC

If you find something interesting you want to download to your PC, view the item. Then choose File⇨Save As from the menu bar. AOL lets you specify the directory and filename for the new file and then automatically downloads the information. Way cool and dead easy!

Searching all of Gopherspace

Because there are (it seems like) billions of Gopher menus to wander among, some kind soul wrote a program that searches all the menus for keywords. You can run the program, called Veronica, by clicking the Search All Gophers button in the Gopher & WAIS window.

Enter a word in the top box and click the Search button. Veronica lists all the Gopher menus that include the word you suggested. You can then view the Gopher menus by double-clicking them as usual. When you are finished, close all the windows by double-clicking in their upper left corner.

Coming Soon

AOL hasn't finished setting up its Internet connection. It's taking some time because it wants to have nice Windows dialog boxes for each Internet service so that everything stays easy to use and consistent. Services that will be set up soon in AOL include telnetting to other computers, FTP-ing files from remote computers, and possibly the World Wide Web (WWW).

Doing Other Things

America Online offers tons of information that has nothing to do with the Internet, so after you are signed up, you might as well check it out. The Computing & Software department lets you exchange messages with others about the software you use or download shareware. The Learning & Reference department offers all kinds of on-line reference materials, including the Library of Congress database of books, Compton's Encyclopedia, Webster's dictionary of computer terms, and information about educational software. And the Travel & Shopping department lets you use EAASY SABRE to make and check your own airline reservations.

Overall, AOL has one of the nicest *front ends* (as we say in the software biz — it means the way a human being actually uses the system) of any of the Internet shell providers. For all but the most seasoned hackers, all these nice icons and menus make the system easy to use! AOL has been slow at times, especially evenings and weekends, but it keeps promising to speed things up soon. Because the trial membership is free, try it out!

What about CompuServe?

Yeah, what about CompuServe, the venerable on-line service that most serious PC nerds use? Well, they've been a little slow at getting connected to the Internet, but they are on the move now.

You've been able to send Internet mail to or from CompuServe for ages. If your CompuServe account number is 12345,678 then you can receive mail from anyone on the Internet at the address 12345.678@compuserve.com (note that the comma in your number has transmogrified into a period).

From within CompuServe, type INTERNET: followed by the Internet address. For example, to send mail to Internet for Dummies Central, you'd address it to INTERNET:midummies@iecc.com. You have to limit the length of your messages to two million characters each — not too big a problem — and the same limit applies for incoming messages.

To *discuss* the Internet, you can use the new Internet forum. Type Go INETFORUM. There are sections for discussing how to get connected, e-mail, Usenet newsgroups, FTP, and all the other usual Internet services.

As of this writing, you can use telnet to connect to CompuServe. Enter compuserve.com as the host name, and the usual port (23). Tell your telnet program to pretend to be a VT-100 terminal, if you can. You have to have a CompuServe account to log in, though, so that CompuServe knows how to bill you. If you don't have one, CompuServe asks if you want to sign up for an account on the spot, including some free hours of usage.

By the time you read this book, CompuServe will probably have added other services. Check on the Internet forum, or use the FIND or HELP commands, to find out what's cooking.

The 5th Wave   By Rich Tennant

Part III
Windows on the Internet

The 5th Wave   By Rich Tennant

RECYCLING CENTER

DOS MANUALS
1. TURN LEVER CLOCKWISE
2. GRIP HANDLE
3. PULL FORWARD
4. DEPOSIT REFUSE

WINDOWS MANUALS
1.
2.
3.
4.

In this part . . .

*I*f you use a PC and run Windows, the Internet is a happening place. This part of the book talks about how to get your PC onto the net in a whole new way, so that it's actually a *full-fledged node* on the Internet. Once you do that (as described in Chapter 8), you can use spiffy Windows-based programs to read your e-mail, browse through Usenet newsgroups, and the like. No more ugly, outmoded, character-based programs for you! And the *best* thing is that most of this fancy new software is free, and you can get it right off the net! Chapter 9 tells you how to grab software from the net, and the rest of the chapters in this part of the book explain how to use our favorite Internet access programs.

Chapter 8

Getting Your Windows Machine on the Net

. . . .

. . . .

What Is SLIP Again?

We knew that you weren't listening when we explained this SLIP stuff in Chapters 2, 3, and 4, so we had better go over it again here. The SLIP (Serial Line Internet Protocol) system allows your PC to connect to the Internet, not as a terminal but as a full-fledged member of the net, at least while your computer is on the phone to its Internet provider. CSLIP (Compressed SLIP) involves the same idea as SLIP, but it's a little faster. PPP (Point-to-Point Protocol) is a fancier system that does more or less the same thing — because they are identical for our purposes, we just refer to them all as SLIP. (If you care about the differences, which you don't, see Chapter 2.)

They are all cool because many network operations are much simpler when your own computer is on the net instead of acting as a terminal to someone else's big computer and because programs running on your own computer can do much nicer sound, graphics, and animation than a terminal can.

The really cool thing about running SLIP software on your PC is something called WinSock. *WinSock* (which stands for *Windows Sock*ets — don't you love these names they come up with?) is a standard way for Windows programs to work with SLIP. If your SLIP software does WinSock, you can run any WinSock application, including nice ones for reading e-mail, checking out newsgroups, telnetting, FTP-ing, and using Gopher and WAIS. Remarkably, many of the best WinSock applications are available for free on the net.

When you are on-line with your Internet SLIP provider, you are on the net. Conversely, when you hang up with your provider, your computer drops off the Internet. If someone wants to telnet to your computer or FTP a file to you and you're not on the phone, it won't work. This isn't a big problem for most people, however.

The way you use SLIP is shown in this list:

- ✔ Install some SLIP software on your computer.
- ✔ Get an account with a SLIP Internet provider.
- ✔ Call up the provider with your SLIP software.

In this chapter, we explain how to get your computer on the Internet by using SLIP and the Trumpet WinSock shareware SLIP package. After you are connected, we describe how to use telnet and FTP, the basic applications you need in order to get started. In the next few chapters, we talk about other nifty Windows-based software your SLIP connection allows you to use, including programs for reading your mail, reading newsgroups, and using Gopher.

SLIP connections are easy enough to use, but they can be tricky to set up. Installing and setting up SLIP software requires entering lots of scary-looking numeric Internet addresses, host names, communications ports — you name it. If this subject makes you nervous, consider starting slow and easy with an Internet shell provider, as described in Chapters 5 through 8. Still with us? This might also be a good time to find a local Internet expert and ask for some help in getting SLIP set up.

Having in hand a plate of cookies, particularly freshly baked ones, when you ask for help is never a bad idea.

A bunch of different TCP/IP network packages are available for DOS and Windows. (See Chapter 28 in *The Internet For Dummies* for a list.) All the Windows packages support WinSock, and most support SLIP also. What this means for you is that if your Windows computer is already set up with a different package, the rest of the chapters in this section apply equally to you because all the WinSock programs work the same no matter which network package is running underneath.

SLIP and e-mail, a digression

When you use SLIP to communicate with your Internet SLIP provider, your lowly PC becomes a full-fledged node on the Internet. That is, your PC is now a *host* computer. This elevated status entitles it to a name. For one PC, for example, we chose the name of our favorite three-year-old, meg. The full network address of your PC is its host name followed by the name of your Internet provider. We use a local provider, for example, TIAC (The Internet Access Company), whose Internet address is tiac.net. So the address of the PC is meg.tiac.net.

The PC is not on the net all the time, however — when the computer is turned off, for example, or when we aren't connected to the SLIP provider. Normally, incoming Internet mail is delivered directly to the recipient's computer. (See Chapter 2 for the gory details.) But when our PC is not connected to the net, what happens to our incoming mail? Do you really have to keep your computer on the phone 24 hours a day just to get your mail?

A good question, and we're glad you asked. No, you don't. SLIP Internet providers receive your mail for you and hold on to it until you next log in, at which point you can move it to your own computer. As long as your SLIP provider's computer is connected all the time (and it's a pretty poor provider if it isn't), mail flows unimpeded.

This arrangement means that, as far as the rest of the Internet can tell, your mailbox is on your Internet provider's computer, not on your own PC. Your e-mail address is usually your login, followed by an at sign (@), followed by your provider's address. We have a login called margy on TIAC, for example, whose address is tiac.net. So mail can come to margy@tiac.net. (But don't send us mail there — you get better results from midummies@iecc.com, which connects you to *The Internet For Dummies* Central, which is in fact on the net continuously.)

Getting a SLIP-ed Disk

OK, you are raring to go. Here's what you need:

- A modem that connects your computer to a phone line. The faster the modem, the better. Try to get one that talks at 9600 BPS (bits per second) or even 14.4K BPS. Otherwise, things are sluggish.

- A phone line (you probably guessed that). Make sure that your phone line doesn't have call waiting, or refer to Chapter 4 to learn how to disable it temporarily while your computer uses the phone.

- Software that does SLIP or one of its variants. We tell you how to install it later in this chapter.

- Software for getting your mail, reading newsgroups, and so on. We talk about these things in the rest of the chapters in this part of the book.

- An account with an Internet SLIP provider and a bunch of technical information about the account (described in gory detail in the next section).

See the coupons in the back of this book for a range of SLIP providers. The cost varies from provider to provider, but is usually in the range of $20 to $50 per month, depending on how much time per month you plan to be connected. It is also worth checking the ads in the business section of your newspaper and talking to friends about their experiences with Internet providers in your area.

 If your PC is on a local area network, things get confusing. You have to talk to your network administrator to find out how to get connected to the Internet, with or without SLIP. Rather than connect your individual PC, your network may need a gateway to connect the entire local area network to the Internet.

Ask Your Provider

Before you can use SLIP, you need a bunch of scary-looking technical information. Ask your Internet provider for the information in Table 9-1 and write it down:

Table 8-1	Information About Your SLIP Connection	
Information	*Description*	*Example*
Your own Internet address	Your PC's own numeric Internet address. Although it is for your computer, you get this number from your Internet provider.	123.45.67.89
Your own host name	The name of your own computer. When you get an account with an Internet provider, you usually get to choose this name. Make it short and spellable, and perhaps cute.	meg
Your domain name	The name of your Internet provider's domain. It looks like the last part of an Internet address and usually ends with .net or .com (in the U.S., anyway).	plebney.com
Your communications port	The communications port on your own computer to which your modem is attached, usually COM1 or COM2. Even if your modem lives inside your computer and doesn't look as though it is connected to a port, it is.	COM1
Your modem speed	The fastest speed that both your modem and your Internet provider's modem can go. If your modem can go at 9600 or 14.4K BPS, for example, but your Internet provider can handle only 9600 BPS, choose 9600 BPS. Conversely, if your modem can do only 2400 BPS (which will seem really slow when you get connected), choose 2400 BPS.	9600

Table 8-1 *(continued)*

Your modem	The kind of modem you have. Actually, WinSock packages are only dimly aware of the details of different kinds of modems. If you have a regular PC-type modem, it's probably similar enough to a Hayes model to fool the programs we're using here.	Hayes
Phone number	The number you call to connect to your Internet provider, exactly as you would dial it by hand. If it is long distance, include the *1* at the beginning. If you have to dial 9 and pause a few seconds to get an outside line, include *9,* at the beginning (each comma tells your modem to pause for about a second, so stick in extra commas as needed to get the timing right).	1-617-637-1234
Username	The name on your account with your Internet provider, also called a *login* name.	myoung
User password	The password for your account.	friedrice
Startup command	The command your Internet provider should run when you call in. Your Internet provider can tell you this command. If the provider starts SLIP right away when you log in, you may not need a start-up command, so you may be able to leave this entry blank when the time comes to type it in.	SLIP
Domain name server	The numeric Internet address of the address computer that can translate between regular Internet addresses and their numeric equivalents (between iecc.com and 140.186.81.1, for example). Your Internet provider should give you this address.	123.45.67.99
Interface type	The exact type of interface used by the provider. The three choices are SLIP, CSLIP, and PPP. Trumpet WinSock handles only SLIP and CSLIP. If your SLIP software and SLIP provider handle it, use PPP; the next-best choice is CSLIP; and the worst (but still OK) choice is SLIP.	PPP
MTU	Some providers limit the sizes of individual packets of data sent over the SLIP link, the maximum transfer unit (MTU). If your provider has an MTU, it lets you know.	NA

There's a Place for Them

Skip this section if you already have a directory in which you like to put little utility programs.

Before you begin filling your computer's disk with network software, you have to make a directory in which to put these new programs. You can use this directory for the programs you download in this chapter in addition to useful little programs you find on the net.

Here's what to do, assuming that you use a PC running DOS and Windows:

1. **Make a directory called** util **or** utility **or** tools **or something.**

   In Windows File Manager, move to the directory in which you want to create the new directory (probably the root), and choose the File Create Directory command from the menu bar. In the rest of the book, we call it \util.

   To make it truly useful, you have to include this directory in your DOS PATH so that DOS can find any programs you store there. (Oooh, sounds yecchy.) This involves changing your autoexec.bat file, so let's make a backup copy first.

2. **In File Manager, copy the** autoexec.bat **file and name the new copy** autoexec.bak **(that's** *bak* **for** *backup***).**

3. **To run Windows Notepad to edit your** autoexec.bat **file, double-click the Notepad icon in Program Manager.**

4. **In Notepad, choose File➪Open so that you see the Open dialog box.**

5. **Choose** C:\ **for the Directory (or the root of whatever disk you start your computer from), enter** autoexec.bat **for the File Name, and then click OK.**

   You see a bunch of apparent nonsense like this (yours is probably somewhat different):

   ```
   @C:\SW\STACKER\CHECK /WP
   LH /L:0;1,45488 /S C:\DOS\SMARTDRV.EXE
   PROMPT $p$g
   PATH C:\DOS;C:\WINDOWS;c:\
   SET TEMP=D:\windows\temp
   LH /L:1,13984 C:\DOS\SHARE.EXE /L:200
   LH /L:1,56928 C:\DOS\mouse /y
   LH /L:1,6384 C:\DOS\doskey /insert
   ```

   Don't panic — you don't have to know what all this stuff means. Find the line that begins with the word *PATH* or *path*.

6. **Carefully, without deleting anything on the line (or anywhere else, for that matter), add a semicolon (;) to the end of the PATH line, and then type the full name of the directory you created in step 1.**

Don't type any spaces. If you created a directory named util in C:\, for example, you add the following line to the end of the PATH line:

```
;c:\util
```

It doesn't matter whether you use capital or small letters.

7. **Choose File⇨Save from the menu bar to save your changes.**

8. **Choose File⇨Exit from the menu bar to leave the Notepad program.**

9. **Exit from Windows by choosing File⇨Exit from the Program Manager's menu bar. Choose OK to tell it that you really want to leave.**

10. **Restart your computer. If you have a reset button, use it. Otherwise, press Ctrl+Alt+Del (so that all the keys are down at once).**

Your computer restarts and then DOS does. If you usually have to type something to get Windows started, do it.

Now you have a place to put your new programs, and you have told DOS to look in this new directory when it looks for programs.

Where Does All This Software Come From?

You can find WinSock software in several places:

- ✔ Your Internet provider may offer it on a disk. That's certainly the easiest way to get it.

- ✔ Your Internet provider may make it available from a shell account. You use Windows Terminal (or a better terminal program, such as ProComm, if you have it) to download it.

- ✔ You can get it from a BBS. We've arranged with Channel 1, a large BBS, to make available at no charge the basic files for Trumpet WinSock (a widely used shareware WinSock).

We authors are lazy typists, and Trumpet WinSock is an awfully long name, so from here on we refer to it as TWS, pronounced "TWS."

A Channel 1 sandwich

Strange but true: The offices of the Channel 1 BBS are on the third floor of a building down the street from Harvard University, and about a mile from *Internet For Dummies* Central. The offices of Del-phi are on the second and fourth floors *of the very same building.* Can this be a coincidence?

Yes, but we're sure that if we think hard enough, we can invent a conspiracy to explain it.

Is that really a newt?

You may have available full or sampler versions of commercial Windows TCP/IP packages from vendors such as NetManage's Chameleon or Frontier's SuperTCP. As this book went to press, Microsoft had released a beta-test version of its own TCP/IP for Windows for Workgroups 3.11, and eventually for the next version of Windows, currently code-named Chicago.

If you have one of these products available, you might as well use that rather than TWS because the commercial versions tend to be somewhat better supported and sometimes faster. Part of the charm of WinSock is that it is an actual standard, so no matter which version of WinSock you have, you can install and run the other applications in Chapters 9 through 14.

What if I'm already on a network?

If your PC is already connected to a network via a modem, you can still use TWS to communicate by way of SLIP. Just be sure that no other program is trying to use your modem at the same time as TWS does.

It's also possible to configure TWS to use a real Ethernet network rather than a modem, but the instructions for that are, unfortunately, way be-yond what we can print here. The details depend on the type of network, the particular brand and model of network card installed in your computer, and what (if any) other network software is already installed.

Whoever runs your existing network is the right person to talk to, to find out whether it makes sense to install TWS also.

Socket to Me, BBS Version

We give the instructions for downloading the software from a BBS because we know that they work if you have a computer and a modem. If your provider offers you the software, you can presumably get some advice from it about what's required to get it into your computer.

The big picture, SLIP-wise

The way you get your Windows PC set up for SLIP or PPP is shown in these steps:

1. **Arrange for a SLIP or PPP account from a local provider.**

   See the coupons in the back of this book for a few possibilities. Or ask your local Internet nerd for advice about this step (bring munchies).

2. **Get the basic SLIP or PPP software loaded into your computer somehow, either from a disk or over the phone.**

   Use the software your SLIP provider gives you, if any, or follow the instructions later in this chapter to get TWS.

3. **Type about a thousand setup parameters (discussed in Table 8-1 earlier in chapter).**

4. **Crank up SLIP or PPP and fiddle with it until it works.**

After you've done that, you can go on to load the swell applications later in the next chapter.

The many phone numbers of Channel 1

Any large BBS has a zillion phone numbers. If you want to download the software from there, you have to use at least one of these numbers. (In case it's not obvious, use the number that corresponds to the fastest speed your modem can handle.) If you don't happen to be a local call away from Cambridge, Massachusetts, prefix each number with 1-617 (assuming you are in the U.S.).

2400 bps	354-7077 or 354-8873
14,400 bps	354-3230 or 354-5776
28,000 bps	349-1370
HST modems	354-3137 or 354-2505

Downloading the basic files

Assuming that you're using the basic shareware TWS, you need three files to get going:

✔ The TWS file that contains the actual SLIP and PPP code, called TWSK10A.ZIP for version 1.0A

✔ The basic accessories file that contains a few WinSock applications you need to get going, called WINAPPS.ZIP

✔ An unzipping program, such as WinZip (our favorite, because it works with Windows), PKUNZIP, or UNZIP, because both the preceding files in this list are in zipped format (if you don't have one, we'll tell you how to download UNZIP from a BBS)

If you already have the requisite files on disk, you can skip the next section on downloading them from a BBS.

Calling the BBS

We assume that your Windows computer is plugged in and turned on, as is your modem (if it's the kind of modem with its own on-off switch), and that they're connected. If not, consult *Modems For Dummies,* by Tina Rathbone (IDG Books Worldwide), which discusses the secrets of modems in far more detail than we can do here.

Follow these steps to call the BBS:

1. **In Windows, if you haven't already done so, create a directory called** \UTIL **by using the File Manager.**

   All your WinSock utility programs and files go here.

2. **From the Accessories window in the Program Manager, run Terminal, the World's Most Generic Terminal Program.**

   (To be fair, it's the World's Most Generic Windows Terminal Program.) If you have another terminal program you like better, feel free to use it instead.

3. **From the Terminal menu, choose Settings⇨Phone Number and set the phone number to something appropriate (1-617-354-3230 if you have a 14,400 bps modem, for example).**

   If you have to dial something special before the number (a 9 for an outside line, for example), put that before the number. If you're making a long-distance call, change the Timeout field from 30 to 60 seconds.

4. **Choose Settings⇨Terminal Emulation and be sure that it's set to DEC VT-100.**

5. **Choose Settings⇨Terminal Preferences and set the Terminal Font to Terminal.**

   If you don't, some of the BBS menus will be unreadable.

6. **Choose Settings⇨Binary Transfers, and be sure that Kermit is selected.**

   If you are using a better communications program than Windows Terminal, select ZMODEM if possible, otherwise YMODEM, and otherwise Kermit.

7. **On the Settings⇨Communications menu, be sure that the parameters are set appropriately for your modem.**

   The baud rate (really *bits per second*) should be 19200 unless your modem runs at 2400 bps or slower, in which case you should use the actual modem speed. Flow Control should be Hardware, Connector should be COM1 unless your modem is attached to a different port, and Carrier Detect should be checked.

8. **On the Settings⇨Modem Commands menu, you can be as creative as you want in fiddling with dialing commands, although the default settings are usually OK.**

   Choose the Hayes default unless you have one of the other kinds of modem listed.

9. **If your phone line uses click rather than tone dialing, change the dial prefix from ATDT (short for *Ahoy There, Dial the Telephone*) to ATDP (short for *Ahoy There, Dial the Phone*).**

   At this point, save the setup parameters so that you don't have to do all this again if you have to call back. Choose File⇨Save As and name your configuration CHANNEL1. The next time you use Windows Terminal, you can choose File⇨Open and double-click CHANNEL1, and all the settings are restored.

10. **From the menu, select Phone⇨Dial.**

   Terminal should dial the phone and connect to Channel 1. If not, check the phone number. If your modem has a speaker, what you hear should give you a clue about what went wrong. (Did you need an initial 9? Forget the area code? Get a busy signal?)

   You may well get a busy signal. Try a few times, then try another number, and then try again later (choosing an off-peak kind of time).

   When you connect, Channel 1 gives you a list of languages in which you can work.

11. **If you find English adequate for your computing needs, press Enter. Then it asks whether you want color prompts. Press Enter again for No.**

    (They're cute, but they're slow.)

    Finally it gets around to asking for your first and last names. You have to register to use Channel 1, although it allows limited access, including downloading all the WinSock files you need, without charge. (If you like what you see, you might consider signing up for a regular paid account, as we have.)

12. **Type in your first and last names.**

    It should notice that it doesn't know your name and ask whether it should Continue and sign you up.

13. **Press C and Enter.**

    Then it asks for a bunch of registration information, such as your address and type of computer. Yes, you want to register, and no, you don't have to pay anything unless you decide to use Channel 1 beyond the introductory offer. Most of the questions are pretty self-explanatory, like your phone number.

14. **For the Default Transfer Protocol, enter K for Kermit.**

    (It warns you that it's slow. Don't worry about it.)

    If you are using a better communications program than Windows Terminal, feel free to choose a faster transfer protocol. Our preferred protocol is ZMODEM. Choose the same one your communications program is configured to use.

15. **Lots of introductory screens appear. Press Enter after you have looked at each one.**

    When it asks Channel 1 Command?, you're in business — you have logged in as a valid user.

16. **Type J FREE to join the free files area where WinSock files are found.**

17. **Press Enter after each screen until it asks Free Conference Command?**

    At long last, you're ready to download something. This is actually the easy part.

18. **Press D (for download) and Enter. When it asks for the filename, enter TWSK10A.ZIP.**

    It should tell you a few things about the file, such as how long it will take you to download it, and then say something like this:

    ```
    , Sz* @-#Y1~^
    ```

    which means "hello" in Kermit-ese.

19. **From the menu, choose Transfer⇨Receive Binary File. In Directories, move to your \UTIL directory. In the File Name box, type the name of the file to receive, the same name you just told Channel 1 to download (TWSK10A.ZIP, in this case), and then press Enter.**

   Yes, it's stupid that you have to type it twice. Lucky for us we're downloading this stuff only once.

   Windows Terminal should display a bar at the bottom of the window saying that it's downloading the file, with a counter that begins counting the amount of data received. The warnings that Kermit is slow are indeed true, so this would be a good time to run down the hall for a cup of coffee or other beverage of your choice.

20. **Download WINAPPS.ZIP, the same way you downloaded TWSK10A.ZIP.**

21. **If you don't already have an unzipping program like WinZip or PKUNZIP, download UNZIP.EXE.**

   You're finished downloading.

22. **Press G for Good-bye to hang up and then leave Windows Terminal.**

Basic installation, Part I

With luck, you now have the distribution files TWSK10A.ZIP and WINAPPS.ZIP copied to your \UTIL directory.

A note to people who skipped the preceding section because they have a floppy disk with the software: Now would be a good time to copy the ZIP files from the floppy to \UTIL on the hard disk.

Unzip the two distribution files. If you have WinZip installed (see Chapter 9 for more about that), you can use it to extract all the files into \UTIL.

If you don't have WinZip yet . . .

. . . you need UNZIP or PKUNZIP, which run in MS-DOS, not in Windows:

1. **Start the MS-DOS prompt from Windows.**

2. **Type** cd \util.

   Or whatever directory you put the downloaded files in.

3. **Type** unzip twsk10a.

   (If you have PKUNZIP, you can type pkunzip twsk10a instead.) UNZIP should extract all the TWS files.

4. **Type** `unzip winapps`.

(If you have PKUNZIP, you can type `pkunzip winapps` instead.) UNZIP extracts all the basic WinSock application files. If it asks whether it should replace `readme.msg` and other files, type **y** to replace all of them.

5. **Type** `exit` **to return to Windows.**

Making icons

Because several of these programs are actually useful, it's worth making a Program Manager group and icons for them.

1. **In the Windows Program Manager, choose File⇨New from the menu.**

2. **Click Program Group and then OK.**

You see the Program Group Properties dialog box.

3. **For Program Description, type** `WinSock Programs` **(or anything else you want). Click OK.**

A new program group containing no files should appear.

4. **Now switch to the File Manager (clicking its icon in the Program Manager should do the trick) and show the `\UTIL` directory. Arrange the screen so that you can see both the files in the `\UTIL` directory and the empty WinSock Programs group window.**

5. **Click on the EXE files of interest in the File Manager and drag them into the WinSock Programs group window.**

Files to drag include `FTPW.EXE`, `TCPMAN.EXE`, `PINGW.EXE`,, `WINARCH.EXE`. Your group window should end up looking more or less like Figure 8-1.

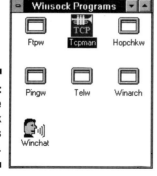

Figure 8-1:
The
WinSock
Programs
group.

This all seems awfully complicated

By this time, you're probably wondering whether all this clicking, typing, and installing will ever end and whether there might perhaps be a simpler way.

The answer to the first question is yes, it will. This stuff is a pain in the neck to get set up, but after it's set up, it's pretty easy to use — two or three clicks to start a network connection, and later another two or three to shut it down.

The answer to the second question is, um, well, yeah, it could be considerably easier. Ideally, there *should* be a nice full-screen setup program that prompts you through the standard questions. (Although, in defense of TWS, we have installed many commercial TCP/IP packages and they aren't a heck of a lot better.) So for the moment, you just have to keep slogging.

Any minute now, you'll use TCPMAN to connect to the network. Then you'll use Pingw to test your connection. In the next chapter, we explain how to use Ftpw (a FTP program) to download software from the net. (WinArch is an Archie client program. Chapter 19 in *The Internet For Dummies* explains how to use Archie — we don't say more about it here.)

Basic installation, Part II

Okay, now you should have an attractive Trumpet icon labeled TCPMAN in your Program Manager. Double-click it to start it. You should see a window like the one in Figure 8-2.

Here's how to tell it about your particular Internet SLIP provider and who you are.

1. **Click the box called Internal SLIP.**

   This step tells it that you'll be communicating by using SLIP over a modem, instead of than using a hard-wired Ethernet. It thoughtfully grays out the fields that don't matter when you're using SLIP. (Amazing, huh?)

   Now you can fill in the fields based on information from your SLIP provider.

2. **Enter your IP address.**

   That is, enter your computer's numeric Internet address. If your system uses "floating" addresses assigned each time you connect, leave this as zeros.

3. **Enter your name server.**

   Enter the numeric Internet address of the provider's computer that handles the decoding of computer host names.

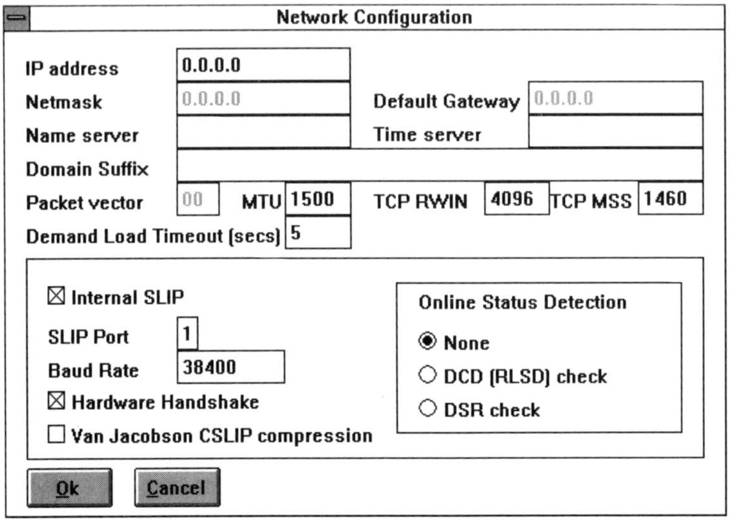

Figure 8-2:
The TWS
configuration
screen.

4. **Leave the time server box blank.**

   It doesn't do anything useful in this version of TWS.

5. **Enter your Domain suffix.**

   Type the name domain in which your computer will live, which is your computer's name but omitting the first part. For example, because one of our computer's names is *chico.iecc.com,* its domain suffix is *iecc.com.*

6. **Enter your MTU.**

   Enter the maximum data packet size your provider can handle efficiently. If your provider doesn't give you an MTU, use the MSS (described in step 8, coming right up) plus 40, so if the MSS is 512, the MTU is 552, and if the MSS is 255, the MTU is 295.

7. **Enter your TCP RWIN, whatever that is.**

   Yes, it's another magic parameter. Leave it as 4096 unless your provider gives you a different value.

8. **Enter your TCP MSS.**

   This is a third magic parameter. Unless your provider gives you a different value, use 512 if you have a SLIP connection and 255 for CSLIP connections.

9. **Leave the Demand Load Timeout as 5 seconds.**

10. **Leave the Internal SLIP box checked.**

11. **Enter your SLIP Port.**

Enter the number of the COM port to which your modem is attached: 1 for COM1, 2 for COM2.

12. **Enter a Baud Rate.**

    Enter 38400 if you have a 486 or Pentium, or 19200 if you have a 386.

13. **Leave the Hardware Handshake box checked unless you have a really cruddy old modem that doesn't properly signal the computer when the remote end connects.**

14. **Choose whether to use Van Jacobsen CSLIP compression.**

    (Does this sound arcane or what?) If your provider uses CSLIP, check this; if uses SLIP, don't.

15. **Select your Online status-detection method.**

    Select DCD unless you have a cruddy old modem.

16. **Recheck all those settings to be sure that they're right and then click OK.**

    A box appears, warning you that you have to restart WinSock for your changes to take effect. (Just WinSock, not all of Windows.)

17. **Click OK.**

    The regular WinSock window, which we'll consider in a moment, appears.

18. **Choose File⇨Exit to leave WinSock and then double-click its icon in the Program Manager to restart it (cognizant of all and the swell things you've told it).**

If you have to go back and change any of these things, you can get back to this screen by choosing File⇨Setup from the TWS menu.

Actually making an actual SLIP connection

Thought this moment would never come, eh? Well, it's about time. There are two ways (one way would be too simple — computers are involved here) to tell TWS to dial and make a connection: the manual way and the automatic way. The manual way is extremely manual: You type commands directly to your modem to make the connection and start the SLIP or CSLIP session and then tell TWS to go ahead. The automatic way involves a script that tells TWS what to send to the modem, what to expect from the remote system, what to type next, and so forth until the connection is made. The manual way works perfectly well if you don't mind doing the typing every time, although we find that it's worth the effort to set it up the automatic way.

Dial ho!

"All right already," you're doubtless saying. "Let's cut to the chase." Okay. Your TWS window should look like this:

```
Trumpet WinSock Version 1.0 Rev A
Copyright (c) 1993,1994 by Peter R. Tattam
All Rights Reserved.
THIS IS AN UNREGISTERED SHAREWARE VERSION FOR EVALUATION ONLY
SLIP ENABLED
Internal SLIP driver COM1 Baud rate = 38400
Hardware handshaking Compression enabled
My ip = 199.0.65.90 netmask = 0.0.0.0 gateway = 0.0.0.0
```

The baud rate, handshaking, compression, and IP numbers should reflect what you told TWS when you typed the zillion setup numbers.

1. **Choose Dialler⇨Manual login from the menu.**

   TWS should say:

   ```
   AFTER LOGGING IN, TYPE THE <ESC> KEY TO RETURN TO NORMAL
           SLIP PROCESSING.
   SLIP DISABLED
   ```

   Not being clairvoyant, you might not be able to guess that this message is TWS's way of telling you to begin typing.

2. **So type whatever your modem needs in order to make the connection.**

   For our modem, we get its attention by typing AT and then typing a command that tells it always to use the port connection speed we programmed in (&B1) regardless of the connection speed at the other end and to use hardware modem flow control (&H1). Sorry to say, modem command settings are among the least well-standardized features of the PC biz. You can probably get by with whatever settings your modem comes with. Failing that, try the ones we use (AT&B1&H1) or — gasp — see whether the modem manual makes any suggestions. For example, type:

   ```
   AT&B1&H1
   ```

   and press Enter. The modem says *OK*.

3. **Tell the modem *Ahoy There, Dial the Telephone!* and give it our provider's phone number.**

   For example, type:

   ```
   ATDT555-2368
   ```

It dials the phone, and when it makes the connection it says:

```
CONNECT 14400/ARQ
```

Holy Digital Data Stream, Batperson! We're connected. Now our provider greets us, and we type our login name and password. (No, we're not going to tell you what it is. We're not totally stupid. Almost, but not totally.)

4. **Type in your login name and password.**

Your Internet provider displays some kind of message, like this:

```
Welcome to the Internet Access Co. Type 'new' at login and
      'new' for password to register for a new UNIX
      shell account. login: dummies
Password: ********
SL/IP session from (199.0.65.12) to 199.0.65.90 beginning....
```

Hey, how about that? SLIP started.

5. **Now tell TWS that the connection has started, by pressing Esc.**

You see a message like this:

```
SLIP ENABLED
```

That's it — you're connected.

Testing your connection

Later, we come back and look at more details of making a connection, but first let's check and make sure that the connection works. You can use a program called Pingw, a little program that pings remote hosts to make sure that you can in fact reach them. Pingw is one of the programs that was contained in the winapps.zip file you downloaded and that you made an icon for in your WinSock.

1. **Go back to the Program Manager and fire up Pingw.**

Pingw asks for you to type in the name of the host to ping.

2. **Either type the name of your provider's name server computer or use a well-known system like** `internic.net` **and press Enter.**

If it works, you should see a list of responses like the ones in Figure 8-3. The rtt numbers are the *round-trip* time it took for the ping to travel from your host to the other one and back (we bet that you expected it to be more obscure than that). The round-trip time is reported in milliseconds

(1/1000 second), so a round-trip time of 219 is 219/1000 seconds, or about a fifth of a second. This is a reasonable round-trip time for a SLIP message; if it's consistently more than 350, there's probably a setup problem. (In particular, make sure that your setup has MTU and MTS set to 512 or less, not the default 1500.)

```
─                        C:\UTIL\PINGW.EXE                     ▼ ▲
Trumpet PING - Copyright (c) 1992 by P.R.Tattam, all rights reserved ◆
host : internic.net
Trying 198.41.0.5
198.41.0.5      id=      1 rtt =       384ms period =    1000
198.41.0.5      id=      2 rtt =       219ms period =    1000
198.41.0.5      id=      3 rtt =       220ms period =    1000
198.41.0.5      id=      4 rtt =       219ms period =    1000
198.41.0.5      id=      5 rtt =       220ms period =    1000
198.41.0.5      id=      6 rtt =       274ms period =    1000
198.41.0.5      id=      7 rtt =       275ms period =    1000
198.41.0.5      id=      8 rtt =       220ms period =    1000




                                                              ◆
◆                                                             ◆
```

Figure 8-3:
Pinging the
InterNIC.

3. Exit from Pingw when you are done.

More About Connections

If you're satisfied with manual dialing, you can skip the rest of this chapter and go on to Chapter 9, in which we tell you how to set up a bunch of other useful Internet software. Or you can skip it for now and come back when you get tired of typing the commands all the time.

For our example, here's a slightly more complex login setup at another regional provider, ClarkNet (what we typed is in boldface):

```
atz
OK
at&c1&b1
OK
ATDT5551212
CONNECT 14400/ARQ Annex Command Line Interpreter   *   Copy-
```

```
               right 1991 Xylogics, Inc. Checking authorization,
               Please wait...
Connecting to port 37 using AT&T Paradyne V.32bis/V.42bis
               modem
Welcome to ClarkNet! Log in as "guest" for ClarkNet info and
               registration.
ClarkNet Username: dummies
ClarkNet Password: *******
Permission granted
       ClarkNet's Menu
   Now using Class B network address.
   1)   Enter clarknet host (UUCP users only)
   2)   Enter explorer host (All users and guest)
   3)   SLIP (SLIP users only)
   4)   PPP (PPP users only)
   5)   Hosts? (All users)
   6)   Who? (All users)
   7)   telnet (IP users only)
   8)   Exit (All users)
Enter Number (1-8): 3
Switching to SLIP.
Annex address is 168.143.0.4.  Your address is 168.143.1.87.
```

It's all in the script

TWS supports *scripts,* which are not altogether unlike the script for a play. The
script describes what you (or the computer on your behalf) type, what the
modem or remote computer responds, what your computer types next, what
the next response should be, and so on. In the preceding example, the computer types a couple of modem commands, with the modem replying OK
after each one. Then the computer dials the phone, and the modem says
CONNECTED and some other junk. The remote system prompts you with
Username, the computer types the login name, the remote system prompts you
with Password, and the computer types the password. Then there's a long
menu from the remote that ends with a request to enter the number to choose,
and the computer types 3. The script has to automate all that typing.

TWS uses two scripts that are stored in files: login.cmd, which logs you in, and
bye.cmd, which hangs up the modem, and it comes with sample versions of
both. Fortunately, the way you hang up a modem is now standardized well
enough that the bye script always works, so we concentrate on the login script.
From the Dialler menu (it's not misspelled — the author's from Australia),
choose Edit⇨Scripts and then double-click login.cmd to start the Windows
Notepad working on that script.

Here's the script for ClarkNet login (we go through it bit by bit afterward):

```
#
# initialize modem
#
output atz\r
input 10 OK\n
#
# set modem to indicate DCD
#
output at&c1&b1\r
input 10 OK\n
#
# send phone number
#
output atdt5552368\r
#
# now we are connected.
#
input 30 CONNECT
#
#  wait till it's safe to send because some modems hang up
#  if you transmit during the connection phase
#
wait 30 dcd
#
#  wait for the username prompt
#
input 30 name:
output dummies\r
#
# and the password
#
input 30 word:
output hahaha\r
#
# we are now logged in
# so start SLIP
input 30 (1-8):
output 3\r display \n
display Connected. \n
#
#
```

```
# now we are finished.
#
online
```

In case it's not obvious, script lines that start with a sharp sign (#) are comments. The computer disregards them, because they're present for the benefit of humans who have to read the script.

This script starts by sending some initialization commands to the modem. In the script, an output line is something to the remote system. (The **\r** is the Enter key, which used to be known as Carriage Return.) An input line is followed by a maximum number of seconds to wait and the message to wait for the modem or remote system to send.

```
#
# initialize modem
#
output atz\r
input 10 OK\n
#
# set modem to indicate DCD
#
output at&c1&b1\r
input 10 OK\n
```

Now we tell the modem to dial the phone. Then we wait as long as 30 seconds for a CONNECT message. Then a wait command says to wait as long as 30 seconds for the modem to turn on the DCD signal, which means that the modem is indeed connected to the remote system.

```
#
# send phone number
#
output atdt5552368\r
#
# now we are connected.
#
input 30 CONNECT
#
#  wait till it's safe to send because some modems hang up
#  if you transmit during the connection phase
#
wait 30 dcd
```

After the modem's connected, we wait for the remote host to prompt us to enter our username. (The input line doesn't have to give everything the remote will send — just enough of it for the computer to figure out when it's time to send the next message.)

```
#
#  wait for the username prompt
#
input 30 name:
output dummies\r
```

We wait for the Password prompt (notice that, as lazy typists, we wait for only the tail end of it) and send the password. No, that's still not our real password.

```
#
# and the password
#
input 30 word:
output hahaha\r
```

In consulting the preceding example, we see that ClarkNet displays a long menu, ending with a prompt that ends with (1-8):. So we wait for that prompt and then type **3**, the entry we want.

```
#
# we are now logged in
# so start SLIP
input 30 (1-8):
output 3\r
```

A display line displays a message merely for the benefit of the user sitting and watching TWS (that is, you). A final online line tells TWS that the connection is made and the script is finished.

```
display Connected. \n
#
#
# now we are finished.
#
online
```

Your login.cmd script is a variation of this script. Make notes of what the remote says and what your computer has to type, and write alternating input and output lines. The modem-dialing lines (other than the phone number) and the display and output at the end should work as is (as are?).

Using your login script

After you've made a stab at creating a login script, save it and leave Notepad and try running it by choosing Dialler Login from the TWS menu. If it works, it should dial the phone, log you in, display Connected, and end with TWS saying SLIP ENABLED. But unless you're incredibly lucky, it doesn't work on the first try. Look to see where the script messed up. Then go back into Notepad by way of Dialler Edit Scripts and fix the lines starting at the place where it messed up. For all but the most horrible dialing situations, you should be able to get it to work on the second or third try. For more hints about dialing scripts, see the install.txt file that comes with TWS.

After your script works to your satisfaction, choose Dialler⇨Options and select Automatic Login on Start Up only followed by OK. This step says that, in the future, whenever you start up TWS from the Program Manager, run the login script immediately so that you get connected right away.

Hanging Up

One last important detail: How do you hang up a SLIP connection? Fortunately, it's pretty easy:

1. **Close any WinSock programs that are running.**

2. **In TWS, choose Dialler⇨Bye to hang up the phone.**

3. **Choose File⇨Exit to exit.**

Don't just tell TWS to exit, because it will, but without hanging up the phone. Be sure to hang up explicitly before you leave TWS.

Don't forget to register

TWS is shareware and pretty darned good shareware at that. If you use TWS regularly, please look at the file install.txt, which includes the registration instructions, including the address (in Australia) to which to send the form and check.

Some of the other programs that you downloaded in the winapps.zip file are shareware, too. If they are worth using, they are worth registering.

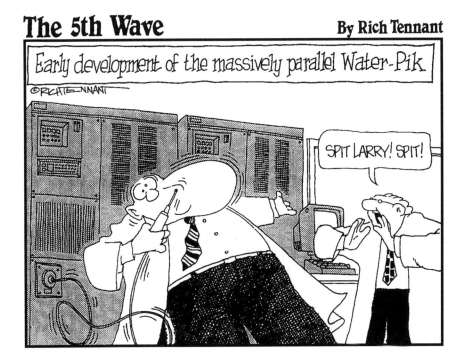

Chapter 9
Grabbing Software over the Net

● ●

In This Chapter

▶ Uncompressing compressed files with WinZip

▶ Checking software for viruses

▶ Installing software in Windows Program Manager

▶ Using FTP to copy programs to your computer

● ●

*A*fter you have installed Trumpet WinSock or something like it and you have an FTP program, you are ready to grab software right off the Internet. All the programs described in the rest of this part of the book, in fact, are available as freeware or shareware by FTP.

Luckily, the winapps.zip file you downloaded in Chapter 9 contains a simple FTP program called Ftpw. It's not the best one around — in fact, we tell you how to get a better one called WS_FTP — but it works.

There are a few things to know, however, about downloading and running software from the net, and this chapter tells you about them. You need a few well-chosen software tools, including a program to uncompress compressed files. Useful little programs like this are usually called *utilities* in the jargon.

The instructions in this chapter and in the rest of the chapters in this part of the book assume that you are using a PC running DOS and Windows. If you are using a Macintosh, you'll be using different unzipping software and a different FTP program. The concepts, however, are the same.

Ready to Decompress: UNZIP and WinZip

You need an unzipping program to deal with compressed files, specifically those with the file extension *.zip* (these are called, amazingly, *ZIP files*). Programs with names like PKZIP, PKUNZIP, and UNZIP have been around for years — if you followed the steps in Chapter 8, you downloaded UNZIP and used it to uncompress the other files you grabbed.

UNZIP and its brethren work fine, but they are DOS programs and not real convenient to use from Windows. It's annoying to use the MS-DOS icon every time you want to run one. Luckily, someone (a guy named Nico Mak) wrote a nice, little Windows program called WinZip that can both unzip and zip things for you, right from Windows.

Grabbing WinZip

To install WinZip, there are three major steps: copy the files, unzip WinZip, and create an icon for WinZip. For now, we use the Ftpw program you got with Trumpet WinSock to do the transferring. Here we go.

If you already have WinZip (which is also available through the mail or from various shareware outlets), skip this entire section. If you have and love PKZIP and PKUNZIP or UNZIP and don't mind running them from DOS, you can skip it too.

1. **Connect to the Internet.**

   That is, run the Tcpman program and choose Connect from the menu bar. Or use whatever program you use to get connected.

2. **When you are connected, run the Ftpw program or another FTP program.**

   Figure 9-1 shows the Ftpw program, asking you for the host name of the FTP server from which you want to snag some files. (The rest of the steps describe using Ftpw. Just follow along if you use another program.)

3. **Enter** `oak.oakland.edu` **as the host name to connect to.**

4. **When it asks for a username, enter** `anonymous`.

   It invents a suitable password to appease the Password Gods at the other end of the connection.

5. **Type** `lcd \util` **to make Ftpw store incoming files in your** `\util` **directory.**

6. **Type** `bin` **to tell it that you are transferring binary files, not text.**

7. **Type** `cd /pub/msdos/windows3`.

   This command moves you to the directory that contains WinZip.

8. **Type** `dir win*.*`.

   Ftpw displays the names of files that begin with *win*. You see a file named something like winzip5b.zip (it may have another name if a newer version exists).

9. **Type** `get winzip5b.zip` **or whatever the current filename is.**

   Ftpw copies the file from the remote system to yours.

10. Type `quit` **to disconnect from the remote system.**

11. **Press Alt+F4 to exit from Ftpw.**

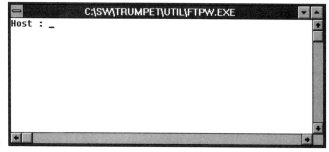

Figure 9-1:
Using Ftpw
to grab a
program
from the
Internet.

If you have trouble getting the files from the `oak.oakland.edu` FTP site, try
FTP-ing to `ftp.uu.net` and looking in the directory `/pub/archiving/zip`.
Alternatively, FTP to `wuarchive.wustl.edu` and go to the directory
`/mirrors/msdos/zip`.

Uncompressing WinZip

Now you can unzip the ZIP file that contains WinZip (say *that* three times fast).
This process requires typing a DOS command, so hold on to your hat. **Note:**
You must have PKUNZIP or similar DOS unzipper to unzip WinZip.

To uncompress WinZip:

1. **In Program Manager, double-click the MS-DOS icon so that you see a
   DOS prompt.**

2. **Type this line:**

   ```
   cd c:\util
   ```

   If you put the WinZip file in a different directory, type that directory name
   instead. Press Enter.

3. **Type** `unzip` **and the name of the ZIP file that contains WinZip, like this:**

   ```
   unzip winzip5b.zip
   ```

   UNZIP unzips (inflates, it claims) the files in that ZIP file, and you see the
   list of filenames as they appear.

4. **When you are finished unzipping, type** `exit` **to return to Windows.**

Now you have the WinZip program, which is contained in several files. No more
DOS commands for you!

Making WinZip easy to run

You want an icon for WinZip in the Program Manager. Also, if you ever run programs from the Windows File Manager, it's a good idea to *associate* WinZip with files that end with the file extension *.zip*. In the instructions in the rest of this book, we assume that you have done this so that double-clicking a ZIP file in File Manager automagically runs WinZip.

To accomplish these two feats:

1. **Arrange your screen so that you can see both the Program Manager program group you want the WinZip icon to be in and the winzip.exe file in File Manager.**

2. **Drag the winzip.exe file into the program group in Program Manager.**

   Poof! A nice little icon appears in Program Manager. Now you are ready to tell File Manager what to do when you click a ZIP file.

3. **In File Manager, choose File Associate from the menu.**

   You see the window in Figure 9-2.

4. **In the Files with Extension box, type** ZIP.

5. **In the Associate With box, type the full pathname of the WinZip program.**

   If it is in a directory called c:\util, for example, type this line:

   ```
   c:\util\winzip.exe
   ```

6. **Click OK.**

Figure 9-2:
Associating
WinZip with
ZIP files.

Associate		
<u>F</u>iles with Extension:	ZIP	OK
<u>A</u>ssociate With:		Cancel
C:\UTIL\WINZIP.EXE		
[None]		Browse...
AmiPro Document [C:\SW\AMIPRO\AMIP[		
Calendar File [calendar.exe]		<u>H</u>elp
Card File [cardfile.exe]		
Media Player [MPlayer.exe]		

Now File Manager knows that if you double-click a ZIP file, it should run WinZip to deal with it. Or you can run WinZip by double-clicking its icon. Very handy!

Running WinZip

Give it a try! Double-click that icon!

The very first time

The first time you run WinZip, it displays a bunch of helpful messages, including asking you about your intention to register your copy (we talk about this subject at the end of this chapter). It also offers to make an icon for itself in the Accessories program group in Program Manager.

One of the dialog boxes you see looks like Figure 9-3.

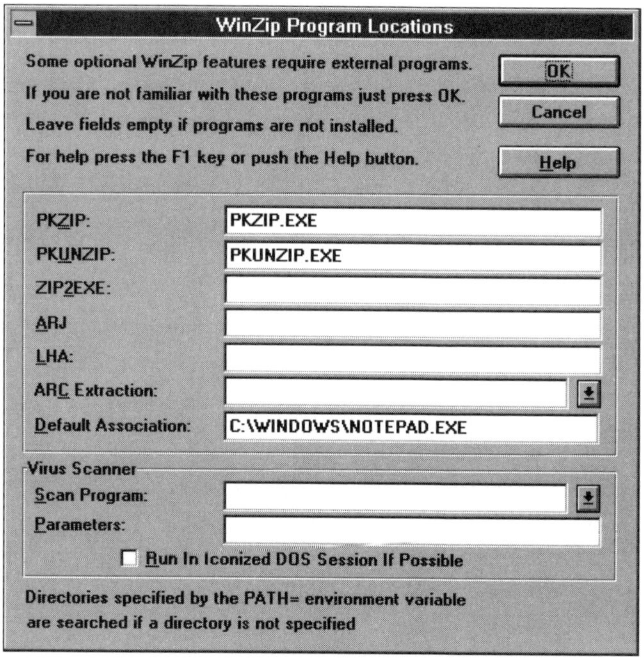

Figure 9-3:
WinZip asks you all kinds of questions the first time you run it.

WinZip looks on your hard disk for other compression programs it might want to use for handling compressed files other than ZIP files. Don't worry — if you don't have any other compression programs, WinZip works just fine by itself. Just click OK.

WinZip's window

After WinZip is finished with its configuration questions, you see a window that looks like Figure 9-4.

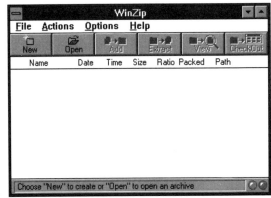

Figure 9-4:
WinZip is
ready to
deal with
your ZIP
files.

To open a ZIP file (which the WinZip folks call an *archive*), click the Open button and choose the directory and filename for the ZIP file. Poof! WinZip displays a list of the files in the archive, with their dates and sizes.

WinZip remembers the last four ZIP files you opened and lists them at the bottom of the File menu. This makes it easy to reopen a ZIP file you used recently.

Unzip it!

Sounds suggestive, we know, but it's not as much fun as it sounds. If you want to use a file from a ZIP file, after you have opened the ZIP file, you *extract* it — that is, you ask WinZip to uncompress it and store it in a new file.

To extract a file:

1. Choose it from the list of files.

You can choose a group of files that are listed together by clicking the first one and then Shift-clicking the last one. To select an additional file, Ctrl+click it.

2. Click the Extract button.

A dialog box asks which directory you want to put the file in and whether you want to extract all the files in the archive or just the one you selected.

3. **Select the directory in which to store the unzipped files.**

4. **Click OK.**

   WinZip unzips the file. The ZIP file is unchanged, but now you have the uncompressed file (or files) also.

Zip it!

To add a file to a ZIP file:

1. **Open the ZIP file by using the Open button.**

2. **Click the Add button.**

   You see the Add dialog box, shown in Figure 9-5.

3. **Select the directory that contains the file (or files) you want to add, by using the Directories/Drives box.**

   To choose the files, select them from the Select Files list.

4. **Choose a setting for the Action box.**

   Decide whether you want WinZip to compress the files into the ZIP file, leaving the original files untouched (Add), or whether you want WinZip to delete the original files after they have been added (Move).

5. **Click the Add button to do the deed.**

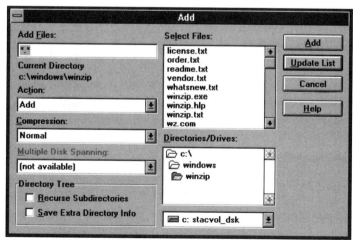

Figure 9-5:
Adding a file
to a ZIP file.

When you choose files, you can select a group of files that are listed together by clicking the first one and then Shift-clicking the last one. To select an additional file, press Ctrl and click it at the same time.

Making your own ZIP file

To make a new ZIP file:

1. **Click the New button in the WinZip window.**

2. **Choose the directory in which you want to store the new ZIP file and enter a name for the file.**

   Make sure that the file extension is *ZIP* (or omit the file extension, and WinZip adds *ZIP* itself).

3. **Click OK.**

4. **Add files to your new ZIP file, as explained in the preceding section.**

Zipped out?

When you are all finished zipping and unzipping, quit WinZip by choose File➪Exit.

Now that you know how to unzip software you get from the Internet, you're ready for the next topic: safe software.

Scanning for Viruses

We all know that you practice safe software. That is, you check every new program you get to make sure that it doesn't contain any hidden software viruses that might display obnoxious messages or trash your hard disk. If this is true of you, you can skip this section.

For the rest of you, it would be a good idea to use a virus-scanning program. You never know what naughty piece of code you might unwittingly FTP to your defenseless computer otherwise!

If you use MS-DOS 6.2 (or later)

DOS 6.2 comes with a virus checker built right into File Manager.

Here's how to use the virus checker:

1. **Run File Manager.**

2. **Choose Tools⇨Antivirus from the menu.**

   You see the Microsoft Anti-Virus window, shown in Figure 9-6.

3. **Choose a disk drive, by clicking it in the Drives box.**

4. **Click the Detect and Clean button.**

   If you are scanning a large hard disk for viruses, this step can take several minutes.

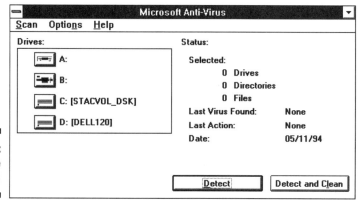

Figure 9-6:
Evict those
viruses!

It's a good idea to run Anti-Virus after you have obtained and run any new piece of software. The FTP servers on the Internet make every effort to keep their software archives virus-free, but nobody is perfect. Don't get caught by some prankster's idea of a joke!

If you don't use MS-DOS 6.2

It costs about $10 to upgrade from DOS 6.0 or 6.1 to 6.2, so we suggest that you just do it. DOS 6.2 has lots of nice little features, and it installs easily and quickly.

If you don't want to do this, many virus checkers are available on the net. Use your FTP program to connect to oak.oakland.edu, and go to the /pub/msdos/virus directory. Follow the instructions later in this chapter for downloading and installing software from the net.

Netting a Program

Now you are ready to grab software from the net, unzip it as necessary, make little icons for it, and check it all over for diseases. This section gives you general instructions for getting a program off the Internet and installing it on your PC. We are assuming that you know which program you want and that you know which FTP server has it.

Luckily, in the rest of the chapters in this part of the book, we tell you which programs we recommend and on which FTP servers you can find them. The programs include mail readers, news readers, Gopher programs, and programs for accessing the World Wide Web.

Getting hold of the program

To copy the file from the FTP server to your own computer:

1. **If you want to make a separate directory for the program, do so.**

   Otherwise, you can store it in your \util directory.

2. **Connect to the Internet.**

3. **Run Ftpw and connect to the FTP server that has the program you want.**

   Or connect to another FTP program you like better; see the section "Over Hill, Over Dale, As We Hit the FTP Trail," later in this chapter.

4. **Choose the directory on the FTP server that contains the file you want, and choose the directory on your computer in which to put it.**

   Use lcd to change to the directory on your computer where you want to store the files you've retrieved. Use cd to change to the directory on the server that contains the files.

5. **Type get** *xxx.yyy***, where** *xxx.yyy* **is the name of a file you want to retrieve.**

   You can do as many "gets" as necessary to get multiple files.

6. **Type** quit **and then press Alt+F4 to leave Ftpw.**

7. **Disconnect from the Internet, to save connect charges.**

Unzipping the program files

Most programs are stored on FTP servers in ZIP files, both to save disk space on the FTP server and to save transfer time while FTP-ing the file. If the program isn't in a ZIP file, skip this section.

1. **In Windows File Manager, double-click the ZIP file.**

   This step runs WinZip and opens the ZIP file. (If is doesn't, see the section "Making WinZip easy to run," earlier in this chapter.) WinZip shows you the files the ZIP file contains.

2. **Click the Extract button.**

   You see the Extract dialog box, shown in Figure 9-7.

3. **In the Extract To box, type the full pathname of the directory in which you want the files to be stored.**

   Alternatively, you can use the directory box to its right to choose the directory.

4. **Choose All Files so that you extract all the files in the ZIP file.**

5. **Click Extract.**

   WinZip begins copying and uncompressing the files from the ZIP file into their new home. As long as WinZip is uncompressing files, the little light in the lower right corner of the WinZip window remains red. When it's finished, it turns green. (it this cute or what?)

6. **To leave WinZip, choose File Exit.**

7. **Now that you have uncompressed the files that are in the ZIP file, you can delete the ZIP file if you need the space on your disk.**

Figure 9-7:
To get the compressed files from a ZIP file, just add water!

If the ZIP file contains any files named read.me or readme.txt or anything else with a *txt* or *doc* extension, read it by using Windows Notepad or your word-processing program. It may contain instructions for installing and configuring the program that are more accurate than what we are about to tell you.

Installing the program

Now the program is ready to run, but there is no icon for it. A few housekeeping tasks remain to be done. If the program uses files as input, associate it with the appropriate file extension. (Remember how you did this for WinZip?) These programs include editors, word processors, draw programs, and other programs that store their data in files. For programs that don't work on input files, you don't need to do this, so skip to Step 5.

1. **In File Manager, choose File⇨Associate from the menu.**

2. **In the Files with Extension box, type the file extension the program uses.**

3. **In the Associate With box, type the full pathname of the program.**

4. **Click OK.**

   Now make an icon for the program.

5. **Open both the Program Manager and File Manager and arrange the screen so that you can see the program group you want to put the icon in (in Program Manager) and the program name (in File Manager).**

6. **Drag the program name from the File Manager into the Program Manager and place it in the program group where you want it.**

   You see a new icon in your new program group.

Configuring the program

Now you can run the program by double-clicking its icon. Hooray!

You may have to tell the program, however, about your Internet address or your computer or who knows what before it can do its job. Refer to the text files, if any, that came with the program or choose Help from the program's menu bar to get more information about how to configure and run your new program.

In Chapters 10 through 14, we'll tell you how to configure each program we describe.

Over Hill, Over Dale, As We Hit the FTP Trail

The Ftpw program is perfectly adequate, but it is a 100-percent totally uncool piece of software that looks like it was designed in about 1978 (because it was). Fortunately, you have much cooler options.

Our favorite FTP program, WS_FTP, is available for free by FTP from the United States Military Academy. And you thought that they only learned how to fight wars!

Using Ftpw for the last time, FTP to `ftp.usma.gov`, change to `/pub/msdos`, and retrieve `ws_ftp.zip`. (Alternatively, FTP to `ftp.usma.edu` and look in the directory `/pub/msdos/winsock`.) Unzip and install WS_FTP, and use that rather than ugly, old Ftpw. Cool features include the ones in this list:

✔ Scrollable and selectable windows for the names of local and remote files and directories

✔ Clickable buttons for such common operations as connect, set binary mode, and so on

✔ Connection profiles, which save the host name, login name and password, and remote host directory of your favorite FTP sites; comes with a bunch of useful profiles already set

WS_FTP is good enough that even when we're using commercial WinSock packages that come with their own FTP programs, we still use WS_FTP because we like it the best.

Dialing for files

Here's how to use the WS_FTP program:

1. **Run the WS_FTP program by double-clicking its icon.**

   You see the FTP Client Connect To dialog box, shown in Figure 9-8. This dialog box lets you enter information about the FTP server you want to connect to. After you've entered this information, WS_FTP saves it so that you can easily connect to the save FTP server again.

2. **In the Config name box, enter the name you want to use for this FTP server.**

   If you want to FTP to `rtfm.mit.edu`, for example, which contains FAQs for all the USENET newsgroups, you might enter **USENET FAQ Central**.

3. **In the Host name box, enter the name of the FTP server.**

   This name can be a regular Internet name (such as `oak.oakland.edu`, another useful FTP server) or a numeric address.

4. **Leave the Host type box set to Auto Detect.**

   This step tells WS-FTP to guess which operating system the FTP server is using.

5. **If you actually have a username on the FTP server, enter your username and password in the User ID and Password boxes.**

   Otherwise, click the Anonymous FTP box. WS_FTP asks for your e-mail address, which it uses as your password (this is the usual thing to do when you FTP anonymously).

6. **Enter your address and click OK.**

   WS_FTP fills in the User ID and Password boxes for you.

   If you want WS-FTP to store the password in the Password box rather than ask you for it every time to connect to the FTP server, click the Save Password box so that it contains an X.

   Leave the account box blank, unless you have your own username on the FTP server and you know which account to enter.

7. **In the Remote Dir box, enter the directory you want to look in on the FTP server.**

   Alternatively, you can leave this box blank and look around yourself.

8. **In the Local Dir box, enter the directory on your own PC in which you want to store downloaded files.**

9. **Click the Save Config button to save this information.**

10. **Click OK.**

    WS_FTP tries to connect to the FTP server.

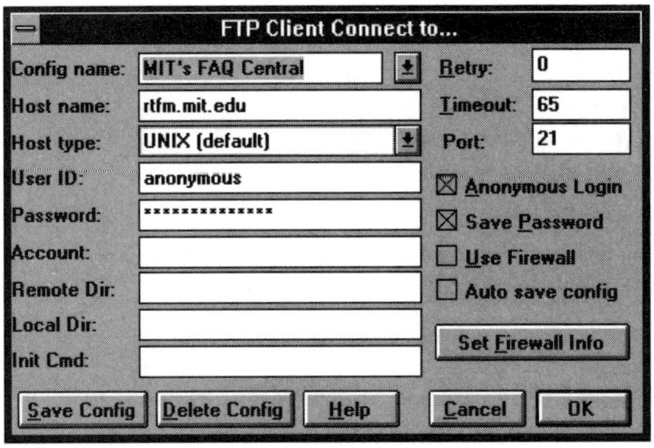

Figure 9-8:
Which FTP
server do
you want to
talk to?

FTP Client Connect to...	
Config name: MIT's FAQ Central	Retry: 0
Host name: rtfm.mit.edu	Timeout: 65
Host type: UNIX (default)	Port: 21
User ID: anonymous	☒ Anonymous Login
Password: **************	☒ Save Password
Account:	☐ Use Firewall
Remote Dir:	☐ Auto save config
Local Dir:	Set Firewall Info
Init Cmd:	
Save Config	Delete Config	Help	Cancel	OK

It won't speak to me!

If you have a problem connecting to the FTP server, messages appear in the two-line box at the bottom of the WS_FTP window. You can scroll this little window up and down to see what happened. For example, **rtfm.mit.edu** is frequently overloaded and doesn't let you log on. But it displays some helpful messages about other FTP sites that might have the information you want. You can see these messages in this box.

If you really want to see the messages the FTP server sent, double-click them. WS_FTP opens a big window so that you can see them better. To close it, click the Close button.

Do you copy?

After you are connected to the FTP server, you see the WS_FTP window, shown in Figure 9-9. WS_FTP displays information about the files on your own computer in the left side of the window (entitled Local PC Info) and the directories and files on the FTP server on the right side (entitled Remote Host Info). On each side are buttons that enable you to change directories (ChgDir), make directories (MkDir), delete directories (RmDir), view files, and so on. Naturally, you don't have permission to delete or change anything on most FTP servers, so don't even try.

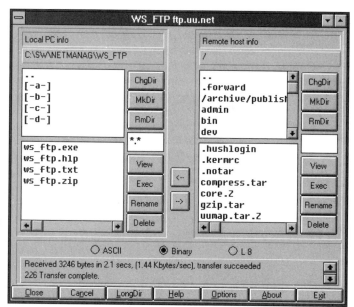

Figure 9-9:
Prepare to
receive
some files!

To move from directory to directory on the FTP server, choose directory names from the list box. Or you can click the ChDir button and enter the full pathname of the directory to go to.

Here's how to copy a file:

1. **Choose ASCII or Binary, using the buttons at the bottom of the window.**

   For files that consist entirely of text, choose ASCII. For anything else, choose Binary.

2. **Choose the file you want on the FTP server.**

3. **Choose the directory to put it in on your own computer.**

4. **Click the left-pointing arrow button in the middle of the window.**

   WS_FTP downloads the file. For large files, this step can take some time, and WS_FTP displays your progress as a percentage completed.

Hang up!

To disconnect from the FTP server after you are finished, click the Close button at the bottom of the WS_FTP window.

Connecting again

To call someone else, click the Connect button. You see the FTP Client Connect To window again. Fill in different information and click OK to make the connection.

To call an FTP server you've called before, click Connect. In the FTP Client Connect To window, click the arrow button to the right of the Config name box. You see a list of the configurations you entered before — choose one and then click OK.

Telnetting with Win QVT/NET: It's a Floor Wax! — No, It's a Breath Mint! — No, It's Both!

Okay now. You have FTP firmly under control. What about the other classic Internet service: telnet? Trumpet WinSock comes with a Telnet program called Telw, but it is a sorry excuse, not even good enough to run the simplest full-screen editor.

None of the freeware or shareware telnet programs available are wildly popular, but the one that most of us use is called Win QVT/NET. It's an all-purpose multifunction program that does telnet and FTP and mail and news and an FTP server and a cousin of FTP's called `rcp`, all in one package. Probably the next version will include a cappuccino attachment. Fortunately, if you just want to use the telnet feature, it's reasonably easy to set up and use.

Grabbing it

Here's how to download and install Win QVT/NET:

1. **This package is big enough to need its own directory, so create one called** \wnqvtnet.

2. **Using the FTP techniques you mastered earlier in this chapter, FTP to** biochemistry.bioc.cwru.edu, **move to the** /gopher/pub/winqvt **directory, and retrieve file** qvtws397.zip.

   (That's version 3.97; when you read this chapter, the version may have changed.)

3. **Extract all the files into** \wnqvtnet.

4. **Make an icon for** wnqvtwsk.exe.

   You don't need a bunch of the files in the ZIP archive if you're using WinSock, most notably wnqvtnet.exe.

Using it

Here's how to use the telnet part of Win QVT/NET:

1. **Connect to the net if you're not already connected.**

2. **Run Win QVT/NET.**

   You see a console window that displays status messages, with buttons below it for applications you can start.

3. **Click the Terminal button.**

   It pops up a window with a Hostname in which you type the name of the host to which you want to connect (ignore the rest of the fields) and click OK. You are connected to the remote host in no time.

   Unfortunately, you also notice that the default setup brings new depth to the term *ugly*. But it's not hard to fix. From the main menu, choose Setup⊅Terminal, adjust the settings to match Figure 9-10, and then click OK. You should have a decent-looking terminal.

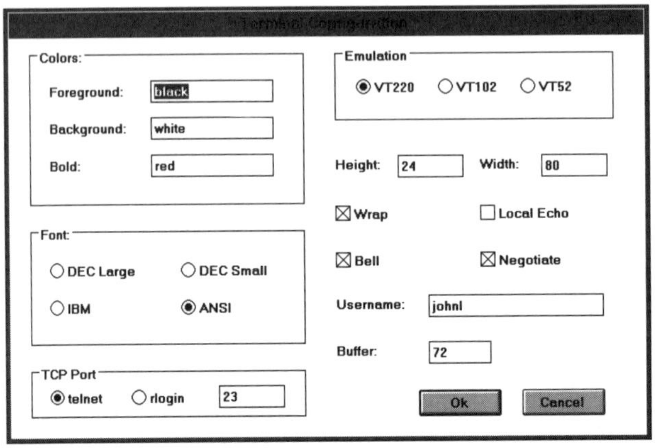

Figure 9-10:
Whipping
Win QVT/
NET's
Terminal
into line.

You can have as many terminal sessions active as you want at the same time. Every time you click Win QVT/NET's Terminal button, you get a new terminal, which you can connect to any host you want.

Feeling trapped?

There's no Exit command on the Win QVT/NET menu. Help! You're stuck in the program forever!

No — there's a way out. Double-click the button on the left side of the window's title bar. This is a standard way to leave any Windows program. Phew!

A program that's not directly useful to humans but that is handy in connection with other facilities, such as Gopher, is TNSTART. It's a little *stub* that tells Win QVT/NET to begin a new terminal session to a host named on its command line. You can create a Program Manager icon for your favorite host, for example, and make the command line something like `\wnqvtnet\tnstart locis.loc.gov` to automatically begin a session to the Library of Congress' LOCIS catalog.

Fingering Your Friends

Finger is a widely used program that lets you find out who's out there. You have to know which computer to look on, but Finger can then tell you whether that person is logged on, her real name, and possibly other information.

In Chapter 9 of *The Internet For Dummies,* we talked about how to use the `finger` command on UNIX systems, and now Windows-SLIP users can get the same information. Just use a program called (simply enough) Finger, which was written by Lee Murach.

Getting it

Finger is available from the FTP server `ftp.cica.indiana.edu` in the directory `/pub/pc/win3/winsock` in a file named `finger31.zip`. (It's version 3.1.)

Here's how to get Finger:

1. **Make a directory to put Finger in.**

   We recommend something like `\util\finger`, but choose any name that makes sense to you.

2. **Connect to your SLIP provider.**

3. **Run your FTP program.**

4. **Connect to the host** `ftp.cica.indiana.edu`.

   This is a busy host, so you may need to do this at an off-peak time.

5. **Change to the** `pub` **directory, then to** `pc`, **then to** `win3`, **and then to the** `winsock` **directory.**

   This step puts you in the `/pub/pc/win3/winsock` directory.

6. **Make sure that you are in binary mode and download a file named** `finger31.zip`.

   Later versions may have other numbers in their filename. Store the file in the directory you created in step 1.

7. **Disconnect from the host and exit from your FTP program.**

Setting it up

Follow the usual procedure to unzip the file and make a Program Manager icon for the Finger program.

1. **In the Windows File Manager, double-click the** `finger31.zip` **file.**

   This step runs WinZip and opens the Finger ZIP file.

2. **In WinZip, extract all the files into your** `\util\finger` **directory.**

   (Or whatever you named the directory in which you plan to put it.)

3. **In File Manager again, drag the** `finger.exe` **file into the Program Manager group where you want its icon to appear.**

You see a little picture of — hmm — maybe it's an angry penguin.

4. **To save disk space, you can delete the** `finger31.zip` **file.**

This program comes with complete source code (the files the programmers used to make it). Unless you plan to do a little programming on your own, you can delete all the files that end in the file extension `.c` or `.h`, in addition to `makefile`, `finger.dlg`, and `finger.rc`.

You're ready to give some Internet host the finger.

Using it

First double-click the icon to get it running. You see the window shown in Figure 9-11. Looks pretty simple — no buttons, no icons, and only one command on the menu: Host.

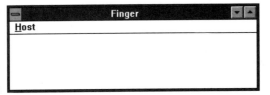

Figure 9-11:
Giving your
host the
finger.

There are two ways to finger: Finger a host computer or finger a particular user on that computer:

✔ When you finger a host computer, it usually tells you who's logged on at the moment. Some hosts tell you lots of stuff — try fingering `mit.edu` to get an idea. Generally, you finger a host to find out who uses it.

✔ When you finger a user on a host computer, it tells you about that person. This capability is useful if you know someone's Internet address and you want to know his real name or other information.

To finger a host, choose Host from the menu, enter the host name (such as `delphi.com`), and click OK. The host computer responds with whatever it sees fit to tell you.

To finger a person, choose Host from the menu and enter the host name (the part of an Internet address that comes after the @) and the username (the part before the @). Then click OK. The host computer responds with whatever information it usually distributes about people, usually their real name and sometimes some text about them.

When you are finished, choose Host⇨Exit. Simple enough!

Doing Your Part

After you've used a new program for a while, perhaps a few weeks, you should begin to feel guilty. Someone has gone to enormous effort to make this wonderful piece of software and you haven't even said thank you. It's time to Do Your Part.

Free versus not-quite-free

Software that comes from the Internet falls into two broad categories:

- ✔ **Freeware:** Given away for free. There may be restrictions on what you can do with it — most freeware owners don't let you resell their programs, for example. The UNZIP program is freeware, as are WS_FTP, Win QVT/NET, and Finger.

- ✔ **Shareware:** Given away for a limited trial period. If you plan to continue to use the program, you are honor-bound to pay for it. PKZIP is shareware. WinZip is shareware.

To find out which category your new program falls into, choose Help About from its menu bar or look for other menu choices that offer information about registering. For example, WinZip has a command called Help Ordering Information.

If you are using a shareware program and you find it to be valuable, go ahead and pay up. It's never a great deal of money, and you become a registered user, entitled to receive information about updates and related programs. Besides, you feel great about what a wonderful, generous person you are. (**Note:** Neither of the authors of this book distributes any shareware programs, so we have no vested interest!)

Registering WinZip

To pay by check, send $29 to Nico Mak, P.O. Box 919, Bristol, CT 06011-0919. To print an order form to submit to your company for payment, choose Help Ordering Information from the WinZip menu bar and then click File Print Topic from the WinZip Help menu bar. To pay by credit card, call the Public (software) Library at 800-2424-PsL or 713-524-6394. You can also mail credit-card orders to PsL at P.O. Box 35705, Houston, TX 77235-5705. To congratulate Mr. Mak on a job well done, you can e-mail him at 70056.241@compuserve.com.

What about PKZIP and PKUNZIP?

If you've been zipping and unzipping files for a while, you probably have and use the PKZIP and PKUNZIP programs. These programs have been around much longer than WinZip has, and they run under DOS. The original version of WinZip, in fact, ran PKZIP and PKUNZIP behind the scenes to do the actual zipping and unzipping.

If you are an old-fashioned kind of person and want PKZIP and PKUNZIP, they are available by FTP too. The FTP site oak.oakland.edu has them in the directory named /pub/msdos/zip, in a file named pkz204g.exe.

PKZIP and PKUNZIP are shareware. To register your copies, send $47 to PKWare, Inc., 7545 N. Port Washington Road, Glendale, WI 53217-3422. You can also register on-line with a credit card on the PKWare Support Bulletin Board System at 414-352-7176.

Chapter 10
Getting Your Mail with Eudora

· ·

In This Chapter

▶ How to get your mail by using a SLIP connection

▶ What is Eudora?

▶ Where does your mail live?

▶ Getting your own copy of, installing, and configuring Eudora

▶ Eusing Eudora

▶ Saving money with Eudora

▶ Creating nicknames for your friends and colleagues

▶ Other mail programs of interest

· ·

SLIP Me Some Mail

After you are connected to the Internet by using SLIP (as described in Chapter 8), you can use any of a number of WinSock mail programs. That is, you can use any mail program that runs under Windows and talks to SLIP by using the WinSock standard.

Several programs are available. Some of the better-known programs are shown in this list:

✔ **Chameleon Mail:** The program that comes in the Chameleon Sampler

✔ **Eudora:** Available for both PCs and Macs

✔ **Trumpet:** Discussed in Chapter 11

Our favorite is Eudora, so that's the one we describe in this chapter. If you want to use the mail program that comes with Chameleon, however, we talk about it a little too, at the end of this chapter. Trumpet's mail capabilities are described in Chapter 11.

What or Who Is Eudora?

Eudora is an easy-to-use mail-reading program that works with WinSock and SLIP. It runs under Windows and lets you write mail messages, read your mail, and reply to and store your messages in folders. It does all the same things other good mail programs do, such as *elm* and *pine*, but it does them with nice Windows menus and mouse clicks. And it stores your mail messages on *your* PC, not on your Internet provider's computer.

Before you can use Eudora, you must be up and running with an Internet SLIP provider, as described in Chapter 8. You also need about 750 KB of space on your disk.

Where Does Your Mail Live?

Before we dive into using Eudora, let's talk for a minute about your Internet address. Chances are that you will choose for your mail to come to your SLIP Internet provider so that your e-mail address is on its host computer. If you have an account named `bclinton` on The Internet Access Company (TIAC), for example, whose host computer is called `tiac.net`, your e-mail address is `bclinton@tiac.net`. The computer on which you get your mail is called your *mail server*.

You can get your mail, however, from anywhere that will let you have a mailbox. One of your authors, for example, connects to the Internet by using TIAC but has a mailbox on `iecc.com`. That works fine—after you're connected to the net, you can get your mail from any computer on the net that has a mailbox for you, not just from your Internet provider's.

If you are a student with an e-mail address at your university or a businessperson with an e-mail address at your work, this applies to you. From your PC at home, you can connect to the Internet by using a SLIP Internet provider. But you can keep your mailbox where it is, at your university or company. You will see how when you have installed Eudora.

So who is Eudora, anyway?

According to the Eudora manual, the program's author was reading Eudora Welty's short story *Why I Live at the P.O.*, and he got inspired. It's nice to know that even nerds read some real books from time to time.

The system your mail lives on (your mail server), however, must be set up to talk to programs such as Eudora. For Eudora and your mail server to work together, the mail server must use something called *POP3,* or Post Office Protocol Version 3. Believe us, you don't care about the internal workings of POP3 (we don't—particularly because one of us spent the better part of a week getting it to work at iecc.com). You just need to know that your mail server can handle it and that Eudora can too.

Getting Eudora

Eudora was written by Qualcomm, Inc., or actually by their QUEST (Qualcomm Enterprise Software Technologies) group. A shareware version is available from ftp.qualcomm.com in the directory /quest/windows/eudora. Or you can buy the commercial version and get a nice manual and technical support. If you have any questions about the commercial version, you can send e-mail to eudora-sales@qualcomm.com or call 800-2EUDORA. (Hmm. If you could send e-mail, you probably wouldn't have to ask the question.)

This chapter describes the shareware Eudora Version 1.4, in case you were wondering.

Grabbing Eudora from the net

This section tells you how to get your own copy of the shareware version of Eudora, assuming that you have already installed Chameleon or something like it.

If you use a different FTP program, fine—just connect to ftp.qualcomm.com, go to the directory /quest/windows/eudora, and grab the files you find there.

1. **Connect to the Internet.**

   That is, run the Chameleon Custom program and choose Connect from the menu bar.

2. **When you are connected, run the Chameleon FTP program.**

3. **In the FTP window, choose Connect from the menu bar. Enter ftp.qualcomm.com as the host name, anonymous as the username, and your e-mail address as the password. Click OK to connect to Qualcomm's FTP server.**

4. **In the Remote part of the FTP window, change to the /quest directory, then to its windows subdirectory, and then to its eudora subdirectory.**

As you do so, if you see any files named `readme` or `README.NOW`, choose ASCII as the Transfer type and copy the file to your own hard disk. Use Windows Notepad or a word processor to read these files. They may contain instructions that are more up to date than what we have written here, including perhaps new version numbers.

5. **In the `/quest/windows/eudora` directory, select a file named something like `eudora14.exe`.**

   It may have another name if the Qualcomm folks have come out with a later version than 1.4. Choose the file.

6. **In the Local part of the FTP window, choose the directory in which you want to put the file, and enter `eudor14.exe` as the filename.**

   The filename is a teeny bit too long for DOS to accept, so you have to shorten it.

7. **Click the button to the left of the Copy label.**

   FTP copies the file from Qualcomm to you!

8. **Copy any other files that look interesting or that you are instructed by `readme` files to copy.**

9. **When you are finished, choose Disconnect and Exit.**

   Now you have a compressed file named `eudor14.exe` that contains the program.

Unwrapping Eudora

The next step is to make a directory to contain Eudora, uncompress its files, and read the `readme` file it contains, if any.

1. **Create a directory for Eudora to live in.**

   Our preferred method is using the Windows File Manager—move to the directory you want the new directory to be a subdirectory of (for example, the root: \), choose File⇨Create Directory, and type a name.

2. **Move the file you just got from Qualcomm into your new directory.**

   In File Manager, you can drag the filename from its current location into the directory you just created.

3. **Uncompress the file by double-clicking it.**

   The file `eudor14.exe` is a *self-extracting file*—that is, when you run it, it uncompresses itself and turns into a bunch of little files. The easiest way to run it is to double-click its filename in File Manager. (This step avoids the need for WinZip to uncompress the file.)

As it uncompresses, the screen goes black and you see the names of the files listed down the side of the screen. Then you return to Windows.

Eudora Version 1.4 consists of the following files: changes, weudora.exe, and readme.txt.

4. **Take a look at the readme.txt file for any late-breaking news about how to use Eudora.**

The easiest way to do this is to double-click its filename in File Manager—this step runs Window Notepad and loads the readme.txt file into it. Alternatively, you can use your favorite word processor.

5. **To make Eudora convenient to run, make an icon for it in Windows Program Manager. First, run the Windows File Manager.**

6. **Arrange the windows so that you can see the weudora.exe file in File Manager and the Program Manager program group you want the icon to be in.**

7. **Drag the file weudora.exe from the File Manager to the Program Manager program group you want the icon in and release the mouse button.**

A nice little picture of a stamped letter appears in Program Manager. There's your Eudora icon!

Whew! You are ready to run Eudora and tell it how to get your mail. This has been a lot of work, we know, but you have obtained a lovely software package for nothing through the wonders of FTP.

If you like Eudora and you want a version with more features and technical support, think about buying the commercial version, which is not very expensive (about $69).

Telling Eudora About You

Before you can use Eudora, you have to tell it about yourself:

1. **Double-click the Eudora icon (the little picture of a stamped letter).**

You see the PC Eudora window. We don't include a picture of it here because it is blank except for the menu bar at the top.

2. **Choose Special Configuration from the menu.**

You see the Configuration dialog box, shown in Figure 10-1.

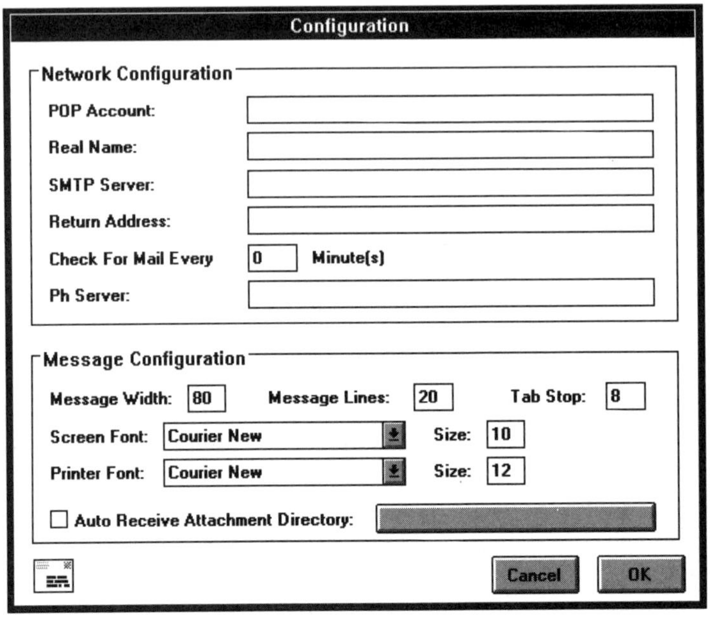

```
┌─────────────────────────────────────────────────────────┐
│                      Configuration                       │
│ ┌─Network Configuration─────────────────────────────────┐│
│ │  POP Account:    [                              ]      ││
│ │  Real Name:      [                              ]      ││
│ │  SMTP Server:    [                              ]      ││
│ │  Return Address: [                              ]      ││
│ │  Check For Mail Every  [0]    Minute(s)               ││
│ │  Ph Server:      [                              ]      ││
│ └───────────────────────────────────────────────────────┘│
│ ┌─Message Configuration─────────────────────────────────┐│
│ │  Message Width: [80]  Message Lines: [20]  Tab Stop: [8]││
│ │  Screen Font:  [Courier New      ▼]  Size: [10]       ││
│ │  Printer Font: [Courier New      ▼]  Size: [12]       ││
│ │  ☐ Auto Receive Attachment Directory: [            ]  ││
│ └───────────────────────────────────────────────────────┘│
│                                   [ Cancel ]  [  OK  ]   │
└─────────────────────────────────────────────────────────┘
```

Figure 10-1:
Telling
Eudora your
life story.

3. In the POP Account box, enter your e-mail address.

This doesn't have to be an address on your Internet provider's computer—it's wherever your mail comes.

4. In the Real Name box, enter your real name as you want it to appear in parentheses after your e-mail address.

5. Leave the SMTP Server box blank to indicate that the same computer on which you receive your mail will handle sending mail too.

Also leave the Return Address box blank, which means that you want the return address on your e-mail to be the same e-mail address you entered in Step 3.

6. In the Check For Mail Every box, enter 30 so that while you are connected to the Internet, Eudora automagically checks your mailbox for mail every 30 minutes.

Enter a larger number to check less often. Don't enter a number smaller than 15 because this will tie up both your own Internet connection and your Internet provider's mail server.

7. Leave everything else as is (for now).

You may want to change some settings later, but these should do.

8. Click OK to save these settings.

Eusing Eudora

Before we get into the details, a word about how to use Eudora: Eudora displays lots of windows, including mailboxes that show lists of messages, message windows that show the text of one message, composition windows for writing your own messages, and others. It's happy to let you display lots of windows at a time, and you can switch among them.

To close a window, double-click the little box with the horizontal bar in its upper left-hand corner. To temporarily minimize (*iconize*) a window, click the downward-pointing triangle in its upper right-hand corner. To turn an iconized window back into a regular window, double-click it.

This is all standard Windows stuff—we just thought that we would point out that it works in Eudora too.

Hello, World!

To try things out, send yourself a message. It's the fastest way to find out whether things are working.

Here's how to send a message:

1. **Choose Message from the menu bar followed by New Message. (Or just press Ctrl+N.)**

   You see a window that looks like Figure 10-2.

Figure 10-2: Composing a message for Eudora to send.

```
┌──────────────────────────────────────────────────────────────┐
│ ─        │      No Recipient, No Subject           │ ▼ │ ▲ │
├──────────────────────────────────────────────────────────────┤
│ (Normal)  ± │ ℋ Signature ± │ BIN HEX BinHex  ± │ QP 🔲 ⇥ ⬚ TXT DOC RR │ Send │
├──────────────────────────────────────────────────────────────┤
│           To:                                              │ ▲ │
│         From: margy@iecc.com (Margy Levine Young)          │   │
│      Subject:                                              │   │
│           Cc:                                              │   │
│          Bcc:                                              │   │
│  Attachments:                                              │   │
│ ─────────────────────────────────────────────────────────── │   │
│ I                                                          │   │
│                                                            │   │
│                                                            │ ▲ │
└──────────────────────────────────────────────────────────────┘
```

2. **Click to the right of the To label in the window and then type the e-mail address to which you want to send a message.**

To send a test message to yourself, enter your own e-mail address.

If you want to send the message to more than one person, you can enter more than one Internet address. Just separate the addresses by commas.

3. Click to the right of the Subject label and type the subject.

You can also press Tab to move from the To field to the Subject field.

4. If you want to send copies to anyone, or *blind* copies, enter the address (or addresses) in the Cc and Bcc fields.

We get to attachments in a minute.

5. Below the gray line, type the text of your message.

You don't have to press Enter at the end of every line — Eudora does word-wrapping to make your message look nice.

6. To send your missive, click the Send or Queue button, whichever appears.

Eudora shows one or the other, depending on whether Eudora is planning to send it out right away or wait a while.

If Eudora is set up to send messages right away, it connects to the mail server on your Internet provider and sends the message as soon as you click the Send button. If Eudora is set up to hold outgoing messages in a queue, nothing seems to happen when you click the Queue button. To send the messages in the queue, press Ctrl+T (or choose File⇨Send Queued Messages from the menu bar).

If you want to save a message and send it later, choose File⇨Save from the menu bar. Then close the window. The message is saved in your outbox, where you can edit and send it later.

Sending Your Messages

Eudora lets you control when your outgoing messages are sent — either right away or when you give the signal. You can save connect-time with your Internet provider if you do as much message reading and writing as possible when you are not connected and then send your messages in a group.

To control when messages are sent:

1. Choose Special Switches from the menu bar.

You see a large window.

The items in the Composition and Send Attachment boxes control the way the buttons appear when you compose a new message (the buttons are described in the sidebar "What are all those buttons?").

2. Choose the Immediate Send box if you want messages sent as soon as you finish them.

What are all those buttons?

At the top of the message window, Eudora displays a row of interesting-looking buttons. You can use them to control a bunch of cool things about your messages:

(Normal): Controls the priority of the message. If you click the button to the right of Normal, you can see the list of priorities.

(Signature): Controls whether your signature file is automatically stuck at the end of the message. (To create a standard signature for your messages, choose Window Signature and type one.)

BinHex: Controls the way Eudora attaches files to your message if the file contains something other than text. To attach a file to your message, you choose the Message Attach Document command from the menu bar and enter its filename. But there are three ways to attach a file in the world of e-mail: *MIME* (use it only for people who also use Eudora or other snazzy mail systems that can do MIME); *BinHex* (for people who use Eudora or Macs); and *Uuencode* (for people who use PCs or UNIX). Don't worry about the details.

QP (Quotable-Printing): Usually pressed and controls the way Eudora attaches text files to your message. Just leave it pressed.

Word Wrap (a page with a curving arrow): Tells Eudora to do word wrap so that you don't have to press Enter at the end of every line.

Tab (a right-pointing arrow): Tells Eudora to type spaces when you press the Tab key. If this button isn't pressed, the Tab key moves you to the next field in the window (usually the To field). Leave it pressed.

Keep Copy (two sheets of paper, one dog-eared): Tells Eudora to keep a copy of your messages in your outbox.

Text as Documents (TEXT/DOC): Tells Eudora more about how to handle attached text files. When it is pressed, attached text files are sent as separate files. When it isn't pressed, the text in the file is stuck at the end of the message.

RR: (Return Receipt): Asks for a receipt when the recipient gets the mail.

The Immediate Send option controls when Eudora sends out messages you compose. If an X is in this box, Eudora displays a Send button when you are composing a message, and it sends the message as soon as you click the Send button. Otherwise, Eudora displays a Queue button, and it holds outgoing messages in a queue. The messages don't get sent until you choose the File⇨Send Queued Messages command from the menu bar (or press Ctrl+T).

If sending a message ties up your PC for a minute or two, you may prefer to keep your messages in a queue and send them every few hours. It's up to you.

3. **Click OK to close the dialog box.**

To send messages right away, press Ctrl+T (or choose File⇨Send Queued Messages from the menu bar).

Here Comes Your Mail!

Well, you've *sent* mail, but how about *getting* the mail that's coming to you? How about the test message you sent earlier, for example?

Getting the mail

Here's how to get your incoming messages from your mail server:

1. **Press Ctrl+M (or choose File⇨Check Mail) to get your mail.**

   If you entered a number in the Check For Mail Every box in the Configuration dialog box (the one you used when you told Eudora your address), Eudora should check your mail automatically at intervals, so you may not need to do this step.

   Eudora asks for your password.

2. **Type the password to the computer on which you get your mail (your mail server). Don't press Enter when you have typed it — click the OK button.**

   The password appears as a row of asterisks when you type it, so type carefully.

   Eudora connects to your mail server, grabs your mail, and copies it to your PC. You see a Progress window showing a series of messages as it does so, starting with logging in to your POP server (that is, your mail server) and then the subject line of each message it finds.

   You see a message saying that you have new mail (click OK to make it go away) and a new window called In, with a list of your incoming messages (see Figure 10-3). Or if no messages are waiting for you, you see the message Sorry, you don't have any new mail.

urhh@cbs.dk	09:32 AM 4/6/94	4	Re: Juggling in Cambrid
ANDY THAMES	09:31 PM 4/14/94	3	Unix For Dummies
Sheila Barrows	06:00 PM 4/22/94	2	The Internet
Judy Kriger	02:41 PM 4/25/94	1	unix scripting
James Mullan	09:02 PM 4/25/94	2	Re: Heartfelt Appeal fo
hy.bender@genie.	05:23 AM 4/27/94	4	Baby!
BRADLEY HARLEN	12:33 AM 4/28/94	1	irc / the book
Scott D Gray	08:54 PM 4/29/94	7	Re: The Sudbury Valley
• Jerry Mintz	09:46 PM 4/29/94	2	Re: The Sudbury Valley
• cook@pandora.sf.	12:52 AM 4/30/94	10	anyone know anything ab
tsaxon@leland.st	11:57 PM 4/29/94	2	Re: Come on out!
Peter C. Torp	04:47 PM 4/30/94	1	Book
• Ed Krol	06:56 AM 5/1/94	2	suggested new members
wu/O=HOWARD KANE	03:57 PM 5/1/94	3	Hi, Dummies authors !

In — 28/113K/8K

Figure 10-3:
Sorting
through the
day's mail.

Streamlining getting your mail

It can be annoying to have to enter your password every time Eudora gets your mail. Unless you are worried about some malefactor sneaking up to your PC and fooling with your mail when you aren't looking, tell Eudora to store your password so that it can remember it and not have to ask you. Choose Special Switches from the menu bar so that you see the Switches dialog box. Choose the Save Password box if you want Eudora to remember the password to your Internet account rather than your having to type it every time you check your mail.

While you are at it, you can choose the Leave Mail on Server box if you don't want Eudora to delete the mail in your mailbox at your Internet provider's account after it has downloaded it to your PC. Choose this option if you want to absolutely, certainly not miss any mail. Sooner or later, however, *someone* is going to have to delete all that mail!

When you are finished making changes in the Switches dialog box, click OK.

You can open the In window at any time by choosing Mailbox In from the menu bar (or by pressing Ctrl+I).

Reading the mail

The In window shows the contents of your In mailbox — messages you haven't read yet. You see one message per line, with the name of the person who sent it (you, in the case of your test message), when it was sent, the number of pages, and the subject. In the leftmost column, you see a black dot or bullet for messages you haven't yet read. It's blank for messages you have read but haven't replied to or deleted.

To read a message, double-click it in the In window. You see a message window that shows the message's priority (usually Normal), subject, and text.

When you are looking at a message, you can easily reply to the message, delete it, forward it to someone else with your comments, or redirect it to someone else.

Sending your response

To reply to a message:

1. Choose Message⇨Reply from the menu bar (or press Ctrl+R).

Eudora shows you a blank message window so that you can compose your reply. Eudora even fills in the address of the person you are replying to and copies the subject from the original message.

2. Write and send the message as usual.

After you have replied to a message, an *R* appears in the leftmost column of the In window, so you know that you have already dealt with the message.

We have assumed that you just read the message when you decide to reply to it. If you want to reply to it later, you can do so without opening it again. Just click once on the message in the In window so that it is highlighted. Then choose Message⇨Reply or press Ctrl+R or click the little Reply icon in the In window.

Getting rid of messages

You can delete a message you have already read. With a message on-screen, choose Message⇨Delete from the menu bar (or press Ctrl+D).

You can delete a message without reading it, in fact, but you might miss something interesting. You can just click once on the message in the In window so that it is highlighted but not open. Then choose Message⇨Delete or press Ctrl+D or click the icon that shows something flying into a garbage can.

Moving along to the next message

When you have read a message, you can close the message window to see the In window again. Then double-click another message to read it.

It's much more convenient to press the down-arrow key, or Ctrl+down-arrow if you prefer, to move to the next message. To tell Eudora that you want this technique to work, choose Special⇨Switches from the menu bar. Click either the Plain Arrows or Ctrl+Arrows setting in the Switch Messages With box. If an X appears in either one of these boxes, the appropriate arrow keys work to move you up to the preceding message in the mailbox or down to the next message. Click OK to clear away the Switches dialog box.

Committing a message to paper

There are two ways to print a message on your PC's printer:

- ✔ When the message is displayed, choose File⇨Print from the menu bar.
- ✔ When you are looking at a mailbox, choose the message and click the little picture of paper coming out of a printer (the rightmost icon in the mailbox window). Choosing File⇨Print from the menu bar works too.

Either way, you see a Print dialog box that lets you choose which pages to print and how many copies. Click OK when you have done so.

Sharing a message with friends

To forward a message to someone else:

1. Choose Message⇨Forward from the menu bar.

Eudora shows you a new message window. The text of the original message appears, indented by the > character (this character shows that you are repeating information you received from someone else). You can delete the part that won't be interesting to the person to whom you are forwarding the message, and you can add your own comments at the end (or anywhere).

2. Type the address of the person to whom you want to forward the message, just to the right of the To label.

If you want to forward the message to more than one person, you can enter more than one Internet address, separated by commas.

3. Then send the message as usual.

After you forward a message, an F appears in the leftmost column of the In window.

You can also forward a message when you are looking at the In window. Click once on the message so that it is highlighted and then choose Message⇨ Forward or click the little Forward icon in the In window.

Oops! This message isn't for me!

Redirecting a message is a concept that most mail programs don't do. If you feel that you got a piece of mail in error and you want to pass it along to its proper recipient, you can redirect it:

1. Choose Message — Redirect from the menu bar.

Eudora displays the message in a new message window, but it doesn't indent the text the way forwarding does. Also, the message is from the person who originally sent it, not from you.

2. Enter the address to which you want to redirect the message.

3. Send it as usual.

After you redirect a message, a D appears in the leftmost column of the In window. The D suggests that you are free to delete it now.

To redirect a message when you are looking at the In window, click once on the message so that it is highlighted, and then choose Message⇨Redirect or click the little Redirect icon.

File It, Eudora

If you are like us, you want to save a certain number of your messages. To keep them organized, we like to save them in different groups, which Eudora calls *mailboxes*. Eudora comes with three mailboxes:

- **In mailbox:** Stores incoming mail until you move it or delete it
- **Out mailbox:** Stores outgoing mail
- **Trash mailbox:** Provides a place for deleted messages to die; Eudora doesn't delete them until you choose Special⇨Empty Trash from the menu bar

You can tell Eudora to delete all the messages from your Trash mailbox when you exit from Eudora. Choose Special⇨Switches from the menu bar and choose the Empty Trash on Quit setting so that it contains an X. Then click OK.

You can create your own mailboxes (for example, one for personal messages, one for a discussion of your department's budget, one for project planning messages, and one for messages about the football pool). After you have made a mailbox and put messages in it, you can read the messages, reply to them, delete them, or move them to other mailboxes exactly as you would if they were in your In mailbox.

Opening a mailbox

To look at a mailbox, choose Mailbox from the menu bar. The menu that appears contains all your mailboxes, including those you have created. Choose a mailbox, and a window for it opens.

When you open your Out mailbox, messages that have already been sent appear with an S in the leftmost column. Those that are queued for sending are marked with a Q.

What are those funky-looking numbers?

In the upper left-hand corner of a mailbox window, you see a box that says something like *5/10K/ 135K*. This is Eudora's cryptic way of telling you that five messages are in the mailbox (the first number), they take up 10 KB of disk space (the second number), and that junk lying around in the mailbox takes 135 KB of disk space (the third number). To tell Eudora to get rid of the junk, click the box (it's really a button). Eudora takes out the trash, and the third number shrinks.

Make me a mailbox

To create a new mailbox and move a message into it, follow these steps.:

1. **In the In window or any window that shows a list of messages, click once on the message you want to put in the new mailbox.**

   Alternatively, you can display the message.

2. **Choose Transfer⇨New from the menu bar.**

   You see the New Mailbox Dialog.

3. **Type the name in the box.**

   The name can contain spaces. Capitalize it nicely so that it will look good on your menus and windows.

4. **Click OK.**

   Eudora makes the new mailbox and moves the chosen message into it.

   Your new mailbox now appears on both the Mailbox and Transfer menus. To see the new mailbox, choose Mailbox from the menu bar and then choose the mailbox name. To move a message into it, select or view the message, choose Transfer from the menu bar, and choose the mailbox name. It's a very convenient system!

If you really want to make several mailboxes, you can organize them into *folders*. Each folder can contain a bunch of mailboxes. First you create the folder by choosing the Make It a Folder box on the New Mailbox dialog box. Then you create at least one mailbox in the folder.

If you want to set up a bunch of mailboxes without moving messages into them, choose Mailbox⇨New from the menu bar.

Saving a message in a text file

What if you want to use a message in a document you are writing? It is easy to save a message from Eudora into a text file. Either view the message or choose it from the mailbox where it lives. Then choose File⇨Save As from the menu bar. You see a Save As dialog box that lets you decide which directory to put the file in and which filename to use. When you click OK, Eudora makes the file.

Alternatively, run your word processor. Display the message in Eudora, highlight the part of the text you want to use in your document, and choose Edit⇨Copy from the Eudora menu (or press Ctrl+C or Shift+Ins) to copy it to the Windows Clipboard. Switch to your word processor and paste the Clipboard text into your document by choosing Edit⇨Paste.

Saving Money with Eudora

You can use Eudora when you are not connected to the Internet. This is a great advantage because it enables you to read your mail and concoct responses at your leisure, without worrying about how much money you are spending on connect-time to your Internet provider. Here's an overview of how it works:

- ✔ Connect to the Internet.
- ✔ Tell Eudora to get your messages.
- ✔ Disconnect from the Internet.
- ✔ Read your messages, reply to them, file them, and so on.
- ✔ Connect to the Internet again.
- ✔ Tell Eudora to send your messages.
- ✔ Disconnect from the Internet again.

Here is how to set up Eudora to work this way:

- ✔ In the Configuration dialog box (choose Special⇨Configuration from the menu bar to see it), don't enter any number in the Check for Mail Every box. This tells Eudora not to check for mail except when you tell it to.
- ✔ In the Switches dialog box (choose Special⇨Switches from the menu bar to see it), don't choose Immediate Send. That is, click its little box so that no X is in it. This tells Eudora not to try to send each message as soon as you have written it. Instead, it waits until you give the word.
- ✔ In the Switches dialog box, select the Send on Check box, which tells Eudora that while is it checking for new mail, it can send any mail that is waiting to be sent.

When you want to read and respond to your e-mail:

1. **Run Eudora.**

2. **Take a look at your In mailbox to see whether there are any messages you want to respond to. Also compose any new messages you want to send (by using the Message⇨New Message command).**

3. **Connect to the Internet.**

    If you use Chameleon, run Custom and choose Connect.

4. **Back in Eudora, choose File⇨Check Mail from the menu bar (or press Ctrl+M).**

    A Progress window tells you what's happening as Eudora gets your new messages and sends the messages that are queued up, waiting to be sent.

5. **Click OK to clear any box that tells you about new mail (or that you don't have any).**

6. **Disconnect from the Internet.**

   If you use Chameleon, switch back to Custom and choose Disconnect.

7. **In Eudora, read your new messages.**

   They appear at the bottom of your In mailbox with a bullet in the leftmost column. Read them, compose replies, delete boring ones, move good ones into other mailboxes, or whatever.

8. **When you are finished with your messages and want to send them, connect to the Internet again.**

   If you use Chameleon, run Custom and choose Connect.

9. **In Eudora, choose File⇨Check Mail from the menu bar again or press Ctrl+M.**

   If you chose the Send on Check box in the Switches dialog box as we told you to, this step checks for new mail *and* sends your queued outgoing mail.

10. **Disconnect from the Internet.**

    If you use Chameleon, switch back to Custom and choose Disconnect.

Kilroy Was Here

You can make a *signature* that Eudora automatically adds to the end of messages you send. A signature usually consists of your full name, e-mail address, perhaps your mailing address or phone number, and maybe some pithy saying. It's a bad idea to make long, flowery signatures because people get tired of seeing them after the first time.

Creating your own personal signature

To make a signature:

1. **Choose Window⇨Signature to open the Signature window (logically enough).**

2. **Type the text of your signature in the window, as shown in Figure 10-4.**

3. **Double-click in the upper left-hand corner of the window to close it.**

   Eudora asks whether you want to save the changes to your signature.

4. **Click Save.**

   Eudora remembers this signature forever or until you change it.

Figure 10-4:
A signature
appears at
the bottom
of messages
you send.

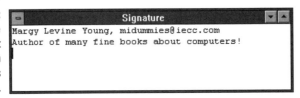

Signature
Margy Levine Young, midummies@iecc.com
Author of many fine books about computers!

Your signature can be as long as you want. It can be really, really long. Some people think that it's incredibly clever to have a signature about 30 lines long with little pictures, quotations, political comments, 14 phone numbers, fax numbers, home address, business address, summer address, winter address—what have you. They are wrong — long signatures are just obnoxious. The rule of thumb is that a signature should be as short as possible and never more than three lines. We manage to get a name, address, phone number, e-mail addresses, and a pithy comment (*"Space aliens are stealing American jobs."* — *MIT Econ Professor*) into 3 lines, and by golly, you can too.

Signing with a flourish

To add your signature to a message, take a look at the window in which you are composing the message. Make sure that the Signature box (the second thingy from the left on the icon bar) says *Signature*. (Actually, it has cursive *JH* and then says *Signature*. We don't know who J.H. is, unless it means *John Hancock*.)

If you don't want to include your signature with a message, click the arrow button to the right of the Signature box. Choose None from the list.

Pass Me That File

When you send a message, you may want to include a file you have stored on your PC. This is called an *attachment* (not an emotional attachment, just an attachment). You can attach a word-processing document, a graphics file, or anything that can be stored in a file on your computer.

You must think about the person on the other end receiving this file, however—what is this person going to do with it? If you send a Microsoft Word for Windows 6.0 document, the person on the other end must have the same program or a program that can read that type of document. If you correspond with folks on different types of computers, especially UNIX and mainframe folks, they may be out of luck. So you may want to find out beforehand which types of files your correspondent can deal with.

Here's an additional twist: The Internet mail system is designed to handle only plain ol' text. No formatted documents, no sound clips, no pictures—nothing fun at all. To get around this restriction, netfolk have come up with several ways of *encoding* these types of file as text. The mail program that sends the files converts them to text, and the mail program that receives the files converts them back. The three most common types of encoding are shown in this list:

- **Uuencode:** Used mainly by UNIX systems
- **BinHex:** Used mainly with Macintosh mail programs
- **MIME:** Stands for Multipurpose Internet Mail Extensions and is used by modern, zippy mail programs, including Eudora, elm, and pine

If you want to send a file that isn't text, any of these encoding systems works fine. But the person receiving the file must have a mail program that can convert it back to its original form. So check with your intended recipient to find out what kind of encoding his or her mail program can do.

Attaching a file

To attach a file to a message:

1. **Compose the message as usual.**

2. **Then choose Message⇨Attach Document from the menu bar (or press Ctrl+H).**

   You see the Attach Document dialog box, which lets you indicate the exact file you have in mind.

3. **Click OK when you have chosen the directory and filename of the file to attach.**

   The directory and filename appear in the header of the message, next to the Attachments label.

   On the icon bar, the third box from the left shows which kind of encoding Eudora plans to use.

4. **To change the encoding, click the arrow button to its right and choose a different type (Uuencode, BinHex, or MIME).**

5. **Send your message as usual.**

The contents of the attached file don't appear as part of the message. The file is "stapled" to the message but remains separate.

If you send an attached file to a Eudora user, it arrives as an attachment, and the person can follow the instructions later in this chapter to detach it and save it. For people who use other mail programs, though, the file appears at the bottom of the message, encoded so that it looks illegible. The person must tell the mail program (or other program, in some cases) to decode that part of the message.

If you change your mind about attaching the document, click the filename in the message header and press the Del key to delete it.

You might think that rather than use the Message⇨Attach Document command, you can just type the directory and filename of the file you want to attach right into the header of your message. But no! Eudora doesn't let you do this, and we don't know why not.

Including information from a document

Another way to send information from a word-processing document as an e-mail message is to copy it from your word-processing program into Eudora. When you do this, the text appears as part of the text of the message, not as an attachment.

In your word processor, highlight the text you want and copy it to the Windows Clipboard (by choosing Edit⇨Copy from the menu). In Eudora, start a new message and put your cursor where you want the text to appear. Choose Edit⇨Paste from the Eudora menu (or press Ctrl+V) to copy it from the Windows Clipboard.

Getting an attached file

When Eudora retrieves your mail from your mail server, it notices immediately whether an incoming message has an attachment. And you will too — Eudora stops in its tracks and displays a Save Attachment dialog box. This dialog box lets you decide in which directory to put the incoming file. Of course, because you can't see the message yet, you may not know what the file contains, so it can be hard to decide where it should go. You may be able to guess by its original filename, which Eudora shows you.

Eudora automatically decodes the attached file, by using Uuencode or BinHex or MIME as appropriate, so it appears just as it did when it left the sender's computer.

If you don't want to be bothered every time Eudora gets an attached file, you can tell Eudora in advance which directory to put attachments in. Choose Special⇨Configuration from the menu bar so that you see the Configuration dialog box. Click the big button to the right of the label Auto Receive Attachment Directory. Eudora displays a dialog box that lets you choose the directory. Click the Use Directory button when you have chosen it. The directory name now appears right in the big button (strangely enough), and an X appears in the box to the left of it. Click OK.

From now on, all attachments will be filed in that directory. You are notified when attachments arrive because the messages to which they are attached show up in your In mailbox.

Quick Ways to Address Your Mail

Typing Internet addresses can be annoying, what with all their strange punctuation. Even more annoying is having to type lists of them when you want to send a message to a bunch of people. To avoid this annoyance, you can use Eudora's *nickname* feature. (They are called *aliases* by many other mail programs.)

What's in a nickname?

A nickname is a short name you can use rather than type an entire Internet address. If you intend to send a great deal of mail to Internet For Dummies Central, for example, it can be a pain to type **midummies@iecc.com** over and over. It's much nicer to type **Dummies** instead.

No problem! Eudora lets you make up as many nicknames as you want and stores them forever. A nickname can be short for one Internet address or for a whole list of them. To fool with nicknames, choose Window Nicknames from the menu bar. You see the Nicknames dialog box.

The Nickname box lists all the nicknames you have created. The Address(es) box shows the actual Internet address(es) for the nickname you have chosen. And the Notes box contains any notes you want to enter about the person or group of people.

Making a nickname

To make a nickname:

1. **Click the new button in the Nickname dialog box.**

    You see the New Nickname dialog box, as shown in Figure 10-5.

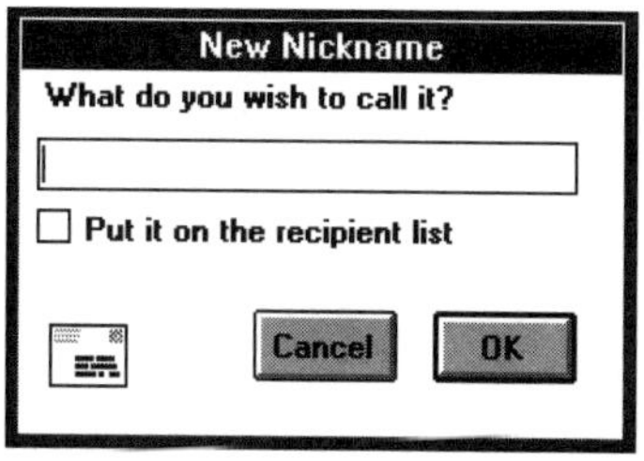

Figure 10-5
Creating a new nickname for one person or for a group.

New Nickname

What do you wish to call it?

☐ Put it on the recipient list

[Cancel] [OK]

2. **Type the nickname you want to create. For example, type** Dummies.

3. **Click OK.**

   The New Nickname dialog box goes away and you return to the Nickname dialog box. The new nickname appears on the Nickname list.

4. **In the Address(es) box, type the actual Internet address to use for this nickname.**

   If this nickname is for a group, enter a list of addresses separated by commas or by Enters.

5. **Press Tab to move to the Notes box and enter any notes about the nickname.**

   If you know which mail program the person (or people) uses, note it here because you might need to know this when you're sending attached files. You might also want to enter any alternative e-mail addresses that people might have (many folks have several).

6. **Repeat these steps for all the nicknames you want to create.**

It is okay to separate the addresses for a list of people by pressing Enter after each address when you type in the Address(es) box in the Nickname dialog box. But you cannot do this anywhere else in Eudora. Instead, you have to separate the addresses by commas.

Using a nickname

We like to keep the Nickname dialog box lying around in our Eudora window so that we can use nicknames whenever we want. When you are composing a message and you want to send it to someone with a nickname, choose the person from the Nickname list in the Nickname window and click the To button. The nickname appears in the To field in the message you are composing.

You can start a new message even more easily, in fact — In the Nickname window, choose the person to send it to and click the To button. Eudora figures that you want to start a new message to that person and opens a new message window, with the nickname in the To field.

You can choose more than one nickname from the Nickname list, if you want. Click one of the nicknames and then Ctrl+click each other name you want to use.

Problems in Paradise

If Eudora cannot connect to your mail server, use the Ping program to see whether the host computer is alive and responding. If your address is lydia@alternet.com, for example, try pinging alternet.com to see whether you get a response.

Sometimes a mail server is unavailable for a moment and comes back quickly. Try checking your mail again after a few minutes.

If you cannot get your mail, make sure that your mail server really uses the POP3 protocol that Eudora requires. Using the telnet program, connect to port 110 of your mail server. (That is, run the telnet program, click Connect, type the name of your mail server as the Host Name and **110** as the Port Number, and then click OK.) You should see a message something like this:

```
+OK CHICO.iecc.com POP3D Version 1.5 11/26/91 by
          wstef@eng.clemson.edu
```

Then tell telnet to disconnect because it requires inhumanly precise typing to do anything useful with the mail server program, which expects to be talking to another computer, not to you.

Commercial Eudora

The commercial version of Eudora has other features, including these two:

- ✔ Two different signatures so that you can use one for friends and the other for business

- ✔ Automatic message filtering so that you can do things automatically according to rules you set up (deleting all messages from someone you don't like, for example, or forwarding all messages from your boss to your secretary)

 If you find that you like the program and use it frequently, think about buying the commercial version. It's not very expensive. After all, if everyone uses the shareware version and nobody buys the real thing, the software division of Qualcomm (which wrote it) will go down the tubes, and the program will never be updated. Be a good citizen of the Internet and buy the software you use. (End of commercial announcement.)

Other Mail Programs

The Chameleon Sampler, the WinSock SLIP program comes with a perfectly usable mail program. It gets installed automagically when you install the sampler software.

Trumpet, a newsgroup-reading program described in Chapter 11, can also send and receive mail.

Writing mail programs is fun, so people do it all the time. A good place to look for mail programs via FTP is sunsite.unc.edu in directory /pub/micro/pc-stuff/ms-windows/winsock/apps. That's a good place, in fact, to look for all sorts of Windows Internet applications. If you're feeling adventurous, look at Win QVT/NET (a Swiss army knife-style combination of telnet, FTP, and mail program), WinElm (a Windows version of the widely used UNIX elm mail program), and WinPanda (a larger Swiss army knife, with mail, newsgroups, FTP, and Gopher). We describe how to get Win QVT/NET at the end of the Chapter 9, in the section "Telnetting with Win QVT/NET."

Chapter 11
Announcing News with Trumpet

- -

- -

What Is Usenet?

As you may recall (from Chapter 11 of *The Internet For Dummies,* to be specific), Usenet is a worldwide system of bulletin boards. Each bulletin board (or *newsgroup*) is devoted to one topic, which can be anything from the care and feeding of tropical fish to arguments about abortion rights.

Anyone can *post* an article (or *posting*) to a newsgroup, and an amazing variety of people do just that. You use a news-reading program (or *news reader*) to read the articles in a newsgroup and to post your own articles.

What Is Trumpet?

Trumpet is the most popular SLIP news reader — that is, it's the program most widely used by people with SLIP Internet connections for reading their favorite Usenet newsgroups. Trumpet runs under Windows or on the Macintosh. After you install it, you can also use Trumpet for reading and sending mail.

Peter R. Tattam of the University of Tasmania (yes, Tasmania, the land of wombats and Tasmanian devils) wrote Trumpet and distributes it as shareware. If you like it, send $40 (in U.S. dollars, even though it's going to Tasmania) to him at Trumpet Software International, GPO Box 1649, Hobart, Tasmania, Australia 7001. Australians can contact him for Australian pricing, he says.

Don't confuse Trumpet, the new reader, with Trumpet WinSock, the SLIP software. We think that Peter should have thought of a different name for one of them, but hey, what's in a name? (Confusion, that's what.)

Who Is Your News Server?

To get newsgroup information, Trumpet uses *NNTP* (*Network News Transfer Protocol*). Your SLIP provider or some other host computer on the Internet to which you can log in must run NNTP so that Trumpet can tap in to it. This computer is called your *news server*.

Your Internet SLIP provider can probably act as your news server. Contact them to make sure that they can handle NNTP. Their news server address may be slightly different from the address you used when you set up your SLIP connection — they can let you know. Either a regular-style Internet address (in words) or a numeric address will do fine.

Enough of introductions and definitions — on with the show! Let's get Trumpeting!

Getting Trumpet

As usual, this program is available by using FTP. After you get it, you unzip it and make an icon for it. (Review Chapter 9 if you don't know what we're talking about.)

Grabbing Trumpet

Here's how to get the program by way of FTP:

1. **Make a directory for your Trumpet program.**

    Call it something like `\util\trumpet`.

2. **Connect to your SLIP provider.**

3. **Run your FTP program.**

   Follow the instructions in Chapter 9 for FTP'ing software.

4. **Connect to the FTP server that stores Trumpet, ftp.utas.edu.au.**

   Yes, you guessed right — you're talking to Australia! (No, you don't have to turn your screen upside down.)

5. **Change to the /pc/trumpet/wintrump directory.**

   That is, change to pc, then to trumpet, and then to wintrump.

6. **Make sure that you are in binary mode and download the ZIP file that contains the program.**

   For the version that runs under Windows (with WinSock), look for a file named wtwsk10a.zip. (This is the filename for Trumpet for Windows, WinSock version 1.00a. The last three characters of the filename may change if Peter offers a new version.)

   Download the file into the directory you made in Step 1.

7. **Disconnect and exit from your FTP program.**

Setting it up

Here's how to unzip the ZIP file and make an icon for it:

1. **In Windows File Manager, double-click the ZIP file you just downloaded.**

   This step runs WinZip and opens the ZIP file.

2. **Extract all the files.**

   (This process is described in Chapter 9 too.) Put them in the directory you made for Trumpet.

3. **Exit from WinZip.**

   Or leave it open if you plan to use it again soon. Whatever!

4. **Make a Program Manager icon for Trumpet.**

   The easiest way is to drag the wt_wsk.exe file from File Manager into a program group in the Program Manager. We stuck ours in our Internet Stuff program group (again, Chapter 9 describes how to create an icon). You get a nice little picture of a trumpet for your efforts.

Tuning Your Trumpet

The first time you run Trumpet, it asks several questions so that it knows how to get in touch with your news server.

To run Trumpet the first time and get it into tune:

1. Double-click the Trumpet icon.

You see a message pointing out that your version of Trumpet is not registered and that you should therefore use it only for evaluation purposes.

The best way to avoid seeing this message every time you start Trumpet is to send in your money!

2. Click OK.

You see the Trumpet Setup dialog box, as shown in Figure 11-1. Trumpet shows this box to you the first time you run it. After that, you can see it at any time by choosing File➪Setup from the menu bar.

Trumpet Setup	
News Host Name	iecc.com
Mail Host Name	iecc.com
E-Mail Address	midummies @ iecc.com
Full name	Margy Levine Young
Organization	IDG Books Worldwide
Signature file name	sig.txt
POP Host name	
POP Username	Password
	☐ Fetch Read-only
Ok	Cancel

Figure 11-1: Telling Trumpet the news about yourself.

3. For the News Host Name, enter the name of your news server.

This server is the Internet host computer from which you get newsgroup information. If you use TIAC (The Internet Access Company in Bedford, Massachusetts), for example, you enter **sundog.tiac.net**, which is TIAC's news server. You can also enter its numeric Internet address. You must use a server that grants you NNTP access. (TIAC understandably provides access primarily to its customers.)

To use a news server, you have to have an account with it or otherwise have wangled permission. Otherwise, you aren't allowed to connect.

4. For your Mail Host Name, enter the name of your mail server.

(See Chapter 10 to find out what a mail server is). Trumpet has to know this name for when you want to post a new article or respond to articles privately by e-mail.

5. For your E-Mail Address, enter your e-mail address (you probably already figured that one out).

Notice that the @ is already there — type the part before the @ in one box and the part after the @ in the other box.

6. For the Organization, type the name of the organization you work for if you feel like it.

You can also leave this part blank.

7. For the Signature filename, enter the name of a file that contains your signature.

Your signature file is a text file that contains a few lines of personal information with which you want to end every article you post.

You can run Windows Notepad right now to make a signature file — don't use a word processor, because this file must have regular ASCII characters with no formatting. The file should be no more than three lines long and contain your name, address (or addresses), and any other info you want to appear at the end of each article you post. Save the file with a filename like sig.txt and enter this name in the Signature filename box.

8. If you plan to use Trumpet for reading your mail, enter the name of your mail server in the POP Host name box and your username on that system in the POP Username box.

Also enter your password in the Password box. If you don't plan to use Trumpet to read your mail, leave these boxes blank.

If you want Trumpet to read your mail but not to delete it from the system with your mailbox so that the next time you use your real mail program, the messages are still there, you can do so. Just choose the Fetch Read-only box so that it has an X in it.

9. Click OK when you have all this information filled out.

The chances of getting it all right the first time are practically zero, but you can choose File⇨Setup whenever you want to make corrections.

10. Trumpet tries to connect to your news server and subscribe you to all the newsgroups.

This step can take awhile! When it is finished, it tells you that There are new news-groups (an understatement — there are *zillions* of new newsgroups).

11. Click OK to clear the message box.

If all is well, you see the News Viewer window (see Figure 11-2).

```
┌─────────────────────────────────────────────────────────────────┐
│ ─            Trumpet News Reader - [News]                   ▼ ▲  │
│ ─  File  Edit  Special  Group  Article  View  Window  Help     ▲ │
│                                                                ▼ │
│ alt.1d                          alt.activism.death-penalty       │
│ alt.2600                        alt.adoption                     │
│ alt.59.79.99                    alt.aeffle.und.pferdle           │
│ ◄                                                            ►   │
│ ┄┄┄┄┄┄┄┄┄┄┄┄┄┄┄┄┄┄┄┄┄┄┄┄┄┄┄┄┄┄┄┄┄┄┄┄┄┄┄┄┄┄┄┄┄┄┄┄┄┄┄┄┄┄┄       │
│                                                                  │
│                                                                  │
│                                                                  │
│                                                                  │
│ ┌────────┐┌────────┐┌──────────┐┌────────┐┌────────┐┌──────┐┌───┐│
│ │   <<   ││   >>   ││ View/list ││ Format ││ Skip all││ Post ││Follow││
│ └────────┘└────────┘└──────────┘└────────┘└────────┘└──────┘└───┘│
│ ┌────────┐┌────────┐                                             │
│ │ Reply  ││ Archive│                                             │
│ └────────┘└────────┘                                             │
└─────────────────────────────────────────────────────────────────┘
```

Figure 11-2:
Trumpet's
Mission
Control.

Now you are ready to read some news. In the future, when you run Trumpet, it connects automatically to your news server, and you see the window in Figure 12-2.

Trumpetshooting

If Trumpet can't connect to your news server, this list shows some things to try:

  ✔ Use the Ping program to see whether your news server is alive.

  ✔ Rather than enter the Internet name of your news server, enter its numeric Internet address. This technique avoids one step in the connection process.

When you think that you have fixed the problem, reconnect to your news server by choosing File Reconnect from the menu bar. If that works, you see a `Connected` message. Then choose Group Subscribe to subscribe to the newsgroups that are available on your news server (subscribing to newsgroups is described later in this chapter).

Choosing a Topic

The top part of the News Viewer window (the part above the scroll bar in the middle) shows a list of the newsgroups to which you subscribe. If you just ran Trumpet for the first time, this list is tremendously long, and you can see only the first few entries. By expanding the Trumpet window vertically, you can see a little more of the list.

To see the rest of the newsgroups on your list:

⌁ Move the cursor up and down the list. The list is in two columns, and when you get to the bottom of the second column, more appear.

⌁ Use the scroll bar in the middle of the window. Click the arrow buttons at the end of the scroll bar to scroll the list. You can also drag the little elevator box along the bar to move faster.

⌁ Press Ctrl+Home to move to the top or Ctrl+End to move to the end.

⌁ Press PgUp or PgDn to move more or less a screenful of groups at a time.

When you see a group that looks interesting, double-click it.

Reading Articles

After you have selected a newsgroup by double-clicking it, Trumpet asks your news server for its articles. A message says Scanning as it downloads them. This process can take a few minutes for a large newsgroup. Just below the menu bar, you see a message that tells you how many lines of text Trumpet has downloaded so far — it can range into the hundreds or even thousands.

Finally you see a list of the articles in the newsgroup (see Figure 11-3), showing the author, size (in lines), and subject of each article.

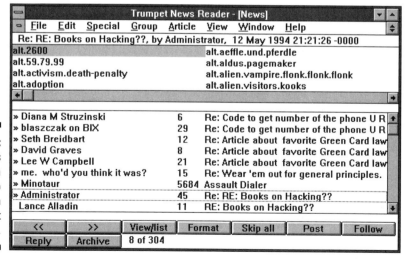

Figure 11-3:
The articles in a newsgroup listed with their subject lines.

To read an article from this list, just double-click it. You see the text of the article (see Figure 11-4).

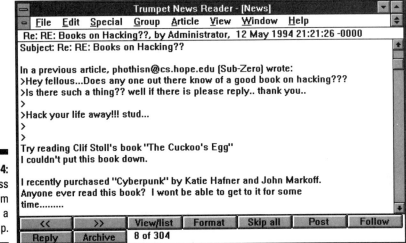

Figure 11-4:
A timeless
article from
a
newsgroup.

When you are looking at an article, you can do a number of things, which are described in the following sections.

Moving to another article

To see the next article in the newsgroup, click the >> button at the bottom of the window (or press F8). To move to the preceding article, press the << button (or press F7).

If you want to see the list of articles again, click the View/list button (or press F9). This step enables you to skim the subjects for article that looks interesting.

Printing the article

You can print the text of the article by choosing File⇨Print from the menu bar. To change the printer, choose File⇨Printer Setup first. You can also change the font by choosing Special⇨Font.

Copying text elsewhere

If you see something interesting in a message, you may want to copy it into your word processor or other program. Select some text in the message and choose Edit⇨Copy from the menu bar. This command copies the text to the Windows Clipboard. You can then paste it into almost any other Windows program.

Alternatively, you can save the entire text of the message to a text file. Choose Article⇨Save to File to create a new file for the message — Trumpet then asks you for the name of the file. To add the text of this message to the end of an existing file, choose Article⇨Append to File (this is useful when you want to save a series of articles together in one big text file).

Saving articles in a folder

You can create an *archive folder* for each newsgroup to which you subscribe. You can put in this folder any articles you want to save. Choose Article⇨Move Article to Folder from the menu bar. If this is the first article you are saving for this newsgroup, you see the message box shown in Figure 11-5. Click Yes to create the archive folder.

Figure 11-5:
Save this
article for
posterity!

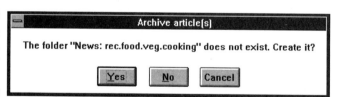

To read the articles you have saved in an archive folder, you have to switch to Trumpet's mail-reading mode (remember that you can use Trumpet as a mail reader, unless you have already fallen in love with Eudora). Choose Window⇨Mail from the menu bar. The top part of the window shows your folders. When you double-click one, the list of articles appears in the lower part of the window, just as it does when you are reading a newsgroup. Double-click an article to see its text.

Gross me out!

To preserve the tender sensibilities of folks on the Internet, dirty, racist, gross, or otherwise offensive articles are usually posted by using a simple code named *rot-13*. (This code is so simple that your six-year-old kid can handle it — you just rotate each letter forward 13 places in the alphabet. In other words, A turns into N, B turns into O, and so on. This code was used by Julius Caesar and was probably broken by the Carthaginians.)

Simple as it is, the code prevents you from inadvertently reading something you might want to avoid. If avoiding a gross posting is the last thing from your mind, you are in luck — you don't have to get your six-year-old to do the dirty work. Just choose View⇨Rot 13 from the menu bar. And if you find the message offensive, don't say we didn't warn you.

Controlling which articles to read

Trumpet (like all news readers) keeps track of which articles you have read so that you don't have to read them again. In the list of articles in the current newsgroup, articles you have read are preceded by >>.

Here are ways to mark articles as read or unread (other than reading them!):

✔ If you have fallen behind in reading a newsgroup, choose Group⇨Read All from the menu bar. This command marks as "read" all the articles in this newsgroup you have retrieved from your news server. (Alternatively, if you feel like reading everything again, you can choose Group⇨Unread All to mark as "unread" all the retrieved articles in this newsgroup.)

✔ If you are *really* way behind in reading the newsgroup, you can tell Trumpet not to bother retrieving more articles in the group. Choose Groups⇨Catch up — the next time you run Trumpet, you receive only articles that arrive starting now.

What if you see the message 502 You only have permission to transfer, sorry? This message means that your news server doesn't think that you have permission to read news articles but instead thinks that your computer is another host system with which it exchanges news. This message usually indicates a minor configuration error at the server, so contact whoever runs the news server, such as your SLIP Internet provider.

Culling the Newsgroup List

If Trumpet automatically subscribed to a billion newsgroups for you, your newsgroup list is cluttered with lots of groups you will never want to read, such as `alt.fan.gilligans.island`. Luckily, you can control which groups appear in your list by subscribing (adding new groups) and unsubscribing (getting rid of groups). Subscribing and unsubscribing don't create or delete groups — they just control which groups *you* deal with.

When you are looking at an article, you may decide, based on the quality of the article, that you have absolutely no interest in the newsgroup. You can unsubscribe to it by choosing Groups⇨Unsubscribe from the menu bar and then clicking the View/list button to see the list of newsgroups again.

To see a list of the groups you have subscribed to and all the groups that are available from your news server:

1. **Choose Groups⇨Subscribe from the menu bar.**

   You see the Subscribe to News Groups window.

2. **To choose which newsgroups to work with, choose a hierarchy from the Top Level Hierarchy list at the top of the window.**

   Newsgroups, as you may know, are organized in a hierarchy based on the first word of their title. All the newsgroups whose names begin with *alt*, for example, are in the `alt` hierarchy. Choose `misc`, for example.

   The Subscribed groups box fills with a list of the groups in that hierarchy you already subscribe to. The Unsubscribed groups box contains a list of those you do not subscribe to.

3. **To subscribe to a newsgroup in the Unsubscribed group box, click it.**

   It jumps into the Subscribed groups box.

4. **To unsubscribe to a newsgroup in the Subscribed group box, click it.**

   It disappears from your Subscribed group list and appears in the Unsubscribed group list.

5. **Keep choosing different hierarchies and sorting through the groups, subscribing and unsubscribing as you go.**

   If you are unsure about a group, you can always decide later — include it in your list and read some messages in it later before deciding.

6. **When you are finished, click OK.**

To unsubscribe from one group quickly, choose it from the newsgroups list and choose Groups⇨Unsubscribe from the menu bar. Poof!

After doing a list of work on your list of subscribed newsgroups, it's a good idea to exit from Trumpet and run it again. This step saves your list of groups, just in case disaster strikes.

Sounding Off

So far, you've just been reading other people's posts. And generally, that's what you do. Enough people run off at the mouth in the world of Usenet newsgroups that you should post articles only when *all* these circumstances occur:

- ✔ You have something interesting to say.
- ✔ You have been reading the newsgroup long enough that you know that someone didn't say it just last week.
- ✔ You have read the FAQ (list of frequently asked questions) for the newsgroup, in case the material is covered there.
- ✔ You aren't angry (very important).

Also, before posting a message, consider replying privately to the message that prompted it. Maybe this person is the only one who is interested in your reply. Why waste everyone else's time?

Replying privately

This is the newsgroup equivalent of "Let's take this outside" except that it is used not only in anger, but also whenever things get personal or not of interest to the general newsgroup reader.

To send a private e-mail message to the person who posted an article:

1. **View the article to which you want to respond.**

2. **Choose Article⇨Reply from the menu bar or click the Reply button or just press Ctrl+R.**

   You see the Mail Article window, as shown in Figure 11-6. Trumpet automatically fills in the address of the person you are responding to, the subject, and your address. (How nice!) It also includes the full article.

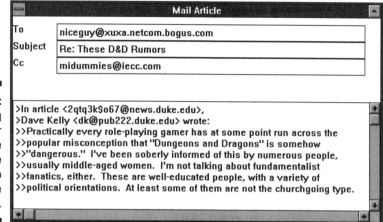

To	niceguy@xuxa.netcom.bogus.com
Subject	Re: These D&D Rumors
Cc	midummies@iecc.com

Mail Article

>In article <2qtq3k$o67@news.duke.edu>,
>Dave Kelly <dk@pub222.duke.edu> wrote:
>>Practically every role-playing gamer has at some point run across the
>>popular misconception that "Dungeons and Dragons" is somehow
>>"dangerous." I've been soberly informed of this by numerous people,
>>usually middle-aged women. I'm not talking about fundamentalist
>>fanatics, either. These are well-educated people, with a variety of
>>political orientations. At least some of them are not the churchgoing type.

Figure 11-6:
Sending
your
message
solely to the
person who
wrote the
article.

3. **Edit the article to include only the part of the article you want to respond to.**

   Make sure to delete all the boring header lines at the top, signature lines at the bottom, and other unnecessary stuff.

4. **Type the text of your message.**

   Check it carefully for quality and wholesomeness.

5. **Double-click the upper left-hand corner of the window to close it.**

   Trumpet asks whether you want to cancel this electronic mail.

6. **To send the message, click the No button. To cancel it, click Yes. To return to editing your message, click Cancel.**

   Yes, this is confusing, but it has its own weird logic.

Tooting your own horn

If you are still sure that you want to post a message to the entire newsgroup, we can't stop you. Here's how you do it:

1. **View the message to which you want to respond publicly.**

2. **Choose Article⇨Follow (short for follow-up) from the menu bar or click the Follow button or press Ctrl+F.**

Trumpet displays the Post Article window. It automatically fills in the name of the newsgroup you are reading, the same subject and keywords used by the article you are replying to, and the suggested distribution (which parts of the world should receive this posting). It also includes the full article to which you are responding.

3. **Edit the copy of the article you are responding to and delete everything except the material you are going to talk about.**

   Delete all headers and signatures and keep just a line to include who wrote the original article.

4. **Type the text of your article.**

   Make it concise and clear and check your grammar and spelling.

5. **When you are finished and you are sure that you want to post your article to the world, click Post.**

   Trumpet spends a few seconds uploading your article to the news server. If you have thought better of it, click Cancel.

Starting a new subject

In addition to replying to articles, you can bring up an entirely new subject — just make sure that it is within the area of the newsgroup.

Here's how you do it:

1. **View the newsgroup to which you want to post the article.**

   It doesn't matter whether you are viewing an article.

2. **Choose Article⇨Post or click the Post button or press Ctrl+P.**

   You see the Post Article window. Trumpet fills in the name of the current newsgroup.

3. **In the Subject box, enter a subject line.**

   Make it short but specific. Never use vague subjects like *I've been thinking* or *Here's an idea*. Give readers enough information to skip the entire article if they aren't interested in your subject.

4. **In the Keywords box, type some words that someone might enter when they search for your article.**

   Some news-reading programs can search through all the articles in a newsgroup looking for keywords.

5. **In the Summary box, you can optionally put a one-line summary of your message.**

6. **In the Distribution box, enter something that tells Usenet how far and wide to distribute your article.**

   Likely entries are **world**, **na** (North America), **usa**, **can** (Canada), **uk**, **ne** (New England), and **ba** (San Francisco Bay area).

7. **In the large, unlabeled box, enter the text of your article.**

   Be clear and to the point. Don't be inflammatory — there's enough of that in newsgroups already! Check your spelling. Stay calm and if necessary use smileys — like this :-) — for a smiling face to indicate emotions.

8. **When you are finished, if you are absolutely sure that you want to post your message where thousands of people will read it, click Post.**

   Otherwise, click Cancel.

Reading and Sending Mail with Trumpet

As we mentioned, you can use Trumpet as your mail reader too. Choose Window⇨Mail from the menu to switch to Trumpet's mail-oriented mode.

The program works in more or less the same way as it does with newsgroups. Your mail is organized into *folders,* with your unread mail in your Incoming Mail folder. If you have saved any newsgroup articles to archive folders, these folders appear here too.

Get set . . .

Before you can get your mail, you must have entered information about your mail server in the Setup dialog box when you first configured Trumpet.

1. **Choose File⇨Setup now to see whether you did.**

   The Trumpet Setup dialog box was shown way back in in Figure 12-1.

2. **For the POP Host name, enter the name of the system on which you get your mail.**

   It's probably the same thing you entered in the Mail Host Name (or SMTP Host Name) box above it in the dialog box. If your e-mail address is dquayle@elephant.com, your POP Host name is usually elephant.com (the part after the @). Your SLIP provider should have given you the name of your POP host.

3. **In the POP Username box, enter your username (the part of your address before the @).**

4. **In the Password box, enter the password you have to enter when you log in to get your mail.**

   It appears as asterisks, for security reasons.

5. **If you don't want Trumpet to delete your mail from the mail server after it downloads it to your PC, choose the Fetch Read-only box.**

   This step is useful when you usually use another program (such as Eudora) to read your mail and you want the mail to stick around until the next time you run Eudora.

6. **Click OK.**

. . . to get your mail

To tell Trumpet to get your mail, choose File⇔Fetch mail from the menu bar. Trumpet connects to your mail server and grabs your mail. To read it, choose Incoming Mail from the list of folders in the top half of the Trumpet window. Then read the messages listed in the bottom half of the window, just as you would read articles.

Limitations of Trumpet

Trumpet is pleasant to use because of its Windows interface, but it's not particularly powerful as news readers go. Many news readers show you a list of articles with one line per subject, for example, showing how many articles there are about the subject (including replies, replies to replies, and so on). Trumpet can't do this (yet).

Also, many news readers let you create *kill files,* which are lists of subjects you want to skip right over and people whose articles you don't want to read. This facility is a life-saver in newsgroups that attract *flame wars* (endless sniping between a small number of people about pointless topics). Without kill files, Trumpet doesn't make it easy to block out this stuff.

Discussions of news readers on Usenet (which, of course, you read by using a news reader like Trumpet) can be found in the groups `alt.winsock` and `comp.protocols.tcp-ip.ibmpc`.

Another News Reader: WinVN

We know of only one other WinSock-type news reader, and it's called WinVN (short for *Windows Visual News,* sort of). If you read a great deal of news, you may find that WinVN is a more convenient news reader than Trumpet is. WinVN doesn't have all of Trumpet's fancy features, but one thing it definitely does have is *threading* (that is, messages in each group are collected by topic rather than just listed in the order they arrived). This technique makes it much easier to skip over uninteresting discussions and to follow interesting ones.

You can get WinVN by FTP-ing to `titan.ksc.nasa.gov` and going to the directory `/pub/win3/winvn`. Look for a file named `winvnstd090_6.zip`, where the 090_6 is the version number and will probably have changed by the time you read this. Follow the instructions in Chapter 9 for downloading it.

A program called WinQVT/Net has a news reader built in to it. You can download it by way of anonymous FTP from `biochemistry.bioc.cwru.edu` in the directory `/gopher/pub/winqvt`. Look for a file called `qvtws?.zip`, where ? is the version number.

Installing WinVN

Installing WinVN is simplicity itself:

1. **Use WinZip to extract the ZIP file into your \util directory.**

2. **Make an icon in the usual way, by dragging the file into the Program Manager group window you want.**

3. **Run WinVN by double-clicking its icon.**

   The first time you run WinVN, it pops up a window that asks you the usual questions about your news server.

4. **Tell it the name of your NNTP news server (leave the port alone), your mail server, and your login and password for the NNTP system.**

   Leave the questions about mail alone.

5. **Click OK.**

   WinVN logs into the news server and looks for some new news. (If it complains that it can't find the server, you probably have entered something wrong, so choose Config Comm from the menu to update it.)

   WinVN displays a box with a long list of newsgroups from which you can choose ones to read. If you already have some favorite groups, you can click them now. If not, it's just as easy to subscribe to groups later.

6. **Click the OK button.**

Before you do anything else, choose Config⊅Configure Miscellaneous. The window that pops up shows about a dozen options, most of which aren't important. But tucked away in the second column is Compute Threads, which turns on the article-threading feature that makes WinVN worthwhile. Click the box next to that option and then click OK. On the menu, choose Config⊅Save Configuration to save this important bit of information away.

Reading the news

To read a newsgroup:

1. Double-click its line in the newsgroups window.

WinVN fetches the names of the unread articles in the group and displays them in a window. (If there are many unread articles, it first displays a window asking whether you want to fetch that many articles. If you want to see them all, click Unread. If you're impatient, try clicking 100 to fetch the first 100 and then go back for more if you're interested.)

Here's where WinVN begins doing something Trumpet doesn't: It threads the articles so that you can read all the messages on a topic together, as shown in Figure 11-7. The lines with little blocks under the Cambridge Stunts article are responses to it.

2. To read an article, double-click its header line.

WinVN displays the article in a new window.

3. To read the next article, press Ctrl+N.

Every time you press Ctrl+N, WinVN retrieves the next article in the thread, or the next thread if that thread is complete.

We find that a good way to read news is to click the first article in a thread that looks interesting and then press Ctrl+N through it until we lose interest. Then we scroll down in the list of articles until we see another interesting thread, click that, and so on. When we run out of interesting articles, we close the article list window by pressing Alt+F4 and then pick another group.

Responding to the news

Posting articles, follow-ups, and mail responses works in pretty much the same way as it does with Trumpet, except that the menu choices and control keys are different. (See the cheat sheet in the sidebar "A WinVN cheat sheet.") Before you post anything, choose Config⇨Configure Personal Info to set your name, e-mail address, and organization name.

Figure 11-7:
A thread of
local
interest.

Articles	Sort	Search

```
64987 05/15 Edward Mccreary      14 Re: Internet
64988 05/18 Bernie Cosell        28 Re: MIT stunt
65046 05/18 Tom Galloway         28    I
64989 05/15 C.P. Brown           19 Re: Cambridge stunts (was: Re: MIT stunt)
65026 05/16 djsd100@hermes.cam   19    I
65081 05/16 A.J. Bolt            13    I
65035 05/16 Luke Vaughn          28    I
65053 05/16 A.W. Garrard         39    I
65058 05/16 A.A. Asthana         17       I
65063 05/16 S.A. Mcintyre        22       I
65090 05/16 djsd100@hermes.cam   21    I
64990 05/18 Richard N. Turner    11 Re: What was an 8089 ???
64991 05/18 Richard N. Turner    13 Re: Clothes named after programming lang
64993 05/15 Dave Fischer         11 Re: Streets named after programming languages
64994 05/15 Kent Walker          12 Re: Osborne I
64995 05/15 Steve VanDevender    30 Re: Need info about an HewlettPackard 150
64997 05/16 Mike Holderness      20 Antique corner: RM 480Z info
64998 05/15 David Thomas Richa   16 Re: Streets named after programming languages (was Re: IRIS frame grabber
64999 05/16 William Guido Sohn    1 Re: longest USENET thread ever
```

Choosing newsgroups

To select and deselect newsgroups, you click the name of the group you want to add or delete from your newsgroup list and then choose Group⇨Subscribe or Group⇨Unsubscribe from the menu. You don't have to subscribe to a group to look at its articles; the main reason to subscribe to some groups is that you can tell WinVN when it starts up not to fetch all the info about unsubscribed groups, which saves some time.

The authors of WinVN, who presumably work on it at NASA between Space Shuttle launches, update WinVN frequently. (While we were writing this book, it advanced from version 0.83 to 0.96), so the version you use probably will have lots of swell features beyond what we describe here. Poke around and find out what they are — it's the Usenet way.

You can find out the latest about WinVN on Usenet in the groups `alt.winsock` and sometimes in `comp.protocols.tcp-ip.ibmpc`.

A WinVN cheat sheet

Key	Description	Key	Description
Ctrl+A	Composes a new article (in the newsgroups or article window) or appends a file (in the message-composition window)	Ctrl+R	Displays a ROT13 article (in the message view window) or turns selected text into ROT13 (in the message-composition window)
Ctrl+B	Forwards an article as e-mail	Ctrl+S	Sends message (in the message-composition window)
Ctrl+C	Composes mail to the author of an article	Ctrl+U	Updates article list (in the article window)
Ctrl+F	Finds a string in a group name (in the newsgroups window) or article title (in the article window)	F3	Finds next group (in the newsgroups window) or article (in the article window) that matches a search string
Ctrl+N	Finds next article (in the message view window)		
Ctrl+P	Finds preceding article (in the message view window)		

Chapter 12
Cute Little HGopher

. . . .

In This Chapter

▶ What HGopher is

▶ Getting it from the net

▶ Loading it up

▶ Flying through Gopherspace with HGopher

▶ Searching for stuff in Gopherspace

▶ Using bookmarks for your favorite Gopher menus

. . . .

*G*opher is one of the most popular of the new Internet services. It's the easiest for a user (that's you) to learn to use and the easiest for someone to set up a server, so Gopher servers are all over the net. In this chapter, we look at a popular WinSock Gopher program called HGopher.

What HGopher Is

HGopher is a Gopher client — that is, a program you use to retrieve information from Gopher servers all over the world. There are a bunch of Gopher clients, but here we concentrate on HGopher, which is relatively *mature* (a computer euphemism for *doesn't crash and burn as much as the others do*) and is more widely used.

Getting HGopher from the Net

You can grab the HGopher program by using FTP from an archive on the net. See the section "Netting a Program" in Chapter 9 for general instructions. Here's what you do:

1. **Create on your system a directory in which to put HGopher — maybe call it \hgopher.**

2. **Use your FTP program to connect to** `lister.cc.ic.ac.uk`.

   Yes, that's in the United Kingdom. Aren't we international!

3. **On the remote system, change to the directory** `/pub/wingopher`.

   Note: You can also FTP to `microdyne.com` and change to the directory `/pub/winsock/apps`, which may be faster.)

4. **Tell FTP to use binary mode.**

5. **Retrieve the file** `hgopher2.4.zip` **from the remote system. That's not a valid DOS filename, so give it the name** `hgoph24.zip` **on your system.**

   This is the filename for Version 2.4. When you read this, there may be a newer version, such as 2.5 or 3.1. You may as well get the newest version you can.

6. **Leave FTP.**

7. **Using WinZip or PKUNZIP, extract the files from** `HGOPH24.ZIP` **into your** `\hgopher` **directory.**

   See Chapter 9 for details. If you're short on disk space, you can delete the ZIP file now.

8. **Add an icon for HGopher to your program manager.**

   See Chapter 9 for instructions. You can put it in your Internet Stuff program group (or wherever you put Internet-related programs).

Loading Up HGopher

At this point, you're all ready to run HGopher, although there's some tuning up we spare you until later.

If its real name is WinGopher, why is the program called HGopher?

In a few places in the documentation, HGopher seems to be called WinGopher. Hmm, an identity problem. Took us a while to figure that one out, until we noticed that the author's name is Martyn Hampton. Since he wrote it, you can hardly blame him for naming it after himself (we would have preferred MartynGopher, or maybe Hamster).

Running HGopher

Run it the same way you run any other Windows program — click its Program Manager icon or click its program name (hgopher.exe) in File Manager. Either way, you should see a window like the one in Figure 12-1.

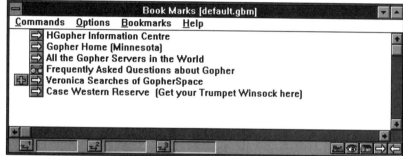

Figure 12-1:
HGopher
starts up.

Help! I'm trapped in here!

For some reason, HGopher sometimes starts up in a teensy little window like the one in Figure 12-2.

Figure 12-2:
We're sure
that
HGopher is
hiding in
here.

We don't know why. If you start up with HGopher in a window like this, just resize the window in the usual way — click the mouse on a corner of the window and drag it out to a useful size.

Flying Through Gopherspace with HGopher

Gopher presents you with lots and lots of menus. Most of the entries in the menus refer to yet more menus, and others show you files and other useful stuff. So there are two things you have to do to get useful work out of Gopher: Find the menus you want and then retrieve the useful stuff from those menus.

Let's take a quick tour of the HGopher screen. (So it's not Hawaii — it's still a tour.) At the top is the usual Windows menu, which we worry about later. In the middle of the screen is the list of Gopher items. At the left of each item is an icon that tells you what kind of item it is, as shown in the following list.

Hgopher icons

Icon	Type of Item
⇨	Another Gopher menu
🔍	A text file
♫	A sound file
📷	A picture
🎞	A movie
🔢	A file containing something else, most often a compressed ZIP archive
💻	A telnet session
🔍	A search item (see "Searching for Mr. Right" later in this chapter)

HGopher comes knowing how to handle menus and a few kinds of files, such as text files, but you have to configure it for everything else. Fortunately, configuring it is pretty easy.

Swoosh!

Enough theory — let's get something from the net. HGopher starts up with a menu containing a few likely starting points. The first is HGopher Information Centre, which we can tell is a menu because there's an arrow to its left.

To look at the contents of a likely-looking menu item, double-click on its line. For example, double-click on the line `HGopher Information Centre`. If you click the line, not the arrow, HGopher highlights it. If you double-click the line, HGopher fetches the menu and shows it to you.

Incidentally, the reason it's spelled *Centre* rather than *Center* is that the server with that menu is in England.

As it fetches the next menu, HGopher reports its progress in one of the boxes in the lower left-hand corner of the HGopher window. The amount of data retrieved so far appears in the box, with the little white light next to it blinking on and off to show network activity. The button with the lightning bolt lets you stop a retrieval that's taking too long; we get back to that subject a little later.

After a few seconds, HGopher shows the new menu, as shown in Figure 12-3.

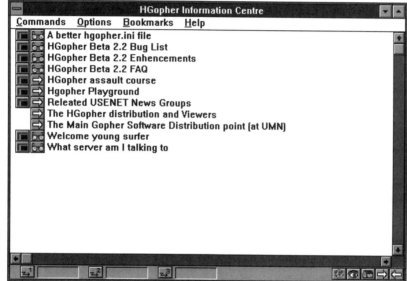

Figure 12-3:
HGopher
has
retrieved a
menu.

Gopher+

The menu in Figure 12-3 is a *Gopher+* (pronounced *Gopher-Plus*) menu. You can tell by the little boxes to the left of the arrows and eyeglasses. Fortunately, Gopher+ is just about the same as Gopher except that you can tell before you retrieve something how big it is by clicking the Gopher+ box. (Gopher+ does a lot of other stuff, but the sizes are by far the most noticeable.

You can move from menu to menu in this way, looking for useful information. Sooner or later, you find a file you want to download or some other information you want to do something with.

Getting a Real File

Near the bottom of the new menu is the item Welcome young surfer, which is a text file (you can tell by the eyeglasses).

I think I've got it

To get a file, just double-click the menu line (the actual line, not the ittle icon in front of it). For example, double-click `Welcome young surfer` (not the eyeglases, the text). HGopher fetches the file for you.

When the file finishes arriving, HGopher starts an appropriate program to let you see its contents. This is a text file, so it starts the usual Windows Notepad, as shown in Figure 12-4.

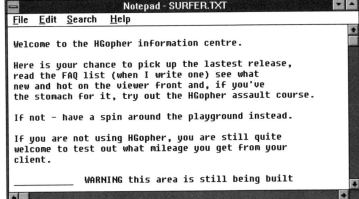

Figure 12-4: HGopher has retrieved a text file.

Within Notepad, you can do any of the usual things you do in it, including scrolling from page to page.

When you leave Notepad (again, in the usual way, by choosing File⇨Exit from the menu or by pressing Alt+F4), HGopher deletes the file.

How to be saved

Unless you tell it otherwise, Gopher retrieves files in what might be called Cruel Joke Mode, because whether you like the file or not, and even if you might want to keep it, after you're done looking at it, it goes away. Poof! (Actually, it's called View mode, but it still can be cruel.)

Fortunately, HGopher's sense of humor is easily tamed. Down in the lower right-hand corner of the window, you notice a little eyeball, which means that you retrieve files just to look at them. Fortunately, you have two other options. If you click on the eyeball (sounds uncomfortable, doesn't it?), the eyeball is replaced by a little folder, known as Copy to File mode. Now whenever you tell HGopher to retrieve a file, it displays the standard Windows Save As box (see Figure 12-5), and you can pick any filename you want to save the file.

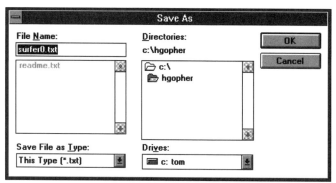

Figure 12-5:
Tell
HGopher
what to call
your file.

The third option, if you click the folder icon, is Copy to Directory mode, indicated by an open file folder. In this mode, whenever HGopher retrieves a file, it puts it in a given directory (normally \tmp, though it's easy to change) and makes up a name for it based on the name it has on the server. This mode can be useful if you want to retrieve a bunch of files, one after another.

If you have trouble remembering what the icons mean, you can get the same effect by choosing Options⇨Copy mode from the menu bar. Its submenu displays View, Copy to File, or Copy to Directory.

Cutting to the Chase

Now you know pretty much all you have to know to navigate around Gopherspace: Double-click a menu item to fetch the data for that menu, which may in turn be another menu.

Here are some other tips:

✔ To return to the preceding menu, either click the top line of the current menu (which should contain the name of the preceding menu) or click the left-pointing arrow in the bottom right corner of the screen.

✔ If you've returned to a previous menu, you can click the right-pointing arrow at the bottom of the screen to go ahead to the place from whence you came. (This process is less confusing in practice than it sounds here.)

Help! I've Clicked and I Can't Get Out!

Sometimes you start retrieving a file and only then discover that the file is 14,000 KB and will take approximately three years to retrieve. Fortunately, you have some options.

Having the last laugh on Cruel Joke Mode

If you told HGopher to retrieve a file and you're looking at it by using the Windows Notepad and want to keep it, there is an easy way around Cruel Joke Mode. Just choose File⇨Save As from the Notepad menu and save the file under a *different* name from the one HGopher used. Then leave Notepad. HGopher deletes the original file, but the copy you've saved is still there.

How to be in two places at a time

HGopher runs *asynchronously,* a fancy computer term which means that it doesn't force you to wait while it does something. If you look carefully at the bar at the bottom of the HGopher window (see Figure 12-6), you notice three little windows and three buttons numbered 1, 2, and 3. That's because HGopher can be retrieving three things — that's three things, yes indeed, three things — at a time. That means that you can start fetching a really big file and then go ahead and continue looking around Gopherspace while it fetches the big file.

HGopher only sort of runs asynchronously. If more than one retrieval is going on at a time, in fact, only the most recent one makes any progress. So if you start retrieving a big file, that is retrieval number 1. Then when you click to move to another menu, that menu is retrieval number 2, and number 1 waits until number 2 is finished, at which point number 1 continues. If you're seriously impatient, you can begin a second file retrieval before the first is finished (that's number 2) and then keep going from menu to menu, with each menu retrieval being number 3 and causing both numbers 1 and 2 to pause.

In practice, we find that it's quite useful to have two things going on at a time, particularly a large "background" file retrieval while looking at other menus, but it's much less useful to have three things going at a time.

If you try to retrieve two large files at a time, the first one has to wait until the second one is finished. Gopher servers, being only subhuman, have limited patience; if the first file has to wait a really long time, like more than a couple of minutes, the server sending it will probably conclude that your HGopher has lost interest and stop sending it. So one large background retrieval at a time is plenty.

Figure 12-6:
Multiple retrievals going on.

Enough, already

Sometimes you start retrieving a file and realize that it was a mistake. You don't want it — forget it. No matter how fast it arrives, suddenly you just don't need another recipe for Pecan Jell-O Fruit Bombe Surprise.

To tell HGopher to stop retrieving something, just click the button next to the box showing the progress of that retrieval. HGopher pops up a box like the one shown in Figure 12-7.

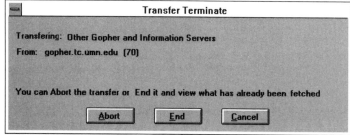

Figure 12-7:
Aborting an
HGopher
retrieval.

You have three possibilities here: Abort, End, and Cancel, names that we must admit seem to be roughly synonymous. But what they do is quite different:

- **Abort:** Stops retrieving the file (or menu or whatever), throws away whatever it has retrieved so far, and pretends that you never asked in the first place.

- **End:** You pretend that it came to the end of the retrieval to show you whatever it already has. This choice can be handy if you're not sure that you asked for the right file, because you can look at what you have so far. If you like it, you can tell it to retrieve the file or menu again.

- **Cancel:** Cancels the cancel — you pretend that you never pushed the button, you love the file, and all is forgiven. This choice is relentlessly logical but baffling — computer naming at its finest. (How many Cancels would a Cancel cancel if a Cancel could cancel Cancels?)

Searching for Mr. Right

One of the nicer features built-in to Gopher is searching. Some Gopher menus offer *search items,* in which you tell it what to look for by typing some keywords.

Using search items

Here's an example of how to use a search item:

1. **Start at the initial HGopher menu.**

   If you're somewhere else, click the little green globe at the bottom of the window. In the next section, we explain what you just did.

2. **Choose Gopher Home (Minnesota).**

   This step should retrieve a screen like the one in Figure 12-8.

   The second and third lines from the end are search items, which you can tell from the little icons to their left, which are supposed to remind you of looking something up in a dictionary.

3. **Click one of these search items.**

4. **HGopher displays the Index Search dialog box, shown in Figure 12-9, in which you type the words to look for.**

   This dialog box is a place where Gopher acts lamentably vaguely. The rules say that you type some words, and the Gopher server to which your words are sent can do with them whatever it wants. All but the most perverse Gopher servers use them to make up a menu of likely-looking entries that match the words you've typed. We typed the word *phone,* for example, and got the menu shown in Figure 13-10.

Coming up with good search words is a black art. Far too often you type a perfectly reasonable word or two and get back an error message that the menu contains no entries, which means that your search words didn't match anything. If that happens, try variants or synonyms — words such as *telephone, phones, directory* (if you're looking for phone books), and the like. In better searching systems, synonyms are handled automatically, but for most Gopher searches, you have to think up synonyms yourself.

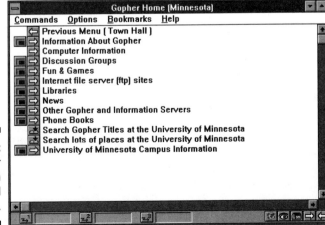

Figure 12-8:
The Gopher
Home in
Beautiful
Minnesota.

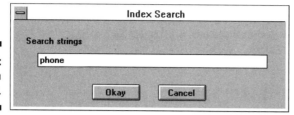

Figure 12-9:
Entering a
search item.

Figure 12-10:
Some
phony-
looking
entries.

Veronica's a busy girl

The most popular Gopher search facility is called Veronica. (She's a friend of Archie's, and Archie is a search program described in Chapter 19 of *The Internet For Dummies*.) Veronica searches through nearly all the Gopher menus in the world, looking for items that match words you enter. She's by far the fastest and easiest (we really should use different words here) route to getting what you want from Gopher.

On the initial screen that comes with HGopher is an entry for Veronica Searches of Gopherspace. Unfortunately, that entry is *stale* (a geek-ese word which means that the computer to which it refers doesn't work anymore). Fortunately, real Veronica is easy enough to find:

1. On the initial screen, choose Gopher⇨Home.

If you've just tried the *phone* example, click the left-pointing arrow in the lower right-hand corner of the screen to return to that menu.

2. Click the Other Gopher and Information Servers option.

3. **Click Search Titles in Gopherspace Using Veronica.**

This step gets you to a page that lists a bunch of Veronica servers all over the world. (In the next section, you even learn how to change the initial screen to refer to this menu rather than to the stale one.)

4. **Choose a Veronica server.**

For each Veronica server, there's one entry for Search Gopher Directory Titles and another for Search Gopherspace By Veronica. The difference is that the first searches only the names of menus, and the second searches every entry in every menu. As you might expect, the second is considerably slower. Also, if you pick search terms for which there are a great deal of matches, the second can come up with so many matches that you can't handle them all.

When you're using Veronica to search, try the directory titles search first, and if that doesn't find what you want, try the slower Gopherspace search.

The procedure for a Veronica search is just the same as any other search — choose the search item for the server you want, type the search terms into the box that pops up, and wait for the result.

We Have to Stop Meeting Like This

As you wander through Gopherspace, you find menus that you particularly like and want to be able to return to. If you are a phenomenally well-organized person, you might be able to remember the exact sequence of menus you went through to get to each of those menus, write them down in a notebook, and carefully re-create the steps to get back to the menu. If you're merely mortal like we are, life is too short for such nonsense. Fortunately, computers are really good at remembering details like this, and HGopher has *bookmarks* that remember your favorite menus for you.

What we have until now been calling the initial screen is in fact the list of bookmarks. (It even says so, right in the window's title.) A bookmark is just like any other Gopher item except that it happens to be stored in a file on your computer rather than out in Gopherspace.

Marking Gopher's greatest hits

You manage your bookmarks primarily by using the Bookmarks menu.

✔ If you're Gophering around and you happen upon a menu you particularly like, choose Bookmarks⇨Mark Menu to add the name of that menu to your bookmarks.

> ✔ If you want to remember a particular item in the current menu, click once on that item to highlight it. (Don't double-click yet.) Then choose Bookmarks⇨Add Item to add that item to your bookmarks.

> ✔ You can create a bookmark yourself if you know the name of a computer that offers Gopher service. Choose Bookmarks⇨Create Bookmark to display the Create/Edit Bookmark dialog box.

For Type, HGopher suggests Menu. Take the suggestion. For Description, type a one-line description of the service that HGopher will use as the menu line. For Host, type the name of the computer. In Port, type the number of the port on which the service is offered. If you don't know the port number, try 70, which is usually correct. Leave the rest of the fields blank and click Okay to add your new item to the bookmarks. Double-click your new bookmark. If the computer does in fact offer Gopher service, you should see its top-level Gopher menu.

Return to Gopher's greatest hits

To show your list of bookmarks, click the little globe at the bottom of the screen. The globe should change to a bookshelf, and you get your list of bookmarks. Choose an entry from the bookmarks in the same way you choose one from any other Gopher menu. Or you can click the bookshelf to go back to the menu you were looking at before you switched to the bookmarks.

If you're extremely lazy and have good finger dexterity, you can click the right mouse button anywhere in the HGopher screen to switch back and forth to your bookmarks.

When you exit from HGopher, if you've made any changes to your list of bookmarks, it asks whether you want to save the changed bookmarks. Click Yes. You can also save your bookmarks directly from the Bookmarks menu.

All Dressed Up and Nowhere to Go

The astute reader (you) may have noticed that we've told you a great deal about how to run HGopher, but we haven't said much about what to do with it. Read Chapter 16 for how to access different types of information with a Gopher program. And check out Chapters 17 through 19 for advice on fun places to visit in Gopherspace.

Chapter 13

Cutting Through the Thicket of WAIS and WINWAIS

● ●

In This Chapter

▶ WAIS of searching

▶ Useful features of WINWAIS and WAISMAN

▶ Useless features of WINWAIS and WAISMAN

▶ Searching tips

● ●

We Have Our WAIS....

WAIS is short for *Wide Area Information Servers.* From its name, it should be obvious what it is and how to use it, so we don't have to write this chapter after all and instead of sitting in front of the computer, we can go outside and finish teaching the dog how to repaint the — what? It's not obvious? Oh, all right, the dog will just have to wait.

Despite its totally generic name, WAIS does a specific thing: It searches for words in documents. If you want to find out about pumpkin pie, for example, you can tell it to look for the words *pumpkin* and *pie* in any of several huge libraries of documents and show you the documents that match the best. (Naturally, you get better results if you tell it to look in libraries that contain recipes, but we get to that.) WAIS can also retrieve pictures and other nontext files associated with the documents it finds, although at this point there aren't a lot of pictures to be found.

You can use one of several Windows programs (called *WAIS client programs*, in Internet-ese) to get into WAIS. Because they all talk to the same WAIS servers with the same sets of documents, they all really do the same thing. This chapter describes two of them:

✔ **WINWAIS:** Written at the U.S. Geological Survey (your tax dollars at play) and has a couple of spiffy features of extreme interest to geographers, like a built-in map of the world

✔ **WAISMAN (or WAIS Manager):** Written at CNIDR, the Clearinghouse for Networked Information Discovery, a North Carolina group that thinks about the sorts of things WAIS does

You use the two programs in almost the same way, but they have enough differences that you might find one of them easier to use than the other. WINWAIS is a little easier to use, but WAISMAN has better multimedia support. (Later, we show you how you can retrieve exciting multimedia documents, such as a sound clip of Bullwinkle the Moose.)

First, we tell you how to install both programs. If you're not sure which one to install, start with WINWAIS. Also, refer to Chapter 9 for an overview of down-loading software from the Internet.

Getting WINWAIS

Setting up WINWAIS is a little tricky because it comes with about three dozen separate files.

Grabbing WINWAIS

The first thing to do is to use FTP to download it to your computer, like this:

1. **Make a directory called \util\winwais.**

   WINWAIS is big enough that its files need their own directory. You can call this directory anything you want — we're just making a suggestion.

2. **Connect to your SLIP provider if you haven't already done so.**

3. **Run the FTP program.**

4. **Connect to host ridgisd.er.usgs.gov by using anonymous FTP.**

   If you use WS_FTP, just check the Anonymous box in the connect window and it fills in the user name and password for you.

5. **In the FTP program, on the remote host, change to the directory software. Then change to the directory wais.**

   This step should put you in /software/wais.

6. **On your own computer, change to the \util\winwais directory.**

   (Or whatever you called it.)

7. **Make sure that FTP is using binary mode and retrieve the file** `wwais24.exe`.

   That's the name for version 2.4. By the time you read this, they may have a newer version named something like `wwais25.exe` or even `wwais30.exe`.

8. **Disconnect and exit from FTP.**

Setting it up

The EXE file you just downloaded is really a ZIP file that knows how to unzip itself.

Here's how to unzip the file:

1. **Start the Windows File Manager, if it's not already running.**

2. **Go to the directory in which you downloaded the WINWIS file and double-click the filename,** `wwais24.exe`.

   This step runs the self-extractor and extracts the files. (Cautious people may want to run WinZip instead and use it to extract the files, in the unlikely event that someone spiked the file.)

3. **If disk space is tight, you can delete some of the extracted files, including** `setup.exe`, `wssetup.exe` **(two setup programs not necessary if you're using WinSock), and** `wwais.exe` **itself.**

4. **Create an icon for WINWAIS in the Program Manager.**

   The easiest way to do this is to drag the file `wais.exe` from the File Manager into one of the program group windows in the Program Manager. If you have done this correctly, the icon should be a little blue globe with a lightning bolt across it.

Getting WAISMAN

Setting up WAISMAN is slightly — but not hugely — more complicated because it's written by using a programming package called Toolbook; it comes with a bunch of pieces of Toolbook in addition to the WAISMAN program.

Grabbing WAISMAN

Use FTP to copy the WAISMAN program to your computer:

1. **Connect to your SLIP provider, if you haven't already done so.**

2. **Run your FTP program.**

3. **Connect to host `ftp.cnidr.org`, by using anonymous FTP.**

   If you use WS_FTP, check the Anonymous box in the connect window, and it fills in the username and password for you.

4. **On the remote host, change to directory `pub`, then to directory `NIDR.tools`, then to directory `wais`, then to directory `pc`, and finally to directory `windows`.**

   They thought that they could hide from you, but you're smarter than they expected. This step puts you in `/pub/NIDR.tools/wais/pc/windows`.

5. **On the local system, change to your `\util` directory.**

   Or change to wherever you are storing your Internet programs.

6. **Make sure that FTP is using binary mode and retrieve the file `waisman3.zip`.**

7. **Disconnect and exit from FTP.**

Setting it up

As usual, you have to unzip the file before you can use it:

1. **In Windows File Manager, go to the directory that contains the file you just downloaded and double-click `waisman3.zip`.**

   This step should start WinZip and open the WAISMAN file.

2. **In WinZip, click Extract.**

3. **In the Extract window, make sure that the Extract To directory is set to `c:\util` and that Use Directory Names is checked. Then click the Extract button.**

   Wait awhile as WinZip extracts all the files. It creates two directories in `\util\winman3` (which contains the actual program) and `\util\wais_src` (which contains files describing WAIS databases you might want to search).

4. **To create an icon for the program, choose the program group in which you want to put the icon in the Program Manager.**

   The usual trick of dragging a file from the File Manager doesn't work with Toolbook programs like WAISMAN.

5. **Choose File New from the Program Manager menu and click OK to create a new program item.**

   You see the Program Item Properties dialog box, as shown in Figure 13-1.

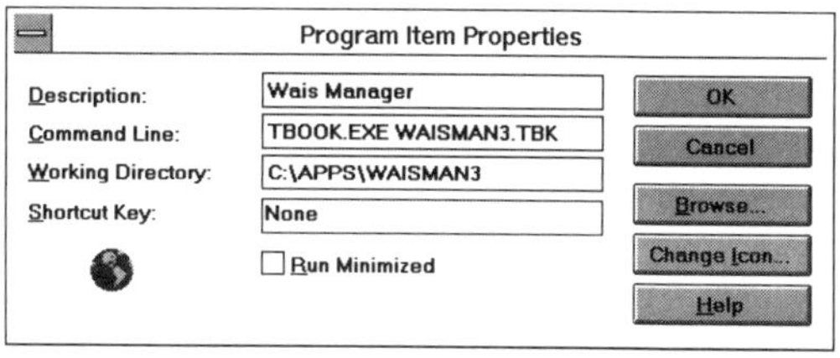

Figure 13-1:
Creating the
Program
Manager
entry for
WAISMAN.

6. **Fill out the dialog box, as shown in Figure 13-1.**

The standard Toolbook icon is kind of grody, so you may want to click Change Icon and enter the name of the icon file thoughtfully provided by the WAISMAN authors (see Figure 13-2). It's yet another blue globe map. (Can't these guys think of anything else? A pile of books? A paper shredder? A cuttlefish? We're tired of globes.)

Figure 13-2:
Setting the
Program
Manager
icon for
WAISMAN.

7. **Click OK to create the icon.**

That's it for basic installation. You can worry about one or two configuration details in the next section.

Your Basic Hand-to-Hand Combat with WAIS

Getting WAIS to cough up some documents starts as a three-step process:

1. **Identify some sources to use.**

2. **Search for some words and get a list of documents.**

3. **Retrieve whichever of the documents looks interesting.**

Hand-to-Hand with WINWAIS

First look at how to find some information with WINWAIS. To run it, double-click its icon (the globe with the lightning bolt) to see a screen that resembles Figure 13-3.

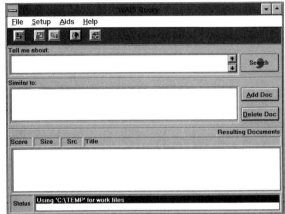

Figure 13-3:
WINWAIS
starts up.

Going to the source

Before you can do any searching, you have to select some *sources*, which are libraries of searchable documents. You can select sources in two ways. WINWAIS comes with two source lists named WAIS and ALLSRC. The WAIS list contains only one source, but fortunately it's the source directory that lists all the other sources. If you're not sure which source you want, you can use the WAIS list to look for likely sources. The other list, ALLSRC, contains a list of all well-known sources. Because new sources appear relatively infrequently, the sources in ALLSRC are pretty much the same ones you can find by searching the directory of sources, so do it the easy way first — use ALLSRC.

To choose some sources:

1. **Click the leftmost button in the row near the top of the window, which switches to the source window.**

2. **To switch to the ALLSRC list, click the mouse on the word** *WAIS,* **which appears in the Source Group window.**

   This step makes a list appear, including the option ALLSRC.

3. **Click ALLSRC.**

   The list of sources appears in the lower window.

4. **Choose one or more sources.**

   You can scroll up and down through that list. When you see a source you like, click it and drag it to the upper window to select it.

5. **Click the Done button.**

You might think that the best way to find what you want is to use every possible source. There's even an All Sources button to select them all. It's usually a terrible idea, in fact, to do that. The problem is that WAIS searches each source separately, so if you have 50 sources and it takes 12 seconds to search each one, the total search takes more than 10 minutes, which is too long to wait unless you are a uniquely patient person. Also, the sources range over an enormous range of subjects, and it seems pointless to include a source containing Australian biological abstracts, for example, if what you're looking for are presidential press conferences that mention the Information Super Collider (a.k.a. the Information Superhighway). Try selecting one or two sources, and if you don't find what you need, select a few more.

Let's look at presidential documents: Scroll down to White-House-Papers and drag that topic to the upper window. Then click the Done button to go back to the main WINWAIS screen.

Are we ever going to do some real searching?

Sure we are (we thought that you would never ask):

1. **Click the mouse in the large top window, the one to the left of the big Search button.**

2. **Type some search words.**

   Type **Iraq sanctions**, for example.

3. **Click Search.**

   WINWAIS goes and does the search for you.

The progress of the search is reported in the tiny window at the bottom of the screen. WINWAIS has to contact the server that contains the source, send it the request, wait while the server performs the search, and then get the answers back. If you're unlucky, it may have trouble contacting the server, in which case you probably see a little window with an inscrutable six-digit WinSock error code. Try the search again, because some of the errors depend on timing and might go away on a second try.

A four-star performance

If the search goes as planned, the list of documents that best match the search words appear in the lower large Resulting Documents window. Each found document is scored as in a movie review, from one star to four. The scoring is specific to the search — whichever document matches best is awarded four stars, even if it didn't match all that well.

To look at any of the documents that were found, double-click the document in the Resulting Documents window. WINWAIS retrieves the document and displays it, as shown in Figure 13-4.

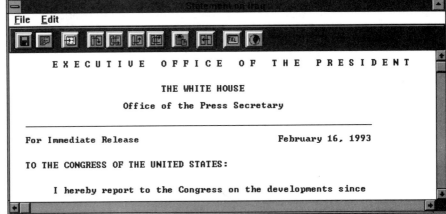

Figure 13-4:
A
presidential
document.

A bunch of buttons are along the top of the document window. Some of them are even useful! (All of them have menu equivalents for button-haters.) This list describes the buttons:

- ✔ **The leftmost (floppy disk) button:** Saves the document to a file. It asks you for the filename before saving.

- ✔ **The second (torn curtain) button:** Prints the document.

- ✔ **The third (arrow stabbing a document) button:** Skips ahead in the document to the first place where your search words occur. Every time you click, it goes to the next place where one of the words occurs.

- ✔ **The next four (various curved lines and boxes) buttons:** Move to the preceding or next document in various orders. The first one (right turn arrow) gets the next document in the order in which the documents are stored on the server. The second (u-turn) gets the next document in the order they're displayed in the list on the search screen (that is, from four stars down to one). The third and fourth (left turn and backward U-turn arrows) get previous documents.

- ✔ **The momma and baby clipboards button:** Copies document text to the Windows Clipboard. You have to select text by using the mouse first.

- ✔ **The last useful button (two boxes pinned together):** Takes text you've selected with the mouse and marks it for relevance feedback, which you learn about next.

By the way, to get rid of the document window, press F3 or double-click the button at the left end of the title bar.

That's irrelevant!

What's large and grey and works in the circus and has a long trunk? Oh, you heard that one back when you were seven years old? Whoops, back to WAIS.

WAIS features relevance feedback, which is when you take the trunk and wrap it all the way around to the — sorry, we forgot again. *Relevance feedback* lets you give a document or a piece of a document back to WAIS to say "find me more documents like this."

On the button

If you use WINWAIS much, you may find that it's easier to control from the keyboard than by using the mouse because you have to type the search strings anyway. So here's a keyboard cheat sheet:

Key (or Keys)	Function
F1	Help
F3	Closes document window
F5	Finds search words in document window
F6	Adds selected text to relevance feedback
Shift+F6	Copies selected text to Clipboard
F7	Gets previous document in source order
Alt+F7	Gets previous document in listed order
F8	Gets next document in source order
Alt+F8	Gets next document in listed order
Arrow keys	Scrolls document up or down

To select an entire document for relevance feedback, from the search screen click the document you want in the Retrieved Documents window and drag it to the middle Similar To window. To unselect the document, just drag it back. You can use the Add Doc and Delete Doc buttons, but dragging is easier and much cooler.

To select part of a document you are viewing in the document window, select the text you like by using the mouse, and click the Relevant button (the one that looks like two bars pinned together.)

After you've set your list of relevant documents, press Search to redo your search, taking into account your relevance list. You may have to add and remove search words and add and remove relevant documents to find what you want.

Back to the source

If you can't find the source you need in the ALLSRC list, you have to search through the Directory of Sources:

1. **In the main screen, click the leftmost button.**

   You see the sources window.

2. **If the ALLSRC list of servers appears, click ALLSRC. When WAIS appears, click that.**

3. **Drag the Directory of Sources from the lower window to the upper one.**

   This step tells WINWAIS that you want to search the directory of sources.

4. **Click the Done button.**

5. **Type some words that describe the kinds of documents you want.**

   To search for patents, for example, type **patent** and **patents**.

6. **Click Search to search for likely sources.**

   The sources appear in the bottom window, scored from one star to four.

7. **Double-click a likely-looking one.**

   You see a special document window, as shown in Figure 13-5. The upper part of the window is the text of the source file, which you can scroll through (slowly) by using the scroll bar. After the computer glop at the top, the file usually has a prose description of the source. If you want to look at other sources in the list, use the buttons at the top of the window to move to the next or preceding source.

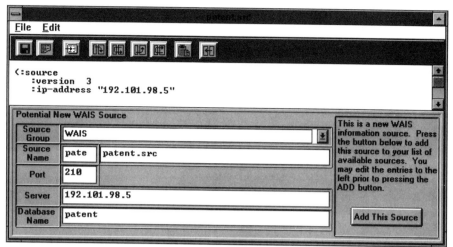

Figure 13-5:
A WAIS
source.

8. **If you find a source you like, click Add This Source to add it to your list of sources.**

9. **Dismiss the window by using F3 or by clicking the button at the left end of the menu bar.**

Now the new source or sources are in your source list and you can use them in future searches just like any other sources.

Be sure to keep in mind the difference between searching for sources and searching for documents. If you want to find patents about banana peelers, for example, you look for sources by using words like *patent*. Then after you've found some sources, you search those sources by using terms like *banana* and *peelers*.

Adding sources by hand

Sometimes you may find a reference to a swell new WAIS source in a mail message or a Usenet news article. If you're a careful typist, you can add a source yourself. From the menu, choose Edit⇨Sources, and you see a Source Editor window similar to the one in Figure 14-7 but that you can fill in yourself. The fields are shown in this list:

Source group: Leave this as *WAIS*.

Source Name: There are two windows. In the first smaller one, type a four-letter code that will be used to identify documents retrieved from this source in the Resulting Documents window. In the second larger one, type a description of the source.

Port: Use the port number given for the source, usually 210.

(continued)

(continued)

Server: Enter the host name or host number of the server.

Database Name: Enter the database name exactly as given and be sure to get the punctuation and spacing the same.

Then click Add to add it to the list of available sources, and Done to leave the window.

If you find that you've messed up in entering a source, you can fix it by coming back to the Source Editor window, clicking the source in question in the list at the top of the window (which fills in the fields with their current values), fixing the values that are wrong, and then clicking Change to store away the changed version.

It isn't very useful, but it sure looks cool

WINWAIS was written at the U.S. Geological Survey, an outfit dedicated to maps, so you may not be amazed to hear that some features in WINWAIS are specifically for mapheads. If you click the globe button in the main screen (the second one from the right that looks like a circle with a big, black smudge), you get a Spatial Data Locator window, like the one in Figure 13-6.

Using the arrows at the top of the window, you can rotate the globe and zoom in, and you can then use the mouse to select regions on the globe. (*Hint:* When you change the rotation or zoom, click Redraw to redraw the globe to your new

specifications.) When you close that window, WINWAIS adds to your current search some search terms that describe the area you have selected. None of the WAIS sources we've ever found can do anything useful with these spatial data terms, but we presume that some nonpublic WAIS servers are chock-full of U.S.G.S. map information you can select geographically in this way.

Warning: Drawing the map can take awhile. On our 486/33DX PC, it takes about five seconds. On a 386SX with no math coprocessor, it takes about 15 minutes. If you have a slow computer, you may want to skip this feature.

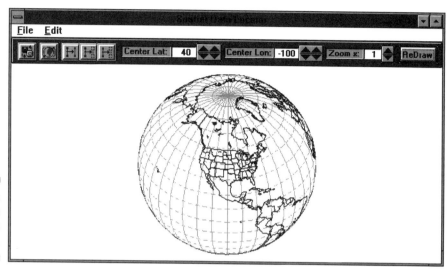

Figure 13-6:
Around the
world in one
click.

WAIS Out, MAN!

The other WAIS program we discuss is WAISMAN (or WAIS Manager). We've
already discussed how to install it, so to run it, click the icon you've made for it
(the globe without the lightning bolt.) First a little window pops up, telling you all the
horrible legal things that happen to software pirates who steal the tools with
which this program was written, but pretty soon you see a screen like Figure 13-7.

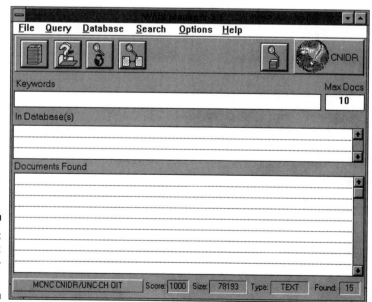

Figure 13-7:
The WAIS
Manager
screen.

Before you do anything else, you have to make one configuration change to WAIS Manager. From the menu, choose Options⇨Configure to get a window that invites you to tell it where your personal WAIS SRC files are. Change its suggestion c:\wais_src to c:\util\wais_src and click OK. (If you installed WAISMAN in a directory other than c:\util, change it accordingly.) Now you're ready to get to work.

Choosing sources from the local list

WAIS Manager comes with a long list of sources. To choose them, click the leftmost button, the one that looks like a pile of paper. You get a list of the sources it knows, like the ones in Figure 13-8.

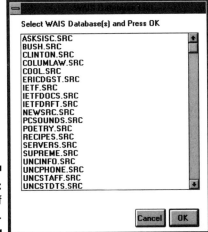

Select WAIS Database(s) and Press OK

```
ASKSISC.SRC
BUSH.SRC
CLINTON.SRC
COLUMLAW.SRC
COOL.SRC
ERICDGST.SRC
IETF.SRC
IETFDOCS.SRC
IETFDRFT.SRC
NEWSRC.SRC
PCSOUNDS.SRC
POETRY.SRC
RECIPES.SRC
SERVERS.SRC
SUPREME.SRC
UNCINFO.SRC
UNCPHONE.SRC
UNCSTAFF.SRC
UNCSTDTS.SRC
```

Cancel   OK

Figure 13-8: The list of sources.

Click the sources you want (unlike on most other lists, you can highlight as many as you want) and click OK.

Choosing sources from the Directory of Sources

WAIS Manager makes this task considerably easier than WINWAIS does:

1. **In the Keywords window, type some terms describing the sources you want.**

2. **Click the third button, the one with a magnifying glass and globe.**

   (We're really, *really* tired of globes by now.) WAISMAN searches for sources. It pops up a window with the search terms, giving you one last chance to edit them.

3. Click OK.

WAISMAN does the search. Cute little windows pop up, showing the progress of making the connection, sending the request, and getting the answer back. (Astute readers will have figured out that the point of the cute little windows is to distract you from the fact that this process can take quite a while.)

The returned documents are listed in the Documents Found window, using names like `patents.src`.

4. Click any document that looks interesting.

WAISMAN displays a window. (This is the same source retrieved with WINWAIS in Figure 13-5.)

In the window, it displays the source in the WAIS *native* format, strange punctuation and all. (See the sidebar called "Getting to the source on sources.") If you like this source, save it.

For some stupid reason, WAISMAN always suggests the filename `newsrc.src` in your `wais_src` directory. You have to change the filename for two reasons:

- ✔ The filename is what shows up in the list of sources, so you need a more memorable name.

- ✔ If you don't change the name, every new `newsrc.src` clobbers the preceding one. So pick a reasonable name (we've edited the name to `patent.src` in the figure) and click OK to save it. Now it's in the sources list, and you can choose it (as you saw earlier) to do your search.

Actual searching, take two

Yes, it is possible to search for stuff in WAIS Manager. Here's how you do it:

1. First you choose some sources, as just described.

2. Type some words in the Keywords line.

3. In the Max Docs box (say that ten times fast — makes a good mantra), type the maximum number of documents you want it to find.

Ten is a good number to use.

4. Click the Search button.

It's the second one from the right with the magnifying glass and the pile of paper. (Disregard the large button with — you guessed it — a globe, which just shows you a box telling you who wrote the program.) Little boxes pop up to distract you while it does the search, and the matching documents are listed in the bottom window, with the best match first.

5. To see a document, double-click its line.

WAIS Manager fetches the document and starts an appropriate program, usually Windows Write, to look at it. If it starts Write, the next thing you see after the time-wasting windows is Write's box, in which it asks whether it should convert the document to Write format. You usually should click No Conversion so that Write leaves the document's contents alone.

WAIS Manager throws each document away after you look at it. If you want to save the document, tell the program through which you're looking at it to save it, usually by choosing File⇨Save As from the menu. Be sure to use a different name from the ugly one WAIS Manager suggests.

Multimedia and other gimmicks

About 99 percent of all WAIS documents are plain text, but the other 1 percent can be any sort of file imaginable. The WAIS system tags every file with a type, such as TEXT, GIF, or AVI. WAIS Manager associates every type of file with a *viewer* program it runs when it retrieves a file for you, much as the Windows File Manger does. To edit the list of which program goes with which file type, choose from the menu Options⇨Default Viewers, which displays a window like the one in Figure 13-9.

Figure 13-9:
WAIS
Manager
viewers
window.

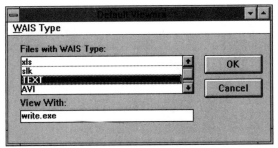

One viewer type it doesn't handle is WAV, which are Windows sound files. Because there happen to be quite a few WAV files in WAIS-land, you should fix this oversight. (Unless, of course, you're unfortunate enough not to have a sound card for your PC, in which case you should raid your children's college tuition fund or other money marked for such frivolous uses and run out and get one because they're tons of fun.)

WAIS's greatest hits

WAIS Manager lets you rerun commonly used searches. Click the button with the yellow folder and question mark, to get a list of interesting queries. Click one of the entries in the list, then click OK to copy that query into the main WAIS Manager screen, and then click the search button (the one with the magnifying glass and the stack of paper) to run the query.

It's supposed to be possible to add new entries to the list of saved queries, but we've never been able to get that feature to work properly.

To add a new viewer type:

1. **In the Default Viewers window menu, choose WAIS type New WAIS type.**

2. **Enter WAIS as the new type.**

3. **Click OK.**

4. **Choose the file type.**

   In the File with WAIS Type window, scroll down to the line that now shows WAV and click it once to highlight it.

5. **In the View With window, enter mplayer.exe, the standard Windows sound player program.**

   If you have another sound program, such as MPLANY or Lotus Sound, feel free to use that instead.

6. **Click OK to dismiss the Default Viewers window.**

If you feel that this is not a really well-designed way to enter and update data, you're not alone.

To test your new viewer — er, listener program — in the list of sources, choose PCSOUNDS, which is a bunch of sounds in PC WAV format. Then, in Keywords, enter **bullwink** and do a search, which should return one document. If you double-click that document, and your computer says "Hello out there in TV land!" in a familiar moosey voice, you can conclude that your multimedia WAIS works.

Other WAIS Programs

Other Windows WAIS programs are available on the Internet, which, if you have lots of time to waste, you may want to investigate. One is EIWAIS, which is available for FTP on host ftp.einet.net, in the directory /einet/pc, in a file called eiwais155.exe (a self-extracting ZIP file.) It's a perfectly decent WAIS client, but because it's somewhat larger than the others and is shareware rather than free, we haven't used it much, but you might want to take a look.

For additional advice about WAIS, consult the Usenet newsgroup comp.infosystems.wais for a running discussion of WAIS.

Chapter 14

Swinging on the World Wide Web

. . . .

In This Chapter

▶ What's the Web?

▶ Getting Mosaic

▶ Using Mosaic

. . . .

The World Wide Web (WWW) is the zoomiest, coolest Internet facility around. It contains lots of information, including pictures and other nontext stuff, in the form of *hypertext.* As you read through the information, therefore, you can click words or buttons to zoom right to related information.

And the best way to read the World Wide Web is by using a *browser* that runs under Windows. (It should really be called a *web reader.* We have already talked about mail readers and news readers, so it seems logical to us.) The two finest browsing programs around are called Mosaic and Cello, both of which run under Windows, work with your WinSock SLIP connection to the Internet, and display WWW information on your screen, including graphics and other types of files. Each has its advantages, so we introduce you to both of them in this chapter.

In addition to using Mosaic, you also need some *viewers,* or programs that can display nontext information. If a page of information from the World Wide Web contains graphics in the form of a GIF file (a standard type of graphics file), you need a GIF file viewer to see it. Don't panic — it's easy to get and install viewers for all the common types of information that WWW pages contain.

For more information about Mosaic and the World Wide Web in general, read the Usenet newsgroups `comp.infosystems.www` or `alt.hypertext`. Also refer to Chapter 22 in *The Internet For Dummies* and Chapter 16 in this book.

Web notes

When you start Mosaic, you can begin with the WWW page it suggests and find your way to the information you want by following the hypertext links. (Don't worry — we tell you how.) Alternatively, you can jump directly to a WWW page if you know its URL.

Every World Wide Web page in the universe has a unique name, so you can jump right to it from any program that displays WWW stuff. This name is called its *URL* (for *Uniform Resource Locator*). In includes information about which machine the page is stored on, the pathname of the file that contains it, and other technical stuff (they look horrendous).

Chapter 16 describes how the URLs for various types of Internet services look. Chapters 17 through 19 list the URLs of some interesting WWW pages, and you may see mentions of other URLs as you wander the net.

Mosaic is available directly from the Internet, by using anonymous FTP. And you need about 1MB of disk space. (You need another 1MB if you don't use Windows NT, because you have to download `win32s.zip` to use with Mosaic — we explain that in the Mosaic installation instructions.)

Mosaic has been subject to frequent improvements by its authors, so the version you get may well have even more and better features than what we describe here. In early 1994 the authors of Mosaic started a company called Mosaic, Inc., and we expect that different vendors will produce a profusion of Mosaics with different bells and whistles. What we describe here is the free version because it works perfectly well and because it's hard to beat the price.

Getting Mosaic

Mosaic is a WWW browser written by Chris Wilson and Jon Mittlehauser of the University of Illinois, at the National Center for Supercomputing Applications. The NCSA also runs a World Wide Web server that provides lots of information about Mosaic in addition to other things.

Or you can try Cello

Cello is a WWW browser written by Thomas Bruce of the Legal Information Institute at the Cornell Law School in Ithaca, New York. Who says lawyers never do anything useful?

Both Mosaic and Cello do pretty much the same thing. The differences are in small details (Cello prints a little better) and in the aesthetics (Mosaic shows links to other WWW pages in color, and Cello underlines them.) Mosaic is by far the more popular program, but if you have the time, it's worth looking at both of them to see which one you prefer.

You can find Cello on the FTP server ftp.law.cornell.edu. If you cannot get through there, you can try the FTP servers princeton.edu (in the directory /pub/mosaic) or gatekeeper.dec.com (in the directory /.f/micro/msdos/win3/winsock). Wherever it is, its filename is cello.zip.

If you see a file named cellofaq.zip, download it too. When you unzip it, it contains cellofaq.txt, a text file with the answers to frequently asked questions (FAQs) about Cello.

Getting Mosaic involves the usual process — copy the zipped Mosaic program file by using FTP and then unzip and install it. The installation involves a big extra step, however: installing Win32s, a Microsoft thing that allows NT-style 32-bit programs to run on your computer. Because Mosaic is such a newfangled NT-style program, you need win32s to be able to run it.

Grabbing it

Mosaic is available by FTP from `ftp.ncsa.uiuc.edu`. That's a *busy* FTP server, so you can also try FTP server `caip.rutgers.edu` (in the directory `/pub`) or `gatekeeper.dec.com` (in the directory `/.f/micro/msdos/win3/winsock`). Look for a file named `wmos20a4.zip`. (As later versions of Mosaic appear, the filename probably will be `wmos` followed by a version number then `.zip`.)

This version and later ones are designed to work with Windows NT or Chicago (the code name for the next version of Windows). If you have regular old Windows 3.1 (like most of us do), you also have to download a file named `win32s.zip`, which sets up your PC up to work with NT-style 32-bit software.

Here's how to get it:

1. **Make a directory to put it in.**

   We recommend `\util\mosaic`, but suit yourself.

2. **Connect to your SLIP provider.**

3. **Run your FTP program.**

4. **Connect to the host `ftp.ncsa.uiuc.edu`.**

   This is a busy host, so you may have to do this at an off-peak time. Or try any of the other FTP servers.

5. **Change to the `pc` directory and then to the `mosaic` directory.**

   This step puts you in the `/pc/mosaic` directory.

6. **Make sure that you are in binary mode and download a file named `wmos20a2.zip`.**

   This is version 2.0 ALPHA 2 (a test version) of Mosaic. Later versions may be available after this book goes to print — go ahead and use them if you want. Store the file in the directory you made in step 1.

7. **If you don't run Windows NT or Chicago, download `win32s.zip` too.**

   It's big — more than 1 MB, so it takes awhile. It contains Microsoft's Win32s program. (It's even legal to download this Microsoft program because the company is distributing it for free. Wow — when's the last time Microsoft *gave away* software?)

8. **Disconnect from the host and exit from your FTP program.**

Getting ready for NT

If you use Windows NT or know that you are already running NT-style 32-bit software, skip to the next section, "Setting it up." Otherwise, follow these steps to install Microsoft Win32s, which is in the `win32s.zip` file you just downloaded.

1. **In File Manager, make a directory called** `\windows\system\win32s`.

   Your computer already has a file called `\windows\system` that contains all kinds of technoid Windows stuff you don't want to think about. Just make a new subdirectory called `win32s`.

2. **Move** `win32s.zip` **into it.**

   You can drag the file in File Manager.

3. **Double-click the** `win32s.zip` **filename.**

   WinZip runs and opens the Win32s ZIP file.

4. **Extract all the files and put them in your** `\windows\system\win32s` **directory.**

   This ZIP file contains three files: `readme.txt`, `w32s1_1.bug`, and `w32s115.zip`. (The numbers may change as new versions appear, and the bug file might disappear.) A ZIP file that contains another ZIP file — how strange! But there it is.

5. **Open the** `w32s115.zip` **file.**

   In WinZip, open this file so that you can unzip it. It contains a bunch of files.

6. **Extract them into the proper directories.**

   Click the Extract button. On the Extract dialog box, choose All Files and User Directory Names (which makes directories as necessary to put the files in). Extract the files to `\windows\system\win32s`. Click OK.

   WinZip extracts the files and puts them in two new subdirectories: `\windows\system\win32s\disk1` and `\windows\system\win32s\disk2`.

7. **Exit from all other Windows programs.**

   The Win32s setup program is going to ask you to do this in a minute, so you might as well do it now.

8. **In File Manager, double-click** `\windows\system\win32s\disk1\setup.exe`.

   This step runs the Microsoft Win32s setup program. The setup program displays a friendly dialog box that tells you to exit from all other programs. If you didn't do so before, do so now because after it is finished installing Win32s, it restarts Windows.

9. **Click Continue.**

   You see a message telling you where your `\windows\system` directory is.

10. **Click Continue again.**

    The setup program installs the Win32s software, showing you how far it has gotten. When it's finished, you see the message `Win32s files successfully installed`.

11. **Click OK.**

    Now the setup program offers to install a solitaire game called Freecell, which incidentally tests to see that Win32s works. In the interests of software testing and reliability and with no thought of sitting around playing Solitaire when you should be working, accept its offer.

12. **Click Continue again.**

    The setup program asks where it should install the Freecell program, suggesting `\winapps\freecell`. If you want to put it somewhere else, edit this path. (Don't worry about it too much — you can always move it later.)

13. **Click Continue again.**

    Freecell gets installed and the setup program tells you so. In the process, it creates a Program Manager program group called Win32 Applications and puts the Freecell icon in it.

14. **Click OK.**

    The setup program bids you *adieu* and says it's about to restart Windows.

15. **Click OK.**

    Windows exits and restarts. (If it doesn't restart properly, you might have to reboot your computer.)

16. **Run Freecell to make sure that Win32s works.**

    Use the help system to find out how it works — it's a challenging game. You don't have to win a game to determine whether Win32s works — just run it for a few minutes. (Frankly, the chances of *us* winning a game of Freecell are one in a million.)

17. **To save disk space, delete** `win32s.zip`, `w32s115.zip`, **and all the files in the** `disk1` **and** `disk2` **directories.**

    You can also delete the `disk1` and `disk2` directories.

Now you are ready to run 32-bit Windows NT applications. Big deal. But because Mosaic is one of them, it may yet be worth all this trouble.

Setting it up

Now you can follow the usual procedure to unzip the Mosaic ZIP file and make a Program Manager icon for it.

The Mosaic ZIP file usually contains a file named `readme.now`. It's a good idea to read this file, by using Windows Notepad or any word processor, in case it contains additional instructions.

1. **In the Windows File Manager, double-click the** `wmos20a4.zip` **file.**

   This step runs WinZip and opens the Mosaic ZIP file.

2. **In WinZip, extract all the files into your** `\util\mosaic` **directory.**

   (Or whatever you named the directory in which you plan to put Mosaic.)

3. **In File Manager again, drag the** `mosaic.exe` **file into the Program Manager group where you want its icon to appear.**

   Poof! A little picture of a fuzzy globe with handy carrying straps appears. (Help! Not another globe!)

4. **To save disk space, you can delete the** `wmos20a4.zip` **file.**

5. **Copy the** `mosaic.ini` **file into your Windows directory.**

   Your Windows directory is probably called `\windows`. To copy the file, in the File Manager, hold down the Ctrl key while you drag the file from its current location in the Mosaic directory to the Windows directory.

At last you're ready to put together the pieces of your Mosaic.

Getting Viewers

World Wide Web pages contain text, small graphics, and attached files. Cello and Mosaic can display text and small graphics just fine, but they need help displaying attached files, which can contain all kinds of stuff.

The easiest place to get some viewers is by way of anonymous FTP from `ftp.law.cornell.edu`, in `/pub/LII/Cello` or from the same place you got Mosaic — `ftp.ncsa.uiuc.edu`, in `/pc/mosaic/viewers`. This section describes some viewers we have heard about or tried, with information about how to get them.

Seeing things

For viewing graphics files, you may need more than one viewer because there are so many types of graphics files. The most common types are GIF and JPEG files.

You can find Lview, which can display both GIF and JPEG files, at `ftp.law.cornell.edu`, in `/pub/LII/Cello` in a file called `lview31.zip`. You can also find it by FTP-ing to `ftp.bio.indiana.edu` and looking in the `/util/ibmpc` directory.

Alternatively, you can get WinGIF for looking at GIF files (from `oak.oakland.edu`, in the `/pub/msdos/windows3` directory in a file called `wingif14.zip`) and WinJPEG for handling JPEG files in addition to GIFs (from the same place as `oak.oakland.edu`, in a file named `wnjp243.zip`).

We have tried Lview, WinJPEG, and WinGIF, and we like Lview the best. Also, Lview is free, and the other two are shareware.

Hearing voices

If your computer has a sound board, you can play sound files (files with such file extensions as WAV, VOC, and AU). You can download WHAM, a good sound player with lots of other features, and WPLANY, a good basic sound player from `ftp.law.cornell.edu`, in `/pub/LII/Cello` in files named `wham131.zip` and `wplny09b.zip`. For WAV files, you can use the `mplayer.exe` program that comes with Windows or WPLANY.

Seeing ghosts

For movie files with the file extension AVI, you can find VIDVUE by FTP in a file named `vidvue10.zip` on the FTP server `wuarchive.wustl.edu`, in a directory called `/systems/ibmpc/win3/desktop`. For movie files with the extension MPG, get a program called MFW by FTPing to `ftp.uwp.edu` and looking in the `/pub/picture.viewers` directory for a file named `mpeg2.zip`.

It takes a great deal of computing power to display a movie. If your computer isn't at least a 486, the movies show so slowly as to be not worth the bother.

After you install Mosaic, we tell you which of these viewers to get and what to do with them.

Putting Pieces Together with Mosaic

Before you can use Mosaic, you still have to configure it — bummer. It doesn't take long.

Configuring it: Do you have an ini?

Mosaic uses an *ini* file to store information about the way it is configured. You may want to edit this file to change your Mosaic configuration. The file, called `mosaic.ini`, is stored in your Windows program directory, usually `\windows`. You can edit this file by using the Windows Notepad or any other text editor.

Don't use a word processor to edit your `mosaic.ini` file because it inserts strange formatting codes that Mosaic can't understand.

It's a good idea to make a backup copy of your `mosaic.ini` file before editing it. You probably also have a copy of the original, factory-delivered file in your Mosaic program directory.

The file is divided into sections, each section starting with a header line in square brackets, like this:

```
[Main]
```

Home sweet home

The most common edit you might want to make is to change your *home page,* which is the WWW page Mosaic loads automatically when you start it and that it reloads when you click the little Home icon (the little button with a picture of a house, below the Navigate command on the Mosaic menu bar).

To tell Mosaic to load the home page automatically when you start Mosaic, change the line that begins with Autoload Home Page to look like this:

```
Autoload Home Page=yes
```

To tell Mosaic *not* to load the home page automatically, change that line to this one:

```
Autoload Home Page=no
```

The home page is usually the one about Windows Mosaic. If you want to change it to another page, you must know that page's URL (its official technical name). Change the line that begins Home Page to list the URL you want, right after the equal sign, like this:

```
Home Page=http://www.ncsa.uiuc.edu/SDG/Software/WinMosaic
             HomePage.html
```

Mail from Mosaic

If you plan to use Mosaic to send e-mail, such as sending feedback to developers or others who provide information about the WWW, tell Mosaic who you are. Change the line that begins with E-mail to contain your correct e-mail address, in quotes, like this:

```
E-mail="midummies@iecc.com"
```

You should also tell Mosaic about your mail server (the Internet host computer through which you send your mail). If you use Eudora, you told Eudora that name of your mail server too (refer to Chapter 10). Change your SMTP Server line, which is in the [Services] section of the file, to contain your mail server, in quotes, like this:

```
SMTP Server="xuxa.iecc.com"
```

Don't use `xuxa.iecc.com` as your mail server — use your *own* mail server!

News from Mosaic

If you plan to use Mosaic to read Usenet newsgroups, you should tell it the name of your news server (the host computer from which you get newsgroup articles). If you installed Trumpet in Chapter 11, you had to tell Trumpet this name too. Change your NNTP Server line, in the [Services] section of the file, to contain the name of your news server, in quotes, like this:

```
NNTP Server="xuxa.iecc.com"
```

Again, substitute the name of your own news server in this line.

Speeding things up

If you find it annoying to wait while Mosaic loads the picture (usually GIF) files that come with many WWW pages, you can tell Mosaic to skip them. Rather than the picture, Mosaic shows the NCSA logo. If you find that you want to see the picture after all, click the logo and Mosaic retrieves the picture for you. To tell Mosaic to work this way, change the Display Inulin Images line to this:

```
Display Inulin Images=no
```

To speed this process up a little more (this is really splitting hairs, so feel free to skip this one), you can tell Mosaic to draw bullets in a faster way. Change the Round List Bullets line in the [Main] section of the file to this:

```
Round List Bullets=no
```

What a view!

The [Viewers] section of the `mosaic.ini` file tells Mosaic which viewer programs to use to view (or listen to) files that are attached to WWW pages. If a page has a GIF file (a standard type of graphics file) attached to it, for example, Mosaic can display the picture only if you have a GIF file viewer. In the "Getting Viewers" section earlier in this chapter, we told you how to get viewers for some common types of files. Now you have to tell Mosaic where you put them.

In the [Viewers] section of the file, skip down past all the lines that begin with TYPE until you get to a line that begins with image/gif. Edit the pathname in quotes to indicate the location and filename of your GIF viewer. (Use File Manager to locate it if you have forgotten.) Leave the %s unchanged after the filename. We use Lview to view GIF files, for example, so our line looks like this:

```
image/gif="c:\util\lview31 %ls"
```

In the same way, edit the image/jpeg line to contain the path and filename of your JPEG viewer (we use Lview for JPEG files too). If you have viewers for other types of files, edit the lines for the file types to include the path and filename of the viewer.

Save that file!

When you are finished making changes to the file, save it. Exit from Mosaic (if it is running) and run it again so that the changes take effect.

We leave the Autoload Home Page line set to no so that we don't have to wait around while Mosaic gets the page every time we start it. The host computer the regular Mosaic home page lives at is usually busy, and there can be a big delay or an error.

Starting it up

When you double-click the Mosaic icon, you see the Mosaic window, shown in Figure 14-1.

Right now you aren't looking at any World Wide Web page.

You can turn on Mosaic's Autoload Home Page feature to tell it to load a World Wide Web page automatically when you start it. To change this option and other options, see the section "Configuring it: Do you have an ini?" earlier in this chapter.

Leaving

When you finish using Mosaic, choose File➪Exit from the menu.

There's no place like home

This empty gray screen doesn't look too interesting. How about getting a World Wide Web page in there?

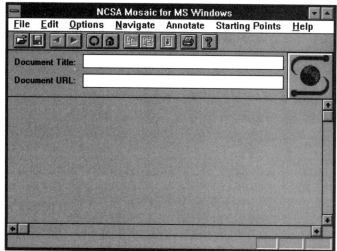

Figure 14-1:
Mosaic
Mission
Control.

Mosaic comes with a list of some interesting pages. To see them, choose Starting Points from the menu. You see a list of suggested WWW pages. For starters, choose Starting Points Document. A message appears at the bottom of the screen, telling you the system to which Mosaic has connected to get the page, and the filename of the page. The little globe icon turns in a flashy way while Mosaic downloads the page. And then — poof! Your page appears and looks like Figure 14-2!

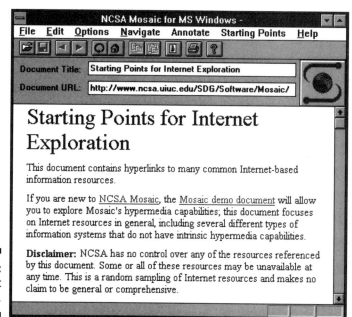

Figure 14-2:
Starting out
in Mosaic.

Jumping around the Web

When you are looking at a WWW page, some words and phrases are underlined and displayed in a different color. These *links* refer to another, related WWW page on that topic. If you see the words <u>National Center for Supercomputing Applications</u> underlined, for example, it is a link to a WWW page about (not surprisingly) the National Center for Supercomputing Applications (NCSA) — the folks who wrote Mosaic.

A link may not necessarily lead to another WWW page — instead, it may connect to a Gopher menu, a Usenet newsgroup, or an FTP site. In any case, the information is related to the topic you click, and Mosaic can display it just fine.

Occasionally you may get an error message when you try to retrieve a page. If that happens, try it again because it frequently works on the second or third try.

You can also use buttons on the icon bar (underneath the menu bar) to move around:

- ✔ The left-pointing triangle button takes you to the previous page you retrieved. If the triangle is gray, there's no page to back up to.

- ✔ After you have backed up by using the left-pointing triangle button, you can click the right-pointing triangle to go forward to the next page you retrieved. If the triangle is gray, there *is* no next page yet.

- ✔ The circular-arrow picture reloads the current WWW page. Click it if Mosaic cannot load a page correctly and you want to try again.

- ✔ The little picture of a house returns you to your home page, which is usually a page about Mosaic for Windows. (To change this, see the section "Configuring it: Do you have an ini?" earlier in this chapter.)

- ✔ Pages can be rather long. A nice feature of Mosaic is its capability to search a page for some text. Click the picture of a page with a downward-pointing arrow on it. Mosaic asks for the text (word or phrase) to look for. Enter it and click Find Next.

Underneath the icon bar, Mosaic tells you the title and URL (technoid name) of the page you are looking at. At the bottom of the Mosaic window is a status line that contains messages from Mosaic about what it's doing.

As of this writing, Mosaic doesn't come with on-line help because we are using an alpha (early testing) release of version 2.0. So clicking the question mark button or pressing the F1 key does absolutely nothing (except display a Windows Help screen which says that it can't find anything). We're sure that when the final version 2.0 is available, it will have lovely on-line help.

Stop everything!

If Mosaic takes forever to retrieve something, you tell it to forget it. Click the spinning-globe Mosaic logo.

Start here

When you install Mosaic, the Starting Points menu contains the following WWW items:

- ✔ **Starting Points Document:** A WWW page with lots of links to pages that contain information about the World Wide Web. It also contains a link to a WAIS starting point, which enables you to use WAIS to search databases (see Chapter 21 in *The Internet For Dummies*) and a listing of FTP sites.

- ✔ **NCSA Mosaic Demo Document:** A WWW page with a list of things that might be interesting for the new Mosaic user.

- ✔ **NCSA Mosaic "What's New" Page:** A WWW page that contains information about recent additions to the World Wide Web and recent changes to Mosaic.

- ✔ **NCSA Mosaic Home Page:** A WWW page that contains information and links about Mosaic, including Mosaic for Windows, the Macintosh, and X Windows.

- ✔ **Windows Mosaic home page:** A WWW page about the Windows version of Mosaic, with up-to-date technical information about it.

- ✔ **World Wide Web Info:** A menu of WWW pages that contain more informa- tion about the World Wide Web.

- ✔ **Home Pages:** A menu of WWW pages that contain the home pages for a bunch of different World Wide Web servers. These home pages usually contain a guide or index to the information on the server.

- ✔ **Gopher Servers:** A menu of Gophers and Gopher-related servers you can use (see the section "Gophers on the Web," later in this chapter).

- ✔ **Finger Gateway:** A way to use a cute finger program (see the section "Keep your fingers off the Web," later in this chapter).

- ✔ **Whois Gateway:** A way to use a whois program to find out about people on the net, by way of a Gopher server at M.I.T. It lists lots of organizations which have whois servers that can provide information about people in those organizations.

- ✔ **Other Documents:** A menu of interesting, offbeat, or even bizarre WWW pages you might like to look at.

- ✔ **Archie Request Form:** A WWW page that lets you run Archie, a service that searches FTP servers for a particular file. If you are looking for a program and know its filename, this is a good way to find it on the Internet. See the section "Searching for files with Archie," later in this chapter.

Changing fonts

You can change the fonts Mosaic uses when it displays most WWW pages, Gopher menus, and other stuff. Choose Options⇨Choose Font from the menu, and you see a list of the different fonts you can define. When you choose one, Mosaic displays a Font dialog box that lets you change the typeface and size of the font. Fool around with the fonts until you like the looks of your pages.

Printing, saving, or copying good stuff

In the version of Mosaic we are using, printing, saving stuff to a file, or copying stuff to the Windows Clipboard doesn't work yet. By the time you read this, it probably will.

To print the displayed page, choose File⇨Print from the menu or click the little picture of a printer.

To save the text of the current page to a file, choose File⇨Save As from the menu or click the little picture of a disk.

To copy some text to the Windows Clipboard, select the text with your mouse. Then choose Edit⇨Copy or click the little picture of two dog-eared pieces of paper.

Remembering good places

When you find a particularly interesting page, you can add it to the Starting Points menu. Choose Navigate⇨Add Current to Hotlist. Now the URL of the current page appears at the bottom of the Starting Points menu.

You can set up your own Starting Points menu or even call the whole menu something else or even add a whole other command and menu of pages you like. Choose Navigate⇨Menu Editor to see a list of the menus that are defined.

A discussion of all Mosaic's menu-editing features is beyond what we have room for in this chapter, but if your version of Mosaic has help, you can figure out how to use the menu editor if you really want to!

Finding other WWW pages

If you know the URL (the official technical name) of a WWW page you want to see, you can tell Mosaic to go directly to it.

1. **Choose File⇨Open URL from the menu (or press Ctrl+O).**

   Mosaic asks for the URL name, by using the confusing dialog box shown in Figure 14-3.

2. **In the URL box, type the URL.**

   With luck, you have the URL in a file on your computer somewhere, so you can copy it by using the Windows Clipboard.

3. **Click OK or press Enter.**

   Mosaic retrieves the URL you requested.

Figure 14-3:
Which URL
do you want,
Master?

The URL of the page you are looking at is displayed in the Document URL box at the top of the Mosaic window. When you point to a link on a Mosaic page, the URL of the link appears on the status line at the bottom of the Mosaic window.

Searching for info

"But where's all this great hypertextual stuff I keep hearing about?" we hear you crying. "I want to find out about pigs in space!" Stay calm — it's out there.

The problem is finding it.

We usually begin searching by looking in CERN's Virtual Library. (CERN is the research lab in Switzerland that invented the World Wide Web.) To see it, choose Starting Points from the menu, then Home Pages, and then CERN Home Page. On this page, click the little picture below the Places to Start Browsing heading — the picture itself is a link.

You see the WWW Virtual Library page. This page shows the library's catalog by subject. Scroll down the list and click the subject areas you want to see — you can find an amazing array of information.

If you think that you will use the Virtual Library much, add it to your Starting Points menu by choosing Navigate⇨Add Current to Hotlist from the menu.

Reading the news

Mosaic isn't a great news reader, but it's usable. Before you can use it to read Usenet newsgroups, be sure that you have entered the name of your news server in your `mosaic.ini` file (see the section "Configuring it: do you have an ini?" earlier in this chapter).

You may see the name of a newsgroup as a link on a WWW page. If you do, you can read the newsgroup just by clicking its link.

Otherwise, here's how to read a newsgroup with Mosaic.

1. **Choose File⇨Open URL from the menu (or press Ctrl+O).**

   Mosaic asks for the URL of the information you want, by using the dialog box shown in Figure 14-3.

2. **In the URL box, enter a URL like this:**

   ```
   news:newsgroupname
   ```

   Substitute the actual newsgroup name for `newsgroupname`. To read `rec.travel`, for example, enter this line:

   ```
   news:rec.travel
   ```

3. **Click OK.**

   Mosaic asks your mail server for the last 20 articles in the newsgroup and displays them as shown in Figure 14-4. Each article is a link.

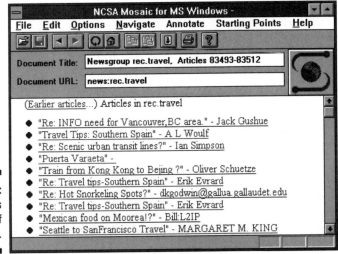

Figure 14-4:
Some news drops out of the Web.

4. Click on any articles you want to read.

If none of them looks interesting, you usually can click an *earlier articles* link. When you click on an article, Mosaic retrieves it from your news server and displays it.

Sometimes you get messages like `Sorry, could not load requested news.` Your news server is probably just a little busy right now. Try again later (assuming that you didn't just misspell the name of the newsgroup you want).

Gophers on the Web

Some of the information you see in Mosaic is actually Gopher menus. If a Gopher menu appears as a link on a page and you click it, Mosaic shows you the menu. You may not even know, in fact, that you have entered Gopherspace.

If you know the URL of a Gopher menu, you can tell Mosaic to go right to it. URLs for Gopher menus look a little odd (but all URLs look strange, so what the heck), like this:

```
gopher://gopher.micro.umn.edu:70/11/
          Other%20Gopher%20and%20Information%20Servers
```

All Gopher URLs begin with the world *gopher,* though. The part after the double slashes up to the second colon is the name of the host the Gopher item lives on (in this example, `gopher.micro.umn.edu`).

Here's how to go right to a page:

1. Choose File⇨Open URL (or press Ctrl+O).

Mosaic asks for the URL of the information you want, by using the dialog box shown in Figure 14-3.

2. In the URL box, enter n URL and click OK.

Good luck typing it correctly! Mosaic fetches the Gopher item, which looks like Figure 14-5. Items with little folders display other menus. Items with little paper pictures are documents you can view.

3. Click on menu item links until you see a document you want.

4. Click on a document you want to see.

Mosaic retrieves the document and displays it.

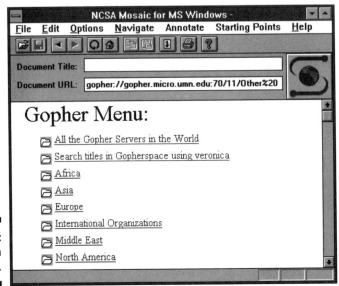

Figure 14-5:
Gophers in
your Mosaic.

Files on the Web

You can use Mosaic to download files from FTP servers. Here's how.

1. Choose File⇨Open URL (or press Ctrl+O).

Mosaic asks for the URL of the information you want, using the dialog box shown in Figure 14-3.

2. In the URL box, enter a URL like this:

```
file://hostmachine/
```

In place of hostmachine, type the name of the FTP server. Don't forget the two slashes before it and one slash after it.

3. Click OK.

Mosaic connects to the FTP server, logs in as anonymous, and displays the root directory of the system, as shown in Figure 14-6.

Items with a little folder icon are directories, and clicking them moves to that directory. Items with little paper icons are text files. Items with a little block of ones and zeros are binary information.

4. Move to the directory that contains the file you want.

5. Choose Options⇨Load to Disk.

This command tells Mosaic to store stuff it retrieves to disk rather than display it on-screen.

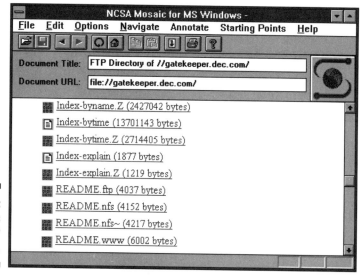

Figure 14-6:
Lots of files
on an FTP
server.

6. **Click the file to download it.**

   Mosaic retrieves the file and stores it to disk, asking you where to put it.

7. **Choose Options⇨Load to Disk again.**

   This command turns off the load-to-disk business so that Mosaic goes back
   to displaying stuff on- screen.

Searching for files with Archie

In Chapter 19 of *The Internet For Dummies,* we told you about Archie, a program
that can search hundreds of FTP servers for a particular file you want. Some
nice person has created a WWW page that lets you enter the filename you want
to search for and some other information and then runs the Archie search for
you. Pretty cool!

Here's how to use it:

1. **Choose Starting Points and then Archie Request Form.**

   You see the Archie Request Form, shown in Figure 14-7.

2. **In the What would you like to search for? box, enter the filename you
   want.**

   If you don't know the entire filename, you can enter just part of it.

3. **If you entered the whole, exact filename, choose Exact Match for the
   type of search. If you entered part of it, choose Case Insensitive
   Substring Match.**

```
┌─────────────────────────────────────────────────────────────┐
│ ─            NCSA Mosaic for MS Windows -           ▼ ▲      │
│ File  Edit  Options  Navigate  Annotate  Starting Points  Help│
│ ┌──┬──┬──┬──┬──┬──┬──┬──┬──┬──┬──┐                            │
│ │  │  │ ◄│ ►│  │  │  │  │ ↓│ ⎙│ ?│                            │
│ └──┴──┴──┴──┴──┴──┴──┴──┴──┴──┴──┘                            │
│ Document Title: │Archie Request Form                    │  ⌐─╮│
│ Document URL:   │http://hoohoo.ncsa.uiuc.edu/archie.html│  (  )│
│                                                           ╰──╯ │
│ Archie Request Form                                          ↕ │
│                                                               │
│ This is a form based Archie gateway for the WWW. If You don't have a browser that│
│ can supports forms, you can still make a search.              │
│                                                               │
│ Please remember that Archie searches can take a long time... │
│ ─────────────────────────────────────────────────────        │
│ What would you like to search for? │            │            │
│ There are several types of search: │Case Insensitive Substring Match│▼│
│ The results can be sorted ● By Host or ○ By Date             │
│ The impact on other users can be: │Not Nice At All │▼│        │
│ Several Archie Servers can be used: │United Kingdom │▼│       │
│ You can restrict the number of results returned (default 95): │     ││
│ Press this button to submit the query: │Submit│ .            │
│ To reset the form, press this button: │Reset│ .              ↓ │
│                                                               │
└─────────────────────────────────────────────────────────────┘
```

Figure 14-7:
Which file
do you want
Archie to
search for?

4. **If you are not in a big hurry, change the impact on other users to Nice or even nicer than that.**

5. **For the Several Archie Servers setting, choose the Archie server nearest you.**

6. **Click the Submit button.**

   This WWW page submits a search request to the Archie server you chose. Prepare to wait awhile. You may want to go to lunch, in fact (it can literally take hours). At long last, Mosaic displays Archie's reply.

Keep your fingers off the Web

Finger is a traditional Internet program that lets you find out about host computers and people who have accounts on the net. To get information about a person, you must know the person's e-mail address.

Here's how to use the WWW to Finger Gateway:

1. **Choose Starting Points and then Finger Gateway from the menu.**

   You see the WWW to Finger Gateway page, shown in Figure 14-8.

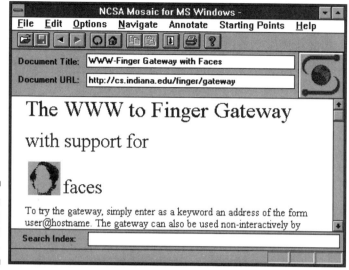

Figure 14-8:
Fingering
friends on
the net.

2. **Enter an e-mail address in the Search Index box at the bottom of the screen and press Enter.**

   Enter your own address, for example. The WWW to Finger Gateway sends off a finger request to the person's host computer and displays the answer when it comes back. The type of information you get back depends on the host computer. Figure 14-9 shows what whitehouse.gov responds with when you finger president@whitehouse.gov.

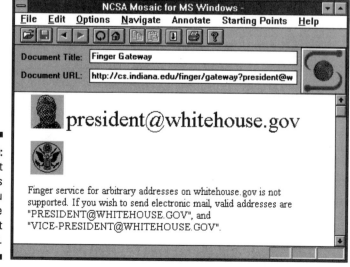

Figure 14-9:
Here's what
happens
when you
give the
President
the finger.

Telnetting with Mosaic

If you are given an URL that begins with `telnet`, you can use Mosaic to run a telnet program for you and look at particular information on other systems. You need a telnet program, like the one in Win QVT/NET (see the section "Telnetting with Win QVT/NET" in Chapter 9 to learn how to get and install it). Then follow these instructions to use it with Mosaic:

1. **Edit the** `mosaic.ini` **file by using Windows Notepad.**

   This step enables you to add a line to your `mosaic.ini` file to tell Mosaic about the telnet program.

2. **Move to the very end of the [Viewers] section of the file.**

3. **Add a new line like this:**

   ```
   telnet="c:\util\ winqvt\tmstart.exe"
   ```

   Make sure that the pathname is correct for your system — you might have stored the Win QVT/NET program in a different directory. This new line should be the last line of the [Viewers] section.

   If you use a different telnet program, enter its path and filename between the quotes.

   If there is already a `telnet` line, just modify it — don't make a second one.

4. **Save the file and exit from Notepad.**

5. **If you are running Mosaic, exit.**

6. **Run Mosaic.**

   You have to do this so that it reads your new, improved `mosaic.ini` file.

7. **Choose File⇨Open URL (or press Ctrl+O).**

8. **In the URL box, enter the URL that begins with *telnet*.**

   Mosaic uses the telnet program you told it about, telnets to the Internet host computer, asks you for the username and password to use, and displays whatever information the URL describes.

Part IV

10,000 Interesting Things to Do on the Net

The 5th Wave

By Rich Tennant

"AND JUST WHAT THE HECK PART OF THE NETWORK DID YOU SAY YOU'RE FROM?"

In this part...

*1*n the year since we wrote *Internet For Dummies,* the Internet has been growing like, like, well, like something that grows really fast. (True fact: A chart of Internet growth in the *New York Times* business section measured the size of the net in *zillions*.) With all those zillions of new hosts on the net, zillions of new services are available, particularly new ones based on Gopher and WWW. So here are a select few of those zillions, to get you started exploring the wonders of the Internet. But first, let's chat a bit.

Chapter 15

Internet Relay Chat: The Ultimate Solution to Free Time

What Is IRC?

In theory, *Internet Relay Chat,* or *IRC,* is a way for individuals around the world to have stimulating, fascinating, on-line discussions. In reality, it's more often a way for bored undergraduates to waste time. But IRC, more than any other Internet service, is what you make of it. If you can find interesting people to have interesting discussions with, it's wonderful. If not, well, kiss your free time goodbye — or stay away from IRC.

Worldwide Gossip-Mongering

Like every other Internet service, IRC has client programs and server programs. The *client* is, as usual, the program you run on your local machine (or perhaps on your provider's system) that you type at directly. An IRC *server* resembles a large switchboard, receiving everything you type and sending it back out to other users, and vice versa. What's more, because the different servers all are in constant contact with each other, stuff you type at one server is relayed to the other servers so that the entire IRC world is one big, chatty family.

Where did IRC come from?

Finland, actually, where it was originally written by written by Jarkko Oikarinen in 1988. It has since spread all over the world and is now one of the standard Internet services.

IRC's most notable hours were in the Gulf War and the 1993 coup in Russia against Boris Yeltsin, as IRC users on the spot sent reports to thousands of other users around the world.

To add some small degree of coherence, IRC conversations are organized into *channels,* with each channel dedicated to a single topic, in theory at least. Any user can create a channel, so you get some pretty funky ones (not to mention downright *dirty*).

Chatting in Theory and Practice

You can use lots of different client programs for IRC that run on lots of different kinds of computers. But, fortunately, the steps to use them are practically identical:

1. **Establish contact with an IRC server.**
2. **Tell it who you are.**
3. **Pick a couple of channels.**
4. **Waste lots of time.**

Setting Up WSIRC (for Windows Users)

TIP

If you're not using Windows, skip ahead to the next section.

Several Windows IRC programs are available, but we like WSIRC (Windows Sockets Internet Relay Chat) because it's a.) easy to use, b.) fairly reliable, and c.) cheap. (You can imagine which of these was our most compelling reason.) It was written by Caesar M. Samsi (be sure to read his bio in WSIRC's on-line help — click the Biography button at the end of the Contents page).

The current version of WSIRC, as we write this chapter, is 1.12-B, so the archive file is called WSIRC12B.ZIP.

Here's how to grab WSIRC from out of the ether:

1. **Connect to your Internet provider, if you haven't already done so, and FTP to one of the hosts in Table 15-1.**

Table 15-1	FTP Servers That Have WSIRC
Host	**Directory**
oak.oakland.edu	pub/msdos/winsock
csa.bu.edu	irc/clients/pc/windows
winftp.cica.indiana.edu	pub/pc/win3/winsock

2. **Log in as anonymous, using your e-mail address as the password.**

3. **Change to the directory on that host where the software is located.**

4. **Set binary mode in FTP and copy wsirc12b.zip to your machine.**

A new version may have been released since we wrote this chapter, in which case the filename may be something like wsirc13a.zip.

The ZIP file for WSIRC is *big*, so it takes a while to download. (The last version we grabbed was 454K.)

5. **Use WinZip to extract all the files in wsirc12b.zip into your \util directory (or wherever you store your Internet-related programs).**

If space is tight, you can delete wsirc12b.zip.

Three versions of WSIRC are available: a free version, a shareware version, and a registered version. The differences are fairly minor: The registered version comes with a better help file, the free version limits you to two simultaneous IRC channels, and the other two versions allow more. If you use WSIRC much, be a sport and register it. The distribution of WSIRC includes wsirc.exe, the shareware version, and wsircg.exe, the free version. If you don't plan to use IRC enough to register it, you can use wsircg.exe and delete wsirc.exe. If you're more serious, use wsirc.exe and delete wsircg.exe.

6. **Make an icon for wsirc.exe or wsircg.exe.**

That is, drag the filename from File Manager to a program group in Program Manager.

Servers, Servers, Everywhere

If you're at a university or use a commercial Internet provider, a server is probably at or near your site. Users at the World, for example (our local Internet shell provider), use an IRC server that World provides. If there is a local server, use it — because it's the polite thing to do and because it probably will respond faster than a server farther away.

If you're sure that there's no local server, Table 15-2 shows a few you can try. Use the one closest to you. There are several dozen public servers other than the ones in this table. Consult the Usenet group alt.irc for more complete and up-to-date lists. Unless otherwise specified, use port 6667 on any IRC servers.

Table 15-2	IRC Servers to Consider
Address	**Location**
csa.bu.edu	Massachusetts
csz.bu.edu	Massachusetts
irc.colorado.edu	Colorado
irc.uiuc.edu	Illinois
ug.cs.dal.ca	Nova Scotia
irc.funet.fi	Finland
cismhp.univ-lyon1.fr	France
disuns2.epfl.ch	Switzerland
irc.nada.kth.se	Sweden
sokrates.informatik.uni-kl.de	Germany
bim.itc.univie.ac.at	Austria
jello.qabc.uq.oz.au	Australia

Connecting to Your IRC Server

If you're a lucky shell user, your diligent system manager has carefully set up IRC for you, so you only have to type **irc** and then IRC starts up and connects to the appropriate server — skip to the next section.

If you've just installed WSIRC, you're not so lucky, and you have to go through a strange little ritual to get WSIRC set up:

1. **Start WSIRC or WSIRCG from the Windows File Manager or Program Manager.**

   It displays a window telling you about your local WinSock.

2. **Whoopee. Click OK.**

   After ten seconds or so, it displays a disconcerting window advising you about a WSA Last Error or something equally disastrous. What it's trying to tell you, in fact, is that it can't figure out which server to use, but because WSIRC is linguistically challenged, it gives you a scary-sounding message instead.

   If you use version 1.13-G or later, you get a much friendlier message (*Please Complete Server Options First*) and the program automatically displays the WSIRC Server Options dialog box. So skip right to Step 5.

3. **Click the OK box to make the message go away, and you should see the WSIRC main window (see Figure 15-1).**

   Before you can do anything else, you have to introduce yourself to your IRC server.

4. **Choose Options⇨Server from the menu.**

   You should see a dialog box like Figure 15-2.

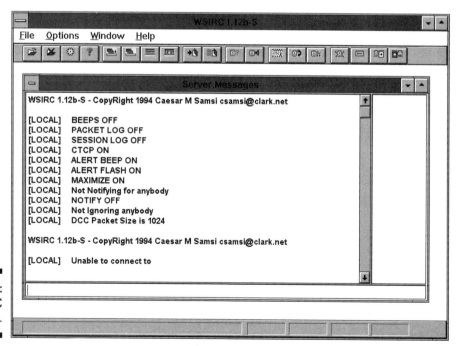

Figure 15-1:
The WSIRC
screen.

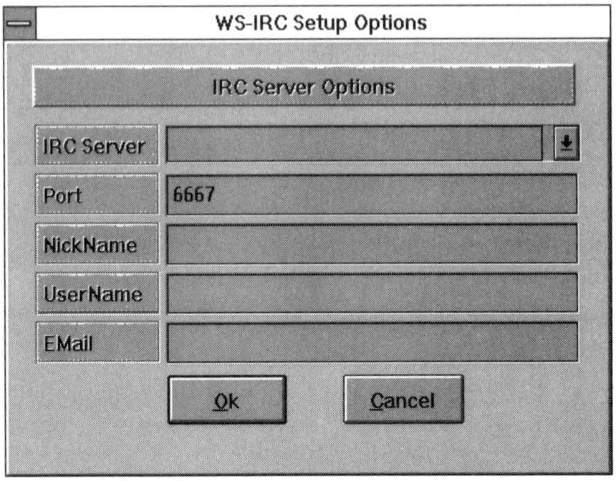

Figure 15-2:
The WSIRC
server setup
window.

5. **In the IRC Server field, type the name of your local server.**

   If you don't have one locally, see the preceding section for some suggestions.

6. **Leave the Port set to 6667.**

   That's the magic number for IRC-ing.

7. **For the Nickname, pick a nickname by which you will be identified to all the other IRC users.**

   All IRC nicknames must be different from each other, so try a peculiar variation on your username.

8. **For UserName and E-mail, enter your username on your provider's system and your e-mail address.**

9. **Click OK.**

   WSIRC pops up a window telling you that the changes will take effect the next time you connect to an IRC server.

10. **Now connect to the server by clicking the open folder icon, the leftmost one in the row of icons at the top of the window.**

    If everything worked okay, you soon see a bunch of welcoming messages from your server (usually with threats about all the naughty things that will get you kicked off). If you get another linguistically challenged error message box, go back to the Options⇨Server command in step 4 and try another server.

After you're connected to a server, you're ready to try some real IRC chatting commands. In the future, when you start up WSIRC, it automatically connects to your server and you don't have to go through this rigamarole again.

The WSIRC window contains a subwindow called Server Messages, which is divided into three parts. The largest part displays messages from the IRC server. At the bottom is a little one-line window. That's where you type commands. To the right is a tall, skinny window used for showing available IRC channels, as you see in a minute.

Talking the Talk, Chatting the Chat

The next step is to choose a channel and begin typing.

For shell users

The client program most commonly used by IRC users is called *IRCII* (that's "IRC two"). It's the one you're most likely to run into if you type **irc** to a shell provider's system. Because it's so popular, most of the other IRC client programs use the same commands, so we can slay a multitude of avians with a single projectolith by telling you about IRCII commands here.

Everything you type to IRCII and its relatives is taken as lines of text. There are two kinds of lines:

- ✔ Commands to IRC
- ✔ Messages to other people

If a line begins with a slash, it's a command. If not, it's a message. (If only computers were this simple all the time.) The following command, for example:

```
/join #hottub
```

says to join the Hot Tub channel, a cheerful and usually crowded hangout.

For WSIRC users

In WSIRC, in most cases you can type a command directly, or you can use a menu or button that types the command for you. The effect is the same either way.

What channels are on?

As mentioned, IRC discussions are organized (if you can call it that) into *channels*. Each channel has a name that begins with a sharp sign (#). We occasionally have a channel called #dummies, for example, for readers of the *Internet For Dummies* books. To find out which channels are available, you can do one of the following:

- IRCII users can type **/list**.
- WSIRC users can click the LIST button (the tenth one from the left, which has four little lines and an open book). WSIRC pops up a box in which you can type listing options. For the moment, just click OK.

Your IRC program gets the list of available channels, which is usually *very* long.

- In IRCII, the list of channels goes zooming by on your screen, probably faster than you can read it. You can make a shorter list — see the next Tip icon.
- In WSIRC, the list of channels is displayed on the right side of the Server Messages window, and you can scroll it up and down. If you click the mouse once in the list of channels, it expands to fill the window, and for each channel you can see its name, the number of users, and sometimes a description of what it is. Notice that most channels have only a single user, which means that it's one person hanging out, hoping that someone will talk to him. Generally, busier channels are more interesting.

In either WSIRC or IRCII, you can limit the list of channels to those with an interesting number of people. Type this line:

```
/list -min 5
```

to see just the channels with at least five people. (In WSIRC, you type this line in the one-line subwindow underneath Server Messages.) That should limit the list to a useful size.

If you use WSIRC and you don't see a list of channels in the lower right-hand corner of the screen, click the List Channels icon (it's the one with the horizontal red lines).

How the heck can I remember what all those WSIRC buttons do?

You can't. Or more precisely, we can't. (You may well be smarter than we are and be able to memorize them all.) Fortunately, a built-in cheat sheet is available. If you move the cursor to any one of the buttons but don't click any, the name of the button is displayed at the bottom of the WSIRC window. So you can move the mouse back and forth until the name shows you that you've found the one you want.

But you've got to admit, they are the most colorful bunch of buttons you've ever seen!

Hey, Aren't We Ever Going to Do Some Chatting?

Oh, all right, we've stalled as long as we can. You join a channel like this:

- ✔ IRCII users can type a **/join** command, followed by the name of the channel (don't forget the #), as shown in this example:

```
/join #dummies
```

IRCII lets you switch rapidly from one channel to another, and it even lets you join multiple channels, but the messages are jumbled together (which makes them hard to follow).

- ✔ WSIRC can let you do the same thing, by typing the same command in the one-line subwindow underneath Server Messages. For lazy typists, WSIRC also lets you double-click the name of a channel in the list in the Server Messages window — much easier! WSIRC opens a new subwindow for every channel you join so that a dedicated IRC-er can have several channels going at a time.

Why do all IRC channel names start with # ?

We don't know. Maybe it means something special in Finnish. In principle, channels can also begin with an ampersand (&) and be limited to a single server, but they're not common.

After you have joined a channel, everything that people on that channel type appears in the window, and everything you type is sent to them. Whenever someone joins or leaves a channel, a message is sent to all the rest of the participants. When you join a channel, everyone else immediately knows that you're there. Stuff that people type appears preceded by their nickname, for example:

```
[JoeBlow] But what do you do with the woodchucks onc eyou
            catch them?
```

In WSIRC, a list of people in the channel is displayed on the right side of the channel's window so that you can tell whom you're up against.

As is so often the case on the Internet, naive users can easily make fools of themselves. When you join a channel, *lurk* for a while. Don't immediately begin typing — wait and see what the tenor of the conversation is. Then type away. If you find that you like IRC, this stage keeps you up all night and well into the next day.

Some other handy commands include the ones in this list:

/names: Lists the people in a channel; plain /names lists all the channels, or you can follow it by the name of a particular channel of interest

/whois: Followed by someone's nickname, tells you something about the person behind the nickname, usually the e-mail address and any other info that's been registered

Enough Already!

If you tire of a channel, you can leave it:

- ✔ IRCII users can type **/leave**.
- ✔ WSIRC users can do the same thing or close the channel's subwindow in the usual Windows fashion by double-clicking its upper left-hand corner.

Then you can join another channel or exit:

- ✔ IRCII users can type **/quit**.
- ✔ WSIRC users can choose File➪Exit from the menu.

Starting Your Own Channel

If you have nothing better to do, you can start your own IRC channel. Just make up a name and join it, as shown in this example (remember that the name must begin with a #):

```
/join #cephalopods
```

In WSIRC, you can click the Join button (the ninth one from the left that has an arrow and an open book), at which point WSIRC pops up a window in which you type the name of the channel. That's all you have to do.

You might as well set a topic line to be displayed to other IRC'ers, by using the /topic command:

```
/topic Squid, cuttlefish, and their cousins
```

Then you wait, perhaps for a long, long time, until someone else joins your channel and starts talking. If you're the first person on a channel, you're considered to be the channel's operator, which gives you the greatly overrated privilege of kicking off your channel any people you don't like (see the sidebar "Operator, is this the party to whom I am connected?").

When you lose interest, you leave your channel the same way as you leave any other, by typing **/leave** or by closing its window.

TECHNICAL STUFF

Attack of the robots

Most participants on IRC are people. Some aren't — some are robots. It turned out not to be difficult to hook up IRC clients to programs, usually known as *bots,* which can participate like a person can. More exactly, like a very, very stupid person can. Some bots are inoffensive and do such things as hold a channel open and send a cheery welcome message to anyone who joins it. Some are really obnoxious and send large numbers of annoying messages to people whom the bot's creator doesn't like.

In many parts of IRC-land, bots are considered to be terminally antisocial, and they aren't the least bit welcome. We don't tell you how to create a bot, but you should keep in mind that a particularly cement-headed user may actually have a microchip for a brain.

Operator, is this the party to whom I am connected?

IRC channels and IRC servers both have *operators*, people with particular authority to give some kinds of commands. The first person on a channel is considered to be the channel's *operator*, and the operator can anoint other users as operators, too. In the /NAMES listing or the list in the WSIRC window, operators' nicknames are preceded by an at-sign (@).

The main command you get to use as a channel operator is /kick, which kicks someone off your channel, at least for the three seconds until he or she rejoins it. It's a thrill, but a rather small one — sort of like finding that you've won 75 cents in the lottery. In WSIRC, the rightmost button is the Kick button.

Server operators manage entire servers and can kick unruly users entirely off a server, permanently. Don't let that happen to you — be a ruly user, please.

Private Conversations

IRC lets you send messages directly to individuals and to channels. To send a message to an individual, assuming that you know his or her nickname, you type this command:

```
/msg nickname your personal message here.
```

For example:

```
/msg johnny Can you believe how dumb that guy is?!!!
```

You can also have a private conversation with someone. When you type **/query**, the nickname and subsequent lines you type are sent to only that person. When you type /query with no nickname, you're back to normal, sending lines to your current channel.

Your "private" conversation will probably be routed through a dozen IRC servers, and the operators of any of them can log all your messages. So don't say anything that has to be really private.

It's a Jungle Out There

The Internet is pretty anarchic, and IRC is one of the more extreme parts of the anarchy. In particular, all you really know about the people you're chatting with is their nicknames and who they purport to be. Unfortunately, some IRC users have a sick sense of humor and delight in offering other chatters "helpful speed-up files" that in fact delete your files or let them crack into your account. Also, many users have a completely different persona in IRC than in they do in real life: They alter details of their age, interests, lifestyle, gender — you name it. In some cases it's fun, and in others it's just strange. So chat all you want, but keep in mind that not all your IRC friends may be who or what they claim to be.

Finally, IRC is a form of virtual reality, and some people find it very addicting. Students have been known to miss entire semesters of classes because they spent every minute on IRC. Remember that IRC can be fun, but it's no substitute for real life.

Chapter 16

Resource, Resource, Who's Got the Resource?

. . . .

In This Chapter

▶ A roundup of resource types and how to get to them

▶ Mysteries of mailing lists and reminders of news

▶ Nibbling on Gopher

▶ Means of WAIS

▶ Strands of the World Wide Web

. . . .

How Many Ways Are There to Get to Internet Information, Anyway?

Roughly a zillion. (That number again.) Among the services are e-mail, Usenet newsgroups, Telnet, FTP, Gopher, WAIS, and WWW. A few items arrive in other hard-to-characterize ways. (An on-line soda-pop machine appears in Chapter 19, for example.) What's more, a great deal of overlap occurs among the various services. You can get to Gopher by way of WWW and telnet. Or you can get to FTP by way of Gopher, WWW, or e-mail. In this chapter, we summarize the various ways to get to different resource types, depending on which sort of hardware and software you have available. For each type, we list the ways in rough order of quality so that a fast and easy-to-use way is listed before a slow and painful one.

The other thing this chapter tells you about is exactly how each type of re-source is described in technical Internet-ese, usually using things called URLs. In the following chapters, you need to know this stuff to access the information we describe.

URL!

In case you missed it in Chapter 14, the World Wide Web brought us the extremely useful concept of *Uniform Resource Locators,* or *URLs.* The point of a URL is to have a simple and consistent way to name Internet resources that tells you both the type of a resource and where to find it. A URL consists of a resource type, a colon, and a location. In most cases, the location is two slashes, the host name where the resource can be found, a slash, and a name on that host.

Commonly used URL resource types are shown in this table:

Type	Description
gopher	A Gopher menu
http	A HyperText Transfer Protocol document (something in native WWW format)
ftp	A directory or file on an FTP server
news	A Usenet news item (unsupported by many WWW client programs)

Some typical URLs are

```
http://www.ncsa.uiuc.edu/demoweb
   demo.html
```

and

```
gopher://wx.atmos.uiuc.edu:70/1
```

The first line is a WWW document, whose URL means that it's accessible by way of HTTP (the standard scheme the Web uses), the host name is `www.ncsa.uiuc.edu`, and the name on that site is `demoweb/demo.html`. The second is a Gopher directory that is on site `wx.atmos.uiuc.edu`, port 70, and its name is `1`.

Although URLs were originally intended as a way for computers to pass resource names around, they have also become widely used as a way to tell people about Internet resources, and that's how we use them in this section of the book.

Put Me on the Mailing List

The oldest way, and still one of the most popular, for people of like interests to get together on the net is mailing lists. You send messages to and receive messages from a mailing list in the same way you do to and from individual correspondents. The great thing about mailing lists is that you can use them even if the only Internet service you have is e-mail (which is true for many people).

The basic operation of a list is simple: Any messages sent to the list are relayed to all the members of the list. As often as not, other people reply, which creates a sequence of back-and-forth comments in a running discussion. Different lists have very different characters. Some are sociable, and others are quite formal. Some have a great deal of traffic — dozens of messages per day — and others may go for weeks or even months without a message.

Immoderation and indigestion

Some mailing lists are moderated, and some are digests. (Many are both.) In a *moderated* list, messages are not automatically relayed, but rather are passed to a human moderator who weeds out the irrelevant ones and passes on the ones he or she approves. Different moderators have different styles — in some lists, practically everything is approved, and in others only a small fraction of the messages make it through. Many lists are quite popular, and the moderator doesn't so much reject inappropriate messages as act as an editor who picks the best submissions to create a high-quality list.

Some people grumble that moderators are petty fascists who pick and choose unfairly to serve their own whims. Well, we (yes, *we,* one of your authors moderates a list on a technical computer topic) do pick and choose to serve our own whims, but it often seems that the ones who grumble the most are the ones whose messages most need to be weeded out.

Some moderated lists are really one-way mail distributors. That is, the messages on the list don't come from the subscribers but from some outside source. One list relays National Weather Service hurricane announcements, for example, and all the messages on that list originally come from the NWS.

When a list sends out more than two or three messages a day, subscribers' mailboxes can fill up quickly. A common way to lessen the mail overload is to collect all the day's messages in a single large message, known as a *digest,* and send that instead so that you get one big message rather than a dozen little ones. Some lists are available only in digest form, and others are available either way.

An open-and-shut case

Most mailing lists are *open,* which means that anyone can send in a message. Others are *closed,* which means that only people who subscribe to the list are allowed to send in messages. If you try to send a message to a closed list to which you don't subscribe, you get back an automatic response telling you about it. Closed lists can sometimes be a pain: If the return address on your e-mail message doesn't exactly match your address as listed in the subscriber list, you can't send messages in. If this happens to you (if your system manager changes the configuration, for example, and your address is improved from `gw@musket.mtvernon.va.us` to `George.Washington@mtvernon.va.us`), send a nice message to the person who manages the list and ask to have your new address added as one allowed to send in messages.

A few lists are open only to qualified subscribers, and you have to apply to belong. A Usenet moderators' list is limited to people who moderate Usenet groups, for example. If you apply to a list with such restrictions, the list manager will probably ask you to show how you qualify.

Mailing list wrangling

You get on and off mailing lists in three major ways (you didn't think that this would be easy, did you?). Fortunately, they're all easy to deal with.

Be sure to remember the difference between the mailing list *manager addresses* you write to in order to get on and off the list, and the *submission address* you write to in order to send messages to the list members. A common newbie mistake (and you certainly wouldn't want to be mistaken for a newbie) is to send a manager message to the list itself. If you want to subscribe or unsubscribe to the list, for example, everyone doesn't have to hear about it — send the message to the manager address. This kind of mistake is particularly embarrassing because it means that everyone on the list can see how you messed up. Don't let this happen to you!

LISTSERV

The most popular mailing-list maintenance software is called LISTSERV. It was originally written to run on giant IBM mainframe computers and has since popped up on other kinds of computers. LISTSERV lists usually have names like SAMPLE-L. The key thing to remember about LISTSERV lists is that all management-type messages, such as requests to subscribe and unsubscribe, should be addressed to listserv, not to the list address. To subscribe to a LISTSERV list that is, for example, the sample-l mailing list on the Internet host sample.org, e-mail a message to listserv@sample.org, which contains this line:

```
sub sample-l George Washington
```

That is, the line contains sub (short for *sub*scribe), the exact name of the mailing list you are talking about, and then your real, human name. (Remember to substitute the real name of the list in this example and send it to the real name of the Internet LISTSERV host computer.)

To get off the list, send to the same address a message containing this line:

```
unsub sample-l
```

If the list has optional digesting (urp!), you can switch between getting daily digests and individual mail messages by sending one of these messages to the LISTSERV address:

```
set sample-l digest
set sample-l mail
```

`digest` gets you the daily digest, and `mail` gets you individual mail messages.

If you have trouble getting on or off a LISTSERV list, you can contact the person in charge of it at `OWNER-SAMPLE-L@sample.org` (the list name prefixed by `OWNER-`).

After you're on the list, send messages to subscribers by mailing to the name of the list, not to LISTSERV (`SAMPLE-L@sample.org`, for example).

Majordomo

Majordomo was originally a LISTSERV wannabe but has now been improved to the point where it's the mailing-list manager that people like the best. Majordomo has escaped the IBM-isms that can be annoying with LISTSERV, such as its TENDENCY TO PUT EVERYTHING IN UPPERCASE and some places where names are limited to eight characters. To get on or off a Majordomo list, send a message to `majordomo@sample.org` (using the actual host name, of course, rather than `sample.org`.)

To subscribe to a list, send this message:

```
sub name-of-list
```

and to unsubscribe, send this one:

```
unsub name-of-list
```

Unlike with LISTSERV, with Majordomo you *don't* put your real name after the list name on the `sub` command. If you do put something after the list name, it is taken to be the mailing address to use rather than the return address on your message, which can come in handy if your mail system puts a bad return address on your outgoing mail.

To contact the human manager for a Majordomo list, send mail to `owner-name-of-list@sample.org`, the same way as with LISTSERV.

Manually maintained lists

A fair number of lists are still maintained manually by humans. To subscribe or unsubscribe to these lists, you send a message to the list maintainer asking to be added or deleted. For manual lists, you concoct the maintainer's address by adding `-request` to the list name; so for a list named `sample`, the maintainer's address is `sample-request@sample.org`.

Human beings, not being computers, sometimes leave their keyboards in order to eat, sleep, or otherwise have a life. (Hard to believe, isn't it?) For a manually maintained list, therefore, it can take as long as a couple of days for the maintainer to get around to acting on your message. We can tell you from experience that sending lots of extra messages to the maintainer doesn't get you attention any sooner and probably won't get you the kind of attention you want.

URLs for mailing lists

Unlike the other types of resources listed in this chapter, you can't get to the contents of a mailing list via Gopher, WAIS, or the World Wide Web. There's no such thing as an URL for a mailing list.

Usenet Newsgroups: The World's Biggest Bulletin Board

The largest volume of public information and misinformation comes flooding in by way of Usenet newsgroups, currently running an astonishing 100 megabytes per day. The only reasonable way to read the news is with a news-reading program such as *trn, tin,* or *nn* on a UNIX system, or Trumpet or WinVN on a PC (see Chapter 11 to learn how to get and use Trumpet).

Almost any system except those that handle only mail provide a news program (or if you're using a PC with SLIP or PPP, provide a news server for your local news program.) If you're unaccountably stuck in a newsfree environment but can telnet out to other systems, you can try telnetting to `cyberspace.org` or `launchpad.unc.edu`, two systems that provide limited public access to news. Some WWW programs provide access to Usenet news also, although because none of the ones we've seen handles topic threads, it's a slow and painful way to read news if you read more than about four articles in a sitting.

Subscribing to a newsgroup

When you find out about a newsgroup of interest, you only have to tell your news program to present it to you.

To subscribe to a group you haven't read in the past, follow the appropriate step in this list:

- ✔ **trn users:** At the newsgroup selection level, press g and the newsgroup name.

- ✔ **nn users:** At the menu listing newsgroups, press G and type the name of the group.

- ✔ **tin users**: At the screen showing newsgroups, press g and type the name of the group.
- ✔ **Trumpet users:** Choose Group Subscribe from the menu and then choose the group you want from the list of unsubscribed groups.
- ✔ **WinVN users:** Just scroll down to the group and double-click its name.

News by way of mail

Some Usenet groups are also available by mail. The group `comp.dcom.telecom` is the same as the e-mail list `telecom@eecs.nwu.edu`, for example, and the group `comp.compilers` is the same as the `compil-l@american.edu` LISTSERV list. Anything that appears in the group is mailed to the list and vice versa. Every few weeks, a message posted to the newsgroup `news.lists` contains a list of groups available by e-mail.

If you're at a site where you can read news but not post it, it is possible to send out Usenet articles by mail by using two public mail-to-news gateways:

- ✔ One gateway, at Digital Equipment in Palo Alto, California, is called `decwrl.dec.com`. To submit an article to a newsgroup, mail the article to the group name with `.Usenet@decwrl.dec.com` added to the end; to submit an article to the `rec.travel` newsgroup, for example, mail the article to `rec.travel.Usenet@decwrl.dec.com`.
- ✔ The other gateway, at the University of Texas, is called `cs.utexas.edu`. The mailing address for a newsgroup is the group name with periods changed to hyphens (`rec-travel@cs.utexas.edu`, for example).

Although it's possible to send messages to groups you can't read, it's really tacky to do so. (This type of message usually ends, "Please send me e-mail because I don't read this group.") If a group's topic is of interest, find a way to read the group. For all you know, the point you are making has been made three times a week for the past year, or the question you are asking was answered yesterday.

URLs for newsgroups

Newsgroups can be described in terms of URLs, a method of naming Internet recources that is defined in the "URLs!" sidebar at the beginning of this chapter. The URL for a newsgroup looks like this:

```
news:news.group.name
```

For example, the `rec.gardens.orchids` newsgroup is called

```
news:rec.gardens.orchids
```

Telnet

Telnet is the classic service that lets you log in to other computers on the net. (It's the next best thing to being there.) Many of the more interesting services offered by telnet are provided on nonstandard network ports. (The standard telnet port is number 23; anything else is nonstandard.) If you use a UNIX-based system, run telnet by giving the host name and, if it's nonstandard, the port number, like this:

```
telnet martini.eecs.umich.edu 3000
```

In Windows and Macintosh telnet programs, you generally have one field in which you type the host name and another for the port, as shown in Figure 16-1.

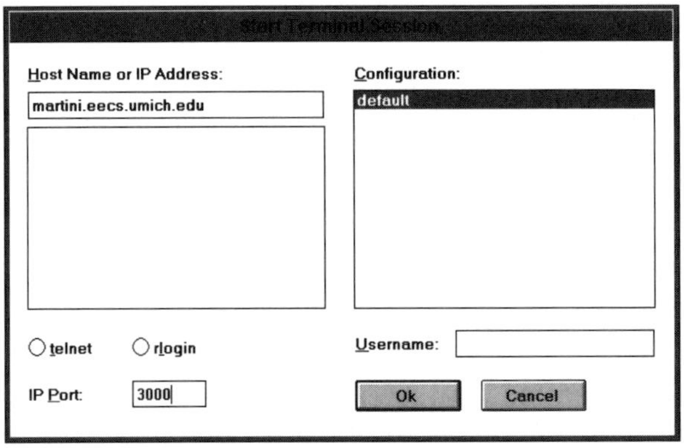

Figure 16-1:
Telnet from
Windows.

URLs for telnetting

Occasionally you also see a telnet address written as an URL, like this:

```
telnet://martini.eecs.umich.edu:3000/
```

You need them in this format if you want to use a World Wide Web browser program for telnetting. See the "URL!" sidebar earlier in this chapter.

FTP

Back in Chapter 9, we talked about using FTP to get WinSock applications. As far as FTP is concerned, those program files are just like any other kind of file, which means that you retrieve other files in the same way as you retrieved those programs.

So if you know how to find programs on the net, you know how to find other files too:

1. **Start your FTP program.**
2. **Connect to the server.**
3. **Log in as anonymous and give your e-mail address as the password.**
4. **Change to the directory that contains the files.**
5. **Set binary mode (unless it's a text file).**
6. **Get the file.**

Refer to Chapter 9 for details.

Sneaky ways to FTP

Let's face it: FTP is getting kind of long in the tooth. I mean, files, directories — it's so totally retro and hopelessly old-fashioned. You can't even tell what type each file is or what's in it. Fortunately, two considerably more convenient ways to get to FTP are available: Gopher and through WWW.

Gophering to FTP

Many FTP servers are also Gopher servers. (It turns out that the extra software required can usually be added by a student in an afternoon, so what the heck.) A frequent clue is the presence of files called .cache, which Gopher uses to speed up some retrievals. If you see files with that name, you can be pretty sure that a Gopher server is lurking nearby.

In any event, it doesn't hurt to try to see whether you can retrieve files with Gopher rather than with FTP. On heavily loaded FTP servers, Gopher is often faster because fewer people are retrieving files by using Gopher than by using FTP. You can also try some name-guessing. If an FTP site is called — for example, ftp.std.com (that's the FTP server for our friends at the World), it's a pretty good guess that gopher.std.com is their Gopher server. See the next section for suggestions about how to use your Gopher program to connect to a particular Gopher host.

WWW meets FTP: URL that file

The World Wide Web, which we discuss in more detail later in this chapter (and also in Chapter 14) has built-in features that make it a good way to get files from FTP servers. Any public FTP server has a WWW URL (see the "URLs!" sidebar at the beginning of this chapter) that lets you look at the available directories and files. If the FTP server is called sample.com and the file you want is called /pub/samplefiles, the URL is

```
ftp://sample.com/pub/samplefiles
```

If you give this URL to your WWW program (most often Mosaic, Cello, or Lynx), it automatically takes care of the details of logging in to the server, retrieving directories, and so on. Conversely, if you have an FTP program and someone gives you this URL, you can fire up the FTP program, connect to `sample.com`, move to the `/pub` directory, and retrieve `samplefiles`. It's more work, but at least you're not stuck.

Going for Gopher

Lots and lots of Gopher pages are available. The reason is partly that Gopher is a highly advanced information-retrieval system, but mostly that the Gopher server software is free and not hard to set up.

Gopher meets WWW and gets the URL

The following line shows the URL for a typical Gopher item:

```
gopher://akasha.tic.com:70/11/bruces
```

This line tells you that the host is `akasha.tic.com`, port 70 (the standard Gopher port, so you could have left out the port number) and that its pathname is `11/bruces`. Who knows exactly what this means, but if you ask Mosaic or Cello to show it to you, they can find it.

As with any URL, you can give this one directly to a WWW program and it scrounges up the menu for you.

You can also use an URL with a Gopher client, but a little surgery on the name is required first. The host name and port number are perfectly okay, but the path needs some work. The problem is that Gopher items have types that are internally remembered as single digits and letters. Most notably, a Gopher menu is type 1, and a plain file is type 0. In an URL, the first character in the path part (the part after a single slash) of the URL is the item type (1, in this case). So this URL refers to a Gopher menu (that's the first 1) whose actual path is `1/bruces` (that's the rest of the path). So what you type for your Gopher path is **1/bruces**.

You can usually get away with leaving out the path on Gopher URLs. In almost every case, an empty path gives you the main Gopher menu for the server, and you can go through a few menus to find the item you want more easily than you can unscramble the path by hand.

UNIX Gopher

If you are using a Gopher program on a UNIX-based Internet system, you can tell it which Gopher item you want to see. When you type the `gopher` command, follow it with the path, host, and port. To start at the Gopher menu discussed earlier, for example, you type this line:

```
% gopher -p 1/bruces akasha.tic.com 70
```

If the path is empty (frequently the case for Gopher URLs), you can leave out the `-p` part, and if the port is number 70, you can leave that out also. So to start at the top-level Gopher menu on that host, you type this line:

```
% gopher akasha.tic.com
```

HGopher

On your Windows machine, you can also start HGopher by giving it a host and path on the command line, but doing anything on the command line in Windows is a pain in the neck. It's much easier to create a bookmark for the resource and then jump to the bookmark.

Here's how you do it:

1. **Start HGopher.**

2. **Display the bookmark page.**

   If it's not already displayed, click the leftmost of the five buttons in the bottom right corner of the screen.

3. **Choose Bookmarks Create and then type the information, as shown in Figure 16-2.**

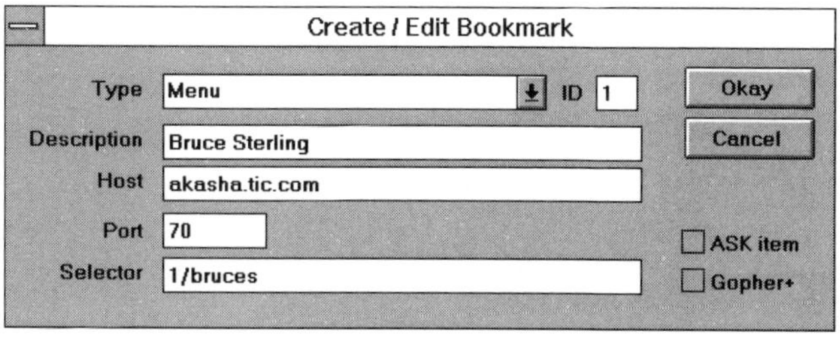

Figure 16-2: Creating a bookmark in HGopher.

Create / Edit Bookmark		
Type	Menu ▼	ID 1	Okay
Description	Bruce Sterling	Cancel
Host	akasha.tic.com	
Port	70	☐ ASK item
Selector	1/bruces	☐ Gopher+

Now you only have to double-click your new bookmark and the Gopher item appears. (If you then decide that you hate it, choose Bookmarks Remove Bookmark to get rid of it.) See Chapter 12 for more details about HGopher.

Means of WAIS

WAIS sources are libraries of documents a server can search for you. WAIS sources are described in a stylized and rather verbose form. For example, here's how the index of U.S. ZIP codes is described:

```
(:source
    :version  3
    :ip-address "192.31.181.1"
    :ip-name "quake.think.com"
    :tcp-port 210
    :database-name "/proj/wais/db/sources/zipcodes"
    :cost 0.00
    :cost-unit :free
    :maintainer "wais@quake.think.com"
    :description "WAIS index of USA Zip Code database"
)
```

For most WAIS client programs, including UNIX *swais* and Windows WAISMAN, you can tell it exactly which file you want by creating a file containing the WAIS document description, punctuation and all. (Usually the description has arrived in a mail or news message, so you don't have to retype the whole thing.) WinWAIS uses a different approach, in which you enter the important parts of the description, the host name, port number, and database name into a form, but you don't need the whole thing. See the sidebar "Adding sources by hand" in Chapter 13.

WAIS, Gopher, and WWW: Strange bedfellows

It is somewhat possible (there's a pair of weasel words) to get to WAIS by way of either Gopher or WWW:

✔ **From Gopher:** If you start up your favorite Gopher program, you should see a menu entry for the Gopher Home in Minnesota. Choose that, and on the menu it retrieves, choose Other Gopher and Information Servers. On that page, you find an entry for WAIS Based Information, which should in theory connect you to a Gopher server that can do WAIS searches. We've almost never found that server to be available, in fact, but you never know — it might come back.

✔ **From WWW:** One WAIS gateway works somewhat more reliably. You can find it from the CERN (the mother of all WWW) home page. Choose Data Sources by Type of Service and then WAIS service, which gives you a long page full of WAIS sources. If you have trouble finding that page, the URL for the WWW page at the WAIS gateway is shown here:

```
http://www.wais.com/waisgate-announce.html
```

Web Walking Wisdom

The World Wide Web is by far the coolest thing mortal Internauts can use. Unlike all the other programs we mentioned, WWW programs use URLs directly.

What do you do if someone tells you the URL of a cool WWW page or if you find one listed in the later chapters of this book? What you do varies a little depending on which WWW program you use. Here are some hints for the most popular ones: Mosaic and Cello.

Getting there by way of Mosaic

If you use any of the many versions of Mosaic, choose File⇨Open from the menu. In the Windows version, you can also click the little open folder near the top of the window; or in the UNIX version, you can click the Open button at the bottom of the window. No matter which version you're using, you type the URL in the window that pops up and then press Enter or click the OK button.

Getting there by way of Cello

If you use Cello, choose Jump⇨Launch by way of URL from the menu. When Cello asks for the URL name, type it in. Then click OK or press Enter.

We often find URLs in Usenet messages we're reading. Lazy typists can avoid typing and pick the URL out of the news message:

✔ On UNIX, if you are reading Usenet news by using trn or another newsreader in an xterm window, use the mouse to select the URL (that is, move the mouse pointer to the beginning of the URL, press and hold the first mouse button, move to the end of the URL so that the URL is highlighted, and release the mouse button). Then move the pointer to the type-in box in the Mosaic Open pop-up window and press the middle mouse button. A friendly gnome types the selected URL into the window.

✔ In Windows, if you are reading Usenet news by using Trumpet or another newsreader, select the URL by using the mouse and press Ctrl+C to copy the URL to the Windows Clipboard. Then switch to Mosaic, choose File⇨Open, and press Ctrl+V to paste the URL in the window. Then click OK or Open to fetch the URL.

WWW by telnet

If you don't have a WWW program such as Mosaic, Cello, or Lynx available locally but you can telnet to other systems, you can telnet to several public WWW systems. Some of these are listed in Table16-1. They don't let you view all the spiffy embedded graphics, but they're much better than nothing.

Table 16-1	WWW Servers You Can Telnet To	
Where	**Name**	**Login**
New Jersey	www.njit.edu	www
Kansas	ukanaix.cc.ukans.edu	www
Netherlands	www.twi.tudelft.nl	lynx
Australia	millbrook.lib.rmit.edu.au	lynx
Switzerland	info.cern.ch	www
Israel	vms.huji.ac.il	www
Slovakia	sun.uakom.sk	www
Taiwan	www.edu.tw	www

WWW by mail, for the desperate

If you just can't find a WWW system and you can't telnet, there is an e-mail server. Using the Web by e-mail is not unlike playing chess by mail, but there are people who do each.

To retrieve a WWW document, send an e-mail to listserv@info.cern.ch. The text of the message should contain a line saying SEND followed by the URL, as shown in this example:

```
SEND http://info.cern.ch/hypertext/DataSources/bySubject/
         Overview.html
```

(That WWW page contains a list of WWW servers.)

It may occur to you that because the WWW gives you access to pretty much every resource on the net, you might be able to use it to retrieve giant binary files, read Usenet groups that aren't available at your site, and otherwise suck down gigabytes of data. Don't do it. The same thing has occurred to the people who run this server (a bunch of physicists in Geneva, Switzerland), and if people start abusing the mail server, it will go away. You can't get giant files anyway because each response is limited to 1,000 lines of text.

Don't Take Our Word for It

The rest of the chapters in this book list the most fun and interesting Internet resources that were available at the time we wrote this book. But the Internet is growing like crazy, and new resources appear literally every day.

The Usenet group comp.infosystems.announce contains nothing but announcements of new Internet resources, almost all of which are new WWW pages, or other resources, such as Gopher menus, you can use by way of WWW. It's strictly moderated, so there are no extraneous messages. Messages are posted only once or twice a week, so it doesn't take much time to monitor the group, and all sorts of interesting new stuff appears there.

Chapter 17

The Net on the Net

In This Chapter

▶ Finding information about the net on the net

▶ Frequently asked questions (FAQs) and their answers

▶ The Usenet urban folklore quiz

▶ The EARN guide to network resource tools

▶ The InterNIC InfoGuide

▶ The Internet Tool List

▶ Entering the World Wide Web: a guide to cyberspace

▶ World Wide Web FAQs and guides

▶ Special Internet connections

▶ The Free for All page

▶ CityScape Internet services

▶ On-line magazines

▶ A list of WWW servers

▶ The Globewide Network Academy

*T*he Internet is such a huge place that no single book can possibly list all the resources and services available. And even if it did, it would be out of date the day it was published. Fortunately, the net itself is the ideal place to find out more about it. (Think of it as looking up the word *dictionary* in the dictionary, except that you're more likely to find something you didn't already know. By the way, have you heard that by lexicographer's tradition, the word *gullible* doesn't appear in any dictionary?)

In this chapter, we look at on-line documents, magazines, maps, and more, which all are ways of finding out about the Internet itself. For each service, we list the URL of the server — that is, its Uniform Resource Locator. Chapter 16 tells you how to use URLs to access stuff by using Gopher, WAIS, and — first and foremost — the World Wide Web. URLs that begin with *http* are World Wide

Web pages; those that begin with *news* are Usenet newsgroups; those that begin with *ftp* are files available from FTP servers; and those that begin with *gopher* are — good guess — Gopher items.

Internet Services Frequently Asked Questions (FAQ) and Answers

URLs:

```
ftp://rtfm.mit.edu:/pub/usenet/news.answers/internet-
               services/faq
```

or

```
news:alt.online.services
```

or

```
news:news.newuser.questions
```

or else (this is not a URL):

```
e-mail to mail-server@rtfm.mit.edu
```

This definitive Usenet document describes the types of services on the Internet, compiled by Kevin Savetz. It has everything from telnet to IRC, and a bunch of other services with names like Prospero that we don't even touch on here. The easiest way to find it is on Usenet in the news.newuser.questions newsgroup or, failing that, by way of FTP. People who have only e-mail access to the net can send a message to mail-server@rtfm.mit.edu that contains this line:

```
send usenet/news.answers/internet-services/faq.
```

The Usenet urban folklore quiz (Part I)

Let's face it — more interesting things exist than chapters full of lists. One of our fellow *Dummies* authors calls them Ten Coffee Pot Chapters. So to perk things up, direct from the world-famous Usenet group `alt.folklore.urban`, it's the Usenet Urban Folklore Quiz.

Each section has ten true or false questions. The answers are at the end of Chapter 19. Don't cheat by looking at the answers first!

Part I: Science

True or false:

1. You can make as much ice faster by starting with warmer water. ___

2. Boiled water freezes faster than ordinary water at the same initial temperature. ___

3. Daylight sky appears dark enough to see stars from the bottom of a deep well. ___

4. Fluorescent lamps light up when held near a high-voltage line. ___

5. Leather saddles used to be treated with llama dung to avoid scaring horses. ___

6. If the entire population of China jumped up at the same time: a.) the Earth's orbit would be disturbed or b.) the entire U.S. would be swamped by a tidal wave. ___

7. You can see glass flow in the windows of old buildings. ___

8. A newspaper once substituted "In the African-American" for "in the black." ___

9. Scientists once concluded that bumblebees can't fly. ___

10. The F-51D fighter plane can flip because of engine torque. ___

The EARN Guide to Network Resource Tools

URL:

```
ftp://ds.internic.net/pub/internet-doc/EARN.nettools.txt
```

or else (this is not a URL):

```
e-mail to listserv@earncc.bitnet
```

EARN, one of the European networks, has written its own guide to network tools. It covers the same stuff as the other on-line guides do (what did you expect?), although it pays more attention to resources available by way of e-mail because EARN has many e-mail-only users.

If you can't get this document by way of FTP, send an e-mail message to `listserv@earncc.bitnet` containing the line `send nettools memo` for the text version or `send nettools ps` for a version that prints beautifully on a PostScript printer but is otherwise inscrutable.

The InterNIC InfoGuide

URLs:

```
http://www.internic.net/
```

or

```
gopher://is.internic.net/ (select InterNIC Information
             Services)
```

The InterNIC is a Network Information Center (NIC), divided into these three parts:

- ✔ **Information Services:** Run by General Atomics in California
- ✔ **Directory Services:** Run by AT&T in New Jersey
- ✔ **Registration Services:** Run by Network Solutions in Virginia, funded primarily (for now at least) by the National Science Foundation

The InterNIC was originally supposed to support the NSFNET (a precursor to the Internet), but as the NSFNET goes away, the InterNIC is still here.

The InfoGuide is primarily a path into InterNIC Information Services, although it also has links to the other two branches. The InfoGuide has useful but not particularly unusual information for new users, including hints about getting on the net, lists of providers, and so on.

The most interesting thing in the InfoGuide is the Scout Report, which comes out each Friday and lists new resources the InterNIC scouts found during the preceding week. To join the Scout Report mailing list, send an e-mail message to `majordomo@is.internic.net`, with the line `subscribe scout-report` in the text of the message. Or read the text of the report on the WWW or Gopher pages referred to in the URLs for the InterNIC.

The Internet Tool List

URLs:

```
ftp://ftp.rpi.edu/pub/communications/internet-tools.txt
            (text file)
```

or

```
ftp://ftp.rpi.edu/pub/communications/internet-tools.html (WWW
                    document)
```

John Arthur December, at the Rensselaer Polytechnic Institute, has an extensive list of tools for Network Information Retrieval (NIR) and Computer-Mediated Communication (CMC). The WWW document has links to most of them, so you can try them out while you wait. If you don't have access to the WWW, the text file version is still quite useful because many of the tools don't need the WWW.

Entering the World Wide Web: A Guide to Cyberspace

URL:

```
http://www.hcc.hawaii.edu/guide/www.guide.html
```

This interesting introductory guide to the WWW is chock-full of pictures and hyperlinks, written by Kevin Hughes, at the Honolulu Community College. The only problem is that it's rather large and can take 15 minutes to retrieve over a SLIP link.

World Wide Web FAQs and Guides

URL:

```
http://cui_www.unige.ch/OSG/FAQ/www.html
```

Oskar Stern, at the Centre Universitaire d'Informatique, University of Geneva, has thoughtfully created a WWW page with references to just about every WWW guide on the net. So this is a great place to start a Web walk.

Special Internet Connections

URLs:

```
ftp://csd4.csd.uwm.edu/pub/inet.services.html (WWW version)
```

or

```
ftp://ftp.csd.uwm.edu/pub/inet.services.txt (text version)
```

or

```
gopher://csd4.csd.uwm.edu/ (select Remote Information
                Services)
```

or

```
news:alt.internet.services
```

Scott Yanoff has been compiling a list of Internet servers and addresses for several years. It's the place we turn to first to find out how to get to a new service or to find the most up-to-date list of servers that let you telnet to services such as Archie and Gopher. The WWW version is the easiest to use, but all the info is also present in the text version you get by way of Usenet, FTP, or Gopher.

Free for All

URL:

```
http://south.ncsa.uiuc.edu:8241/Free.html
```

The Free for All Page is an experiment in cooperative (well, sort of cooperative) hypermedia. Anyone who wants to can put an entry and a picture into the page, so it has everything from biochemical research results to pictures of scantily clad French ladies.

This page contains about 100 images that come from literally all over the world, so it can take an extremely long time (the better part of an hour) to retrieve the whole thing.

CityScape Internet Services

URL:

`http://www.cityscape.co.uk/`

CityScape is a British Internet provider. Its home page has links to several on-line magazines in addition to local businesses and an ever-growing guide to the pubs in Cambridge, England, with a handy locator map, shown in Figure 17-1.

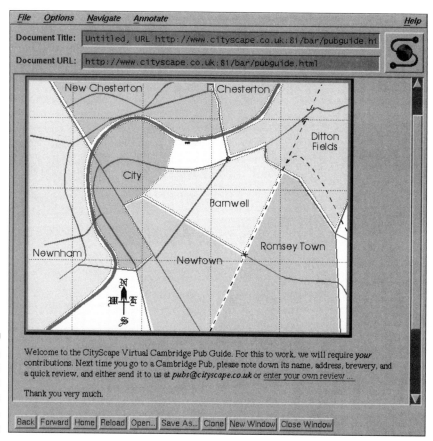

Figure 17-1:
The
CityScape
Cambridge
Pub Guide.

On-line Magazines

In a place as big and busy as the Internet, it can be difficult to keep up with what's new because it changes every day. Fortunately, you're not on your own — lots of magazines, both on paper and on-line, can help keep you up to date. Paper magazines are hopelessly retro, so here we just look at the on-line ones.

Internaut

URL:

```
ftp://ftp.netcom.com/pub/mailcom/internaut/index.html
```

Internaut grew out of a project to write a book about Internet resources. There was too much information for the book, so the overflow turned into *Internaut,* an on-line magazine. Articles discuss the history of parts of the net, various methods of connecting to the net, and discussions of various kinds of Internet software. (One of the articles speaks enthusiastically about the promise of Internet connections by way of cable TV, but even though one of the TV cables on which the Internet is supposed to be available runs right past the window of one of our offices, we don't know anyone who's been able to get connected. Harumph.)

The Global Network Navigator

URL:

```
http://gnn.nearnet.com/
```

The *Global Network Navigator* also grew out of an Internet book and has become the best magazine on the net. Unlike the other magazines, *GNN* is supported by advertising, which gives it a budget to pay writers to write real articles rather than have to scrounge stuff or have the editor write everything. The difference is obvious: The writing is better and the breadth of coverage is much greater than in other on-line magazines.

GNN has sections of feature articles (usually with provisions for reader responses on-line), commentary, collections of clippings from both the net and the regular media, and commercial sections. As *GNN* has evolved, it has grown new sections. In 1993, it gained a section on travel, and in early 1994 a section on personal finance. (We visit the travel section in Chapter 18.) New material appears nearly every day, so it's always worth a visit.

Global On-line Magazine

URL:

```
http://www.gold.net/home.html
```

This on-line magazine was originally intended for subscribers to the IP-GOLD access service, but it is accessible to readers anywhere. This system happens to be in England, so the slant is slightly British.

Matrix News

URL:

```
http://www.tic.com/mids/midshome.html
```

or else (this is not a URL):

```
e-mail to mids@tics.com
```

Matrix News is a monthly newsletter that discusses the Matrix, the totality of all the interconnected networks in the world. Articles address connectivity in various countries, statistics on different networks, and unusual network applications. Unlike the other on-line magazines, this one costs a small amount of actual money — $15 per year for students and $25 per year for humans for an on-line subscription. Issues can be delivered in text or PostScript form and by e-mail or FTP. (We get the PostScript FTP version, so each month the publisher e-mails us a short message giving the code needed to unlock its FTP server so that we can FTP the current issue.)

Few readers are interested in all the articles, but each issue always has something interesting. An article about Internet connections in Brazil, for example, might not be all that interesting to you, but we found it fascinating because one of us will be living there soon.

Fishnet

URL:

```
http://www.cs.washington.edu/homes/pauld/fishnet
```

The Usenet urban folklore quiz (Part II)

Still with us? Amazing!

Part II: Computing and medicine

True or false:

11. Apple used a Cray supercomputer to design hardware systems; Cray used an Apple. ___

12. Bill Gates has a $750,000 Porsche 959 he can't use because it can't be made to comply with emission laws. ___

13. A Russian mechanical translator program translated "out of sight, out of mind" into "blind and insane," and "Spirit is willing, but the flesh is weak" as "the drink is good, but the meat is rotten." ___

14. In 1947 a moth was found in a relay of the Harvard Mark II computer and was taped in to the logbook as the "first actual case of bug being found." ___

15. Computing pioneer Grace Hopper coined the term "bug" as a result of this event. ___

16. A London doctor was fired for inveigling Turkish peasants to donate a kidney. ___

17. Flowers are bad in hospital rooms because they suck oxygen from the air. ___

18. Some people sneeze when they're exposed to bright light. ___

19. Drinking large quantities of deionized or distilled water over a long period of time can screw you up because of ion imbalances. ___

20. You can catch a cold by being chilled. ___

Fishnet is a weekly compendium of odds and ends compiled by Paul Barton-Davis at the University of Washington. It runs mostly to pithy notes and interesting citations, generally short and to the point.

The name comes from "net fishing," or poking around on the network for interesting-looking stuff. If you're looking for fish that swim in the water, try the Usenet groups `rec.outdoors.fishing` and `rec.outdoors.fishing.fly`.

WWW: Wow, It's Big

URLs:

```
http://www.mit.edu:8001/people/mkgray/compre3.html
        (alphabetic)
```

or

```
http://www.mit.edu:8001/people/mkgray/compre.bydomain.html
        (by domain)
```

Matthew Gray, a student at M.I.T., has created a list of all the WWW servers he could find. Wow, there's a lot of them — more than 1,200 — all in one rather large WWW page. Unlike the Free for All page you read about earlier, this one just has references to the other pages (no fancy graphics), so it loads fairly quickly — a couple of minutes over a SLIP link. There are two versions of the page: The first one lists the servers in alphabetical order, and the second one is grouped by domain so that you get some idea of where the servers are. (You find, for example, three servers from Poland and four from Portugal.)

It's often impossible to tell from the names what information you will find on which server, so this is a great place to begin some aleatoric network exploration.

The Globewide Network Academy

URL:

```
http://uu-gna.mit.edu:8001/uu-gna/index.html
```

No global village is complete without an institution of higher learning. The GNA's goal is to create an actual, fully accredited university that exists on the Internet, with teachers and students physically located all over the world. It has or will have a library, a virtual campus on which people can meet, a curriculum, courses — all the things a university needs.

Courses are taught by using whatever Internet services the teacher wants, frequently including real-time course meetings by way of IRC or MOO (a multiuser simulation system).

Some of the Spring 1994 courses included the ones in this list:

- ✔ Introduction to the Internet
- ✔ Introduction to Object-Oriented Programming Using C++
- ✔ Microbial Ecology and Environmental Microbiology
- ✔ Art and Technology
- ✔ Introduction to Screenwriting
- ✔ Renaissance Culture
- ✔ Introduction to C Programming

So drop by its WWW page and see what's up.

Chapter 18

Useful Stuff Is Out There!

● ●

In This Chapter

▶ How's the weather?

▶ Money information from EDGAR

▶ Information about patents

▶ Sending a fax

▶ Looking at census data

▶ Academic information

▶ Books and bookstores on the net

▶ Let your fingers do the shopping

▶ Stock prices by wire

▶ Smithsonian photos

● ●

*D*espite what the preceding chapter might have led you to believe, the Internet does indeed contain information about topics other than itself. This chapter looks at some of the real stuff you can find on the net.

To show that we're not kidding, we begin with some actual useful information that, back in the dark ages, might have required buying a newspaper, visiting the library, or even (gasp!) picking up the phone.

How's the Weather?

Everyone talks about the weather, but nobody does anything about it, right? Well, you still may not be able to do anything about it, but at least you can be well informed.

The National Weather Map

URL:

```
http://www.mit.edu:8001/usa.html
```

The WWW weather map, shown in Figure 18-1, shows the current national weather map. It's up to date; the map in the figure had been issued by the Weather Service only 45 minutes before we snapped a picture of it here at Internet For Dummies Central. When you click on any point in the map, it hunts up the forecast for that place. (We would show you that too, but by the time it made it into print, the forecast would be a little out of date.

WWW Weather World

URL:

```
http://www.atmos.uiuc.edu/wxworld/html/top.html
```

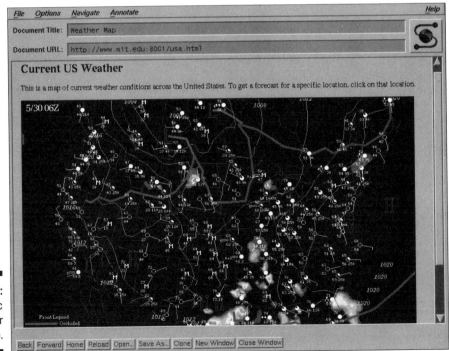

Figure 18-1:
Your basic weather map.

Weather information has been available on-line from the University of Illinois for years. Weather World makes it all available at the click of a button. You can get weather maps, infrared satellite photographs, and visible light photographs. You can also get animations of the last several hours' photographs, just like they do on The Weather Channel. Real weather junkies can leave the map displayed in a window and then every hour or so press the Reload button to refetch the most current image.

The Weather Machine Gopher Server

URL:

```
gopher://wx.atmos.uiuc.edu/
```

The Weather Machine is the Gopher cousin of Weather World. Some of the same maps are available, but it also has much more detailed information, such as forecasts by city and county for most states, in addition to forecasts for Canada, much of the Caribbean, and several other countries.

EDGAR, Prince of Profit

URLs:

```
http://town.hall.org/edgar/edgar.html
```

or

```
ftp://town.hall.org/edgar
```

or (this is not a URL)

```
e-mail "HELP" to mail@town.hall.org
```

Interested in money? We thought so. The U.S. Security and Exchange Commission, the government agency that regulates stock markets, has a system called EDGAR that contains data filed with it by all the thousands of publicly held companies it regulates. Every time a company sneezes, it has to file stuff with the SEC, so from EDGAR you can find out a great deal about your favorite company. Check out companies in which you hold stock, companies in which you might like to hold stock, the company where you work, and the company where you plan to work next. (For those last two, just remember: It wasn't us who suggested you do that.)

The EDGAR server is set up as a WAIS server, so you can get to it by way of WWW, FTP, WAIS, or an e-mail server. You give the company name, and it gives you the facts.

It's Patently Obvious

URLs:

```
http://town.hall.org/patent/patent.html
```

or

```
ftp://ftp.town.hall.org/patent
```

There's been much excitement (and anger) in the computer business about patents issued for software. You can find out about recent software patents and any other patents issued since 1994. Again, the primary access is by way of WAIS or WWW, although if you know the number of a patent you want, you can just FTP it from the server.

Just the Fax, Ma'am

URL:

```
http://town.hall.org/
```

While you're visiting the Town Hall WWW system, click the item called The Phone Company. An experimental e-mail-to-fax gateway lets you send faxes to people all over the world. Coverage is spotty because the faxes are sent by volunteers who have joined the project, so the places you can send faxes to are the places that are a local call from the volunteers' systems. But it's fun to use.

The Phone Company page contains a form on which you can enter that the fax be sent.

The phone number must be entered with the country code. For numbers in North America, it should look like 1 617 936 1234 because our country code is 1.

If you follow the link to Phone Company Information, you find pages explaining the fax system and the way you address mail. Here's the address for the preceding phone number:

```
remote-printer.John_Smith@16179361234.iddd.tpc.int
```

The Census Bureau

URLs:

```
http://www.census.gov/
```

or

```
gopher://gopher.census.gov
```

or

```
ftp://ftp.census.gov/pub
```

The Census Bureau, repository of far more information than it is healthy to have in one place, has recently come into cyberspace. (Actually, that's a cheap shot because the Census Bureau has one of the best records among government agencies for protecting personal privacy.)

On its WWW, Gopher, and FTP servers, you can find statistical and financial data of many varieties. You won't find detailed statistical data (too bulky, evidently), but there are statistical briefs (beautifully formatted in PostScript form, so you have to retrieve them and then print them by using a PostScript viewer) full of interesting info. We found out from one of them, for example, that although Americans of Asian and Pacific Island backgrounds are only slightly more likely to graduate from high school than are whites, they're almost twice as likely to complete college and go on to a graduate degree. At certain kinds of cocktail parties, that sort of factoid can be darned handy.

The Academic Circuit

Most colleges and universities in the U.S. and many of them overseas have connections to the Internet. As people have discovered how easy it is to set up a Web or Gopher server on a spare computer, it has become *de rigeur* for each institution, and frequently each department, to set them up to let the rest of the world know what they're up to and, more important, how cool they are. Figure 18-2 for example, shows a WWW page for a university chosen at random (well, considering that we both graduated from there, maybe not exactly random).

Check out those universities

URL:

```
http://www.mit.edu:8001/people/mkgray/compre.bydomain.html
```

A relatively convenient way to see what's up at a particular institution is from the Wow It's Big page (see the section "WWW: Wow, It's Big," in Chapter 17), particularly the version organized by domain (remember the last part of an Internet host's address, like *com* or *edu* or *gov*). If you scroll down to the edu domain, you find most of the schools in the U.S. conveniently listed in alphabetical order with links to their WWW servers.

Depending on your age, it's a swell way to find out what your alma mater has been up to or to check out a school you or your offspring are considering attending.

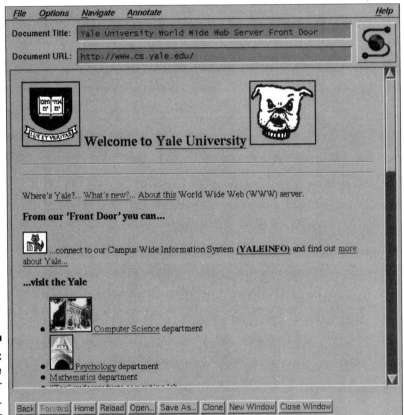

Figure 18-2:
A Web page
from Mother
Yale.

The USENET urban folklore quiz (Part III)

Hey, don't you have anything better to do than this? Well, if you insist:

Part III: The groves of academe

True or false:

21. A professor listed a famous unsolved math problem; a student thought that it was homework and solved it.

22. At some colleges, if a roommate commits suicide, it gets you an automatic *A* for all your courses.

23. A student got his tuition money by asking in a newspaper ad for a penny from each person.

24. A professor allowed students to "bring in what they can carry for exam;" one student carried in a grad student.

25. A student submitted a 20-year-old paper for class. The professor gave it an *A*, saying that he always liked it but that he got only a *B* when he wrote it.

26. Eminent Stanford professor Donald "Art of Computer Programming" Knuth's first publication was in *MAD* magazine.

27. A philosophy professor's one-word exam was "Why?" He gave an *A* to a student who replied, "Why not?"

28. A low-grading professor graded the same exam in successive semesters; he gave it a higher grade each time. The fourth time around, he wrote, "Like it more each time."

29. Science class students took a swab from the inside of their cheek and examined it under a microscope. One group saw odd organisms and called the professor, who looked and declared that it was sperm.

30. Albert Einstein did poorly in school.

Hear ye! Hear ye! Electronic publishing!

Books and magazines have been printed on paper and physically transported from the publisher to the bookstore to the customer for hundreds of years. It's *so* old-fashioned. Isn't it time to put a stop to it? (A fine thing for us to say, eh?) Several mainstream — that is, not written and edited by or for geeks — magazines are now available partly or entirely on the net. This section presents a sampling of them.

Internet Distribution Services

URL:

```
http://www.service.com
```

This *electronic kiosk* in Palo Alto, California, offers, among other things, *Answers,* a magazine for adult children of aging parents.

The Electronic Newsstand

URLs:

```
gopher://enews.com/
```

or

```
telnet://enews.com/  (login as enews)
```

The Internet Company (which, despite its grand name, consists mostly of two guys named Rob and Bill) has developed the Electronic Newsstand, which offers a wide variety of magazines and on-line information services. All magazines offer tables of contents and selected articles and let you order single issues or discounted subscriptions on-line. A few offer the entire magazine electronically. The magazines really run the gamut from *American Demographics* to *Canoe & Kayak* to *The New Yorker* to *Yellow Silk*.

The Literary Life

Until the on-line revolution reaches its final victory, many old-fashioned books will still be made in the traditional way, by pressing ink on thin layers of deceased, dissolved trees. (You have one of these books in your hands now.) In the meantime, a bunch of bookstores are on the net, many with on-line catalogs, and all of which welcome on-line orders. (Wouldn't this be a good time to buy another dozen copies of this book to give to your friends? How about just one or two?)

This section presents a selection of them.

Future Fantasy Bookstore

URL:

```
http://www.commerce.digital.com/palo-alto/FutureFantasy/
          home.html
```

This specialty sci-fi store in Palo Alto, California, holds readings and events in addition to selling books. An extremely cool logo appears on its WWW page. This tiny store gets a large fraction of its orders from the U.S. and overseas by way of the Internet.

Softpro Books

URL:

```
gopher://storefront.xor.com/
```

or (this is not a URL)

```
e-mail to softpro@world.std.com
```

This computer bookseller has stores near Boston and in Denver that carry all the *Dummies* books, of course.

Book Stacks Unlimited

URL:

```
telnet://books.com/
```

This large "virtual" bookstore in Cleveland has a large on-line catalog BBS you can telnet to. It carries *Dummies* books too.

Wordsworth Books

```
email to info@wordsworth.com
```

Wordsworth is a large, general-interest bookstore in Cambridge, Massachusetts, that sells most books at a discount. It carries all *Dummies* books, many autographed by us. (Its book buyer says of one of your authors: "I have to buy all of his books. He's friends with my dog.")

Quantum Books

URLs:

```
gopher://gopher.std.com/  (then select Book Sellers, then
             Quantum Books)
```

or (this is not a URL)

```
email to quanbook@world.std.com
```

Quantum is a specialty computer-book store with stores in Cambridge, Massachusetts, and Philadelphia.

Roswell Electronic Computer Bookstore

URLs:

```
http://www.nstn.ns.ca/cybermall/cybermall.html
```

or

```
gopher://gopher.nstn.ns.ca/1e-mall
```

or (this is not a URL)

```
e-mail to roswell@fox.nstn.ns.ca
```

This large, Canadian computer-book store is located in Halifax, Nova Scotia. It has a large on-line catalog with many thousands of titles, including *Dummies* books.

Computer Literacy Books

```
e-mail to info@clbooks.com
```

Computer Literacy Books is the premier computer-book store chain in the country, with three stores in Silicon Valley and one near Washington, D.C. It goes without saying that it carries all the *Dummies* books.

The World of Commerce

More and more normal businesses are getting connections to the net, usually with Gopher or WWW pages, where you can find out about their wares and, usually, order them.

I don't like Spam!

A few businesses unfortunately have taken to blanketing the net with obnoxious advertisements. Early in 1994, a pair of Arizona lawyers caused an enormous furor by blanketing Usenet newsgroups with thousands of copies of an electronic advertisement offering to file applications in an upcoming U.S. immigration lottery, known as a "Green Card" lottery. They claimed, not very plausibly, that there was nothing wrong with what they had done and that people who objected were just fuddy-duddies who hated all advertisements, and managed for their troubles to get their pictures in the *New York Times* and to get interviewed on CNN.

They also got many, many megabytes of on-line complaints, enough that their Internet provider (who had no advance notice of their plans) had to disconnect from the net for a while. To put it mildly, the lawyers didn't make themselves popular. Internauts all over the world ground their teeth in fury for weeks.

Their technique was quickly dubbed *spamming*, a term inspired by an old Monty Python skit of actors in Viking costume who, with almost no provocation, would break into a song about Spam. (Yes, it's the same stuff that comes in little, blue cans and sort of resembles meat.) With luck, as commercial providers become more sophisticated, spamming will be nipped in the bud and attempted spammers booted off the net.

The Internet Mall

URLs:

```
news:alt.internet.services
```

or

```
ftp://ftp.netcom.com/pub/Guides
```

or (this is not a URL)

```
finger taylor@netcom.com
```

Dave Taylor, who is well known on the net for being the original author of the *elm* mail program, has compiled an extensive list of cybershops on the net, selling everything from culinary herbs to fossils to computer books. The mall is organized into five *floors:*

- **First Floor:** Media (books, magazines, music, video)
- **Second Floor:** Personal items (games, crafts, flowers, promotional items)
- **Third Floor:** Computer hardware and software
- **Fourth Floor:** Services (travel, research, credit checks, real estate, incorporation)
- **Top Floor:** Food court (chocolate, tea, coffee, herbs, beer-making supplies)

The Internet Shopping Network

URL:

```
http://shop.internet.net
```

This WWW page points you to thousands of hardware and software items for personal computers and workstations, in addition to reprints from *InfoWorld*. For Mosaic and Cello users, it has snazzy graphics as well. Most products are sold at a discount. You have to be a member to order, but membership is free. Anyone can browse and look at prices, descriptions, and even reviews of the products.

The Branch Mall

URL:

```
http://branch.com:1080/
```

This is another WWW mall, offering a florist, gift food baskets, and other goodies.

Stock Prices, Almost Live

URLs:

```
ftp://rtp.dg.com/pub/misc.invest/quote-dump
```

or

```
telnet://rahul.net/
```

One of those questions that comes up, oh, about every five minutes, is whether it's possible to get on-line, real-time stock quotes by way of the Internet. That's an easy one: No. Real-time stock information is worth a great deal of money and nobody's going to be giving it away for free. Most commercial services offer nearly real-time 15-minute delayed prices, but usually with a charge.

Here's an Internet source for some relatively up-to-date stock quotes:

1. **Telnet to** `a2i.rahul.net`.

2. **Log in as** *guest* **by typing** n **for the new screen-oriented menu.**

3. **When it asks what your terminal type is, tell it (**vt100 **is a good guess).**

   It shows you a menu.

4. **Choose Current system information and then Market report.**

   (Confused yet? This process turns out to be easier than it sounds.)

You should get a long market-comment newsletter, including several hundred stock, fund, and currency prices.

To get the report every day by mail, drop a note to its author, `Martin.Wong@eng.sun.com`. The daily reports are archived at the FTP site listed as the first URL for this section.

The Smithsonian Photo Archive

URL:

```
ftp://photo1.si.edu/
```

The Smithsonian Institution (which, because it's supported by U.S. tax money, you've probably already paid for) has an enormous photo collection, highlights of which are available on this FTP server. The pictures are in the subdirectory `images/gif89a`. Topics include the sorts of things you find in the Smithsonian museums, such as aerospace and natural history.

Chapter 19
Fun and Silly Stuff

In This Chapter

▶ Fun, adventure, and total silliness!

▶ Travel: metros, trains, cruises, and more

▶ Countries around the world

▶ Comics

▶ Personals and dirty pictures

▶ Just plain silliness

▶ Radio

▶ Fun and games, including juggling and racing

▶ Food, glorious food

*I*n this chapter, we lean back and relax (as though we weren't doing that already) and look at some of the fun and informal resources the net offers.

Travel

Internauts are a peripatetic crowd, always on the move. There's more information about travel than about anything else (except for information about the net itself.) Because the net is truly global, it has tons of information about specific countries available from the countries themselves.

The Global Network Navigator

URL:

```
http://nearnet.gnn.com/gnn/meta/travel/index.html
```

The Global Network Navigator, which we mentioned in Chapter 17, has an entire section dedicated to travel, including a running series written by someone who's heading slowly around the world, filing reports by modem from his laptop. As of May 1994, he had gotten to Nepal, someone had swiped his computer, and he was stuck. We hope that by the time you read this, he's on his way again.

The Navigator also has travel tips, country features, and ads from travel-related businesses.

The Avid Explorer

URL:

```
http://www.explore.com
```

This WWW server is run by a travel agency that offers cruises, expeditions, and other travel services.

U.S. State Department travel advisories

URL:

```
http://www.stolaf.edu/network/travel-advisories.html
```

Wondering how dangerous it is to go to Djibouti? The U.S. State Department publishes for every country in the world (except, for some reason, the United States) a travel advisory that discusses travel facilities, entry requirements, political instability, medical facilities, and availability of U.S. embassies and consulates. (As developing African countries go, Djibouti's not particularly unsafe. You can call the embassy in Djibouti City at 35-39-95.)

This WWW page at St. Olaf College has links to all the current travel advisories, so you can Know Before You Go. Many experienced travelers find these advisories to be a bit alarmist (Egad! You can't get Big Macs in Timbuktu!), so you might also want to take them with a grain or two of salt.

The page also has links to the CIA's *World Fact Book,* which has political and economic information for countries all over the world, and links to home pages for a few countries.

Toot toot!

Railroad lovers will find a wealth of information. This section presents a sample.

The Railroad Page

URL:

```
http://www-cse.ucsd.edu/users/bowdidge/railroad/rail-home
          .html
```

This page displays mailing lists, FTP archives, commercial services, on-line maps — everything for the well-informed rail fan.

The CalTrain Schedule

URL:

```
http://www.commerce.digital.com/palo-alto/CalTrain/form.html
```

This page gives an interactive schedule for the trains between San Francisco and San Jose, California, and all intermediate stations.

The Metro Server

URL:

```
telnet://metro.jussieu.fr:10000/
```

Are you troubled by getting lost on the subway? As long as you live in Vienna, Hong Kong, Montreal, Palermo, Toronto, Mexico City, Lille (France), Amsterdam, Lyon (France), Madrid, Marseilles, London, Paris, Boston, Toulouse (France), New York, Frankfurt (Germany), San Francisco, Munich, Washington (D.C.), or Athens, this is your lucky day. The Metro server figures out your route for you. Telnet in, and you immediately are in the Metro system. You tell it the name of the city and the departing and arriving stations, and it gives you the best route and the travel time.

When the server asks whether you want to use the X Windows system, say no (but see the following section). You can abbreviate stations to the shortest amount of the name that isn't ambiguous.

For once, X Windows is useful

If you're using an X Windows computer (a UNIX workstation, an X terminal, or a PC running X software), you can use a spiffy windowed version of the Metro server. First, you have to tell your local X server that it's OK for the Metro server to draw its windows on your screen. Type this UNIX command:

```
% xhost +metro.jussieu.fr
```

Then telnet to the Metro server and tell it yes, you want to use the X Windows system. It needs to know the name of your display screen, which is almost certainly the name of your computer followed by *:0* (milton.iecc.com:0, for example). Tell it (if its guess isn't correct), press Enter, wait awhile, and a Metro window appears on-screen, as shown in Figure 19-1.

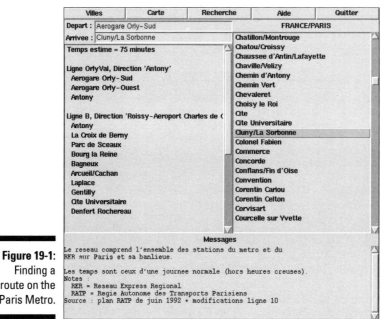

Figure 19-1:
Finding a
route on the
Paris Metro.

1. **Click the Cities menu and choose the city you want.**

2. **Scroll through the list of cities on the right, and click the From station to highlight it.**

3. **Then move to the From box and click the middle button to insert the station name.**

   This is the standard X Windows text cut-and-paste technique.

4. **Do the same thing for the To station.**

5. **Click Search to get the route in the left window.**

6. **When you're finished searching, click Quit to get rid of the window.**

If the Metro server has a map available, click the Map menu item to display it. As you move the cursor from station to station on the map, the station name is displayed at the bottom of the map. It's way cool.

Countries Around the World

This section presents a bunch of informative World Wide Web home pages.

Down Under

Let's begin with places that are farther from home (our home, that is).

Collected New Zealand Information
URL:

```
http://www.cs.cmu.edu:8001/Web/People/mjw/NZ/MainPage.html
```

Here's lots of information about beautiful New Zealand.

Guide to Australia
URL:

```
http://life.anu.edu.au/education/australia.html
```

This page has even more information about equally beautiful Australia: Geography, Environment, Culture (yes, there's more than beer), History, Travel, and Communications.

Europe

Now for some high culture.

The Germany Page
URL:

```
http://www.chemie.fu-berlin.de/adressen/brd.html
```

With typical German thoroughness, this page offers you links to much, much more than any individual would want to know about Germany. Much of it is interesting and useful, of course.

Ireland: The Internet Collection

URL:

```
http://itdsrvl.ul.ie/Information/Ireland.html
```

Here you find news, advice, and opinions from the Emerald Isle.

Slovenia

URL:

```
http://www.ijs.si/slo.html
```

On the sunny side of the Alps, tucked in among Italy, Austria, and Croatia, is Slovenia. It's a nice place; we were there in 1971 for a computer conference. Learn all about its past and present.

Information about the Netherlands

URL:

```
http://www.tno.nl/NL-www/nl-info.html
```

This page has basic Dutch info, largely from the CIA's *World Fact Book*.

U.K. information

URL:

```
http://www.cs.ucl.ac.uk/misc/uk/wfb.html
```

Also from the *World Fact Book*, this page has been enriched with links to other, more specific information about counties and cities. You're only two clicks away from in-depth info about pubs in London.

Basic information about Poland

URL:

```
http://info.fuw.edu.pl/poland-info.html
```

This is the Polish page from the *World Fact Book*.

Switzerland On-line Guide

URL:

```
http://heiwww.unige.ch/switzerland
```

The *World Fact Book* again (gee, it's almost as though nobody but the CIA knows about anyplace), enhanced with attractive photographs and other Swiss stuff.

Austria On-line Guide

URL:

```
http://ravel.ifs.univie.ac.at/austria/austria_info.html
```

Guess what! It's the *World Fact Book* page about Austria! Wow!

The Funnies

Enough travel. Let's relax and read the funnies.

Dr. Fun

URLs:

```
http://sunsite.unc.edu/Dave/drfun.html
```

or

```
news:alt.binaries.pictures.misc
```

The Internet has its own daily cartoon, Dr. Fun, in the tradition of *The Far Side*. It ranges from the strange to the extremely strange; one recent caption was "Silly String and Crazy Glue — a Deadly Combination." (The picture was not unlike what you would expect.)

The Doctor appears every weekday as an attractive, full-color graphic. Don't miss him.

Dilbert and Doonesbury

URL:

```
http://nearnet.gnn.com/arcade/comix/index.html
```

The folks at GNN (the Global Network Navigator, described in a section by the same name in Chapter 17) have a comics page featuring real syndicated comics, which at the moment is Dilbert, every nerd's favorite strip (because everything he says about us nerds is true) and some classic Doonesbury strips about the Internet. You can find Dr. Fun from here too.

The Usenet urban folklore quiz (Part IV)

Holy petunias, you're still here. Let's get this over with.

Part IV: The entirety of human knowledge

True or false:

31. The song "Happy Birthday" is copyrighted.

32. Studies indicate that the majority of U.S. currency has traces of cocaine.

33. A woman had epileptic seizures after hearing "Entertainment Tonight" anchor Mary Hart's voice.

34. Some parents got a video for their children and found that it was recorded over an old porn tape.

35. Unless fast food shakes are marked "dairy," they aren't milk: instead, they're mostly carrageenan (seaweed extract) gel.

36. Lead leaches from lead crystal decanters into drinks, which is not good for you.

37. People have been poisoned by eating food cooked on burning oleander branches.

38. A woman removed the label from a "tuna" can and found a cat-food label underneath.

39. There is a basketball hoop at the top of the Matterhorn replica at Disneyland.

40. There were (are?) Japanese soldiers hiding out on islands in the Pacific who believed that WWII was still on.

41. Gerbils are illegal in California.

Um, It's Personal

Lest we forget that even nerds have personal lives, read on.

Virtual MeetMarket

URL:

```
http://wwa.com:1111/
```

Because people in cyberspace are as sociable as those in real life, sometimes, it was just a matter of time until the personals column appeared, so here it is. Each ad gets a page, as shown in Figure 19-2. There aren't many ads yet, so they're free both to place and to respond to.

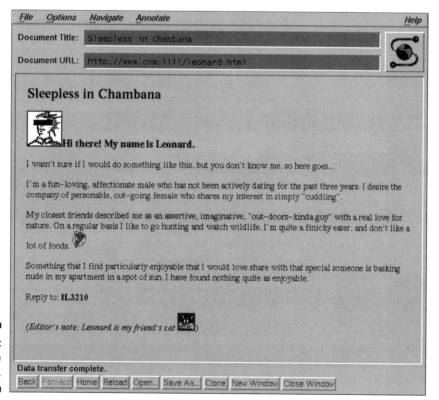

Figure19-2:
Where the
elite meet.

Femmes femmes femmes je vous aime!

URL:

```
http://www.cnam.fr/bin.html/imageWWW
```

This extraordinarily politically incorrect page features pictures from France of scantily clad ladies. It's all pretty innocent; we've seen more salacious stuff in *Vogue*. As one might imagine, it's quite popular. Controversial too.

Just Plain Silliness

It's important to keep in mind that much Internet material is provided for, or used by, college undergraduates. You should therefore not be too surprised to find sophomoric humor, like the items in this section.

WWW Calc

URL:

```
http://guinan.gsfc.nasa.gov/Web/Calc.html
```

Computer geeks have always delighted in making a big, expensive computer act like a greatly overpriced version of a common household or office appliance. (The On-line Internet Toaster was a big hit at a recent trade show.) WWW Calc takes the global resources of the World Wide Web and makes them simulate a $7.95 pocket calculator, only slower.

Try it out. Then forget about it.

Making Gopher harder to use

URLs:

```
telnet://jh.ccs.neu.edu:1709/
```

or

```
ftp://mailbase.ac.uk/pub/lists/unite/files/jays_house.txt
```

Part of the charm of Gopher is that it's easy to use. You just click menu items, and there's your stuff. Some people seem to feel that information is worthwhile only if they have to work to get hold of it. If you're one of these people, MOO Gopher is just the ticket for you. It's a Gopher client hidden inside a Multi-User Dungeon (MUD), so you have to look around and guess where to find things. Some help is available, so it took us only two or three minutes to find some Gopher menus, but doubtless there are more we didn't find.

And Now, Coming to a Network Near You

URLs:

```
http://www.ncsa.uiuc.edu/radio/radio.html
```

or

```
http://www.cmf.nrl.navy.mil/radio/ITR.html
```

or

```
http://juggler.lanl.gov/itr.html
```

or

```
http://www.doc.ic.ac.uk/public/media/audio/ITR/
```

or (this is not a URL)

```
e-mail to info@radio.com or sites@radio.com
```

The global village now has its own radio stations — Internet Talk Radio and Internet Town Hall, produced by the Internet Multicasting Service. Every week, ITR and ITH send out interviews, stories, and the occasional goofy sound clip. (One of them said, over portentous music, "The future . . . is tomorrow.") There's a weekly Geek of the Week interview with a network notable in addition to talks from the National Press Club and the occasional National Public Radio show. Most of it is well worth listening to. Some shows during a week in May 1994 included the ones in this list:

- ✔ **Common Ground:** The director of the special UN/OAS mission to Haiti discusses what went wrong.

- ✔ **HarperAudio:** The poet and novelist Robert Graves reads from *The White Goddess,* a study of anthropology and mythology.

- ✔ **SoundBytes:** "12 Tone Geek," performed by house band Tungsten Maqaque (3 1/2 seconds long).

- ✔ **National Press Club:** Garrison Keillor discusses *Why I Decided Not to Run for President in 1996.*

- ✔ **HarperAudio:** Sci-fi author Frank Herbert reads from his classic *Dune* series.

- ✔ **Professor Neon's TV & Movie Mania:** Robert Justman, who directed and produced shows from "The Outer Limits" to "Star Trek" and "Star Trek: The Next Generation," discusses the production of these shows.

If your computer can play sounds (most workstations, all Macs, and any PC with a sound card of some sort can), you can download the files and play them. By way of the World Wide Web, you can use any of the four URLs at the beginning of this section to get information and schedules.

For actual FTP sites, send a message (contents unimportant) to sites@radio.com. We don't list sites here because they change frequently. For a FAQ message giving a more detailed overview of ITR and ITH, including info about how you can get the programs on cassette, send a message (contents unimportant) to info@radio.com.

Sound files are *really, really big.* One hour of sound fills up about 30 megabytes of disk space. As the Multicasting Service's FAQ message says:

```
Oh my! Do you mean to tell me that you expect me to download
              45 megabytes of data? Are you nuts?
Yes.
```

You can make yourself extremely unpopular if you download 15-megabyte files in the middle of the day from a server on another continent. So don't do that. Check the sites list to find a server close to you, and do your heavy-duty downloading at off-peak times, like in the middle of the night or on weekends.

Rare Groove

URL:

```
http://rg.media.mit.edu/RG/RG.html
```

This magazine is about popular music, with playlists, charts, reviews, and even sound snippets of new songs.

Put up or shut up on the Information Superhighway

Back at the dawn of electronic history, around 1945, someone went around and asked people what they liked to watch on television. The answers were along the lines of classic movies and plays, educational lectures, concerts, and stuff like that. And what did we really watch? *I Love Lucy* and *Queen for a Day*.

So recently someone asked similar questions about what people would want access to on the coming Information Superhighway (known in some circles as the Information Supercollider). What do you know: classic movies and plays, educational lectures — you get the idea. With the Internet Multicasting Service, we got what we asked for. Are we going to take advantage of it or are we really waiting for Internet *Wheel of Fortune*?

Fun and Games

And now for something completely different!

Attention, klutzes!

URL:

```
http://www.hal.com/services/juggle/
```

Ever want to learn how to juggle? The Juggling Information Service features news, advice, pictures, vendors of juggling equipment (flaming Indian clubs have to come from somewhere), software, and lots of gossip.

Horsing around

URL:

```
http://www.inslab.uky.edu/People/stevem/horses/KyDerbyInfo/
      kyderby.html
```

It's the brightest jewel of the Triple Crown, the Kentucky Derby. This page includes the facts you need to know, such as the fact that in 1994, number 6, Go For Gin, paid $20.20, $8.40, and $5.80. There's also news, events, and previous results.

More fun and games

URL:

```
http://wcl-rs.bham.ac.uk/~djh/index.html
```

This page links together Web pages, archived FAQ files, and everything else the author could find about games and gaming. Want to know about playing Bolo on your Macintosh? Here's where to find out.

Food, Food, Wonderful Food

Finally, we get to something that we all can agree is interesting and important.

Where to eat in the hub of the universe

URLs:

```
http://www.osf.org:8001/boston-food/boston-food.html
```

or

```
news:ne.food
```

Hungry in Boston? This page lists hundreds of restaurants, with reviews constantly updated by readers' messages to Usenet. Most listings are linked to longer reviews, as shown in this example:

```
Emporio Armani Express [Italian] — Back Bay
More a scene than anything else, though the food is rather
good. For the men: dress like you're in advertising; for
the women: wear either no makeup or way too much. Feign an
attitude. They hired the most obsequious waiter I've _ever_
had, but you already guessed that. Have a drink in the bar
downstairs first. If you don't feel too alienated, have
dinner upstairs. (4/94)
```

On-line soda machines

Soda machines have been on the net for almost as long as there's been a net. Nothing annoys a hard-hacking nerd more than walking down the hall to get a life-sustaining carbonated sugar beverage only to find out that the machine is empty or — worse — was just filled and the soda is warm. To avoid this unspeakable horror, machines were quickly networked for the benefit of local users. Of course, the net being the net, it's as easy to query a machine from 10,000 miles away as it is from 10 feet away.

The most common way to check on a soda machine is with the `finger` command. The more popular machines on the net are shown in this list:

- ✔ drink@drink.csh.rit.edu
- ✔ coke@cs.cmu.edu
- ✔ coke@xcf.berkeley.edu
- ✔ pepsi or cocacola@columbia.edu
- ✔ coke@ucc.gu.uwa.edu.au

A typical response from the Carnegie-Mellon machine is shown here:

```
[G.GP.CS.CMU.EDU]
Login name: coke
In real life: Drink Coke
Directory: /usrg1/coke
Shell: /usr/cs/bin/csh
Plan:
Thu May 19 08:06:14 1994
M&M validity: 9
Coke validity: 9
   M & M          Buttons
   /—\       C: CC......................
  |   |  C: C........... D: C...........
  |****  |       C: C.......... D: C...........
  |***** |       C: C.......... D: C...........
  |***** |       C: CCC.........
   \—/       S: C...........
   |   Key:
   |   0 = warm;  9 = 90% cold;  C = cold;  . = empty
   |   Leftmost soda/pop will be dispensed next
  _^_
```

A really overimplemented on-line Coke machine

If you are blessed with an X Windows screen (such as a workstation or X terminal), you can see the amazing Rochester Institute of Technology Coke Machine Front Panel, as shown in Figure 19-3.

Figure 19-3:
The R.I.T.
Coke
machine.

1. **Type this line:**

   ```
   xhost +drink.rit.edu
   ```

   This line tells your X server that it's okay to display the Front Panel.

2. **Type this line:**

   ```
   finger hostname:0@drink.rit.edu
   ```

   Substitute the name of your X terminal or computer for *hostname*.

3. **Wait a minute or so for the Front Panel to appear.**

4. **Click a few of the buttons, even though you don't have any money to spend.**

5. **Say hi to Ricardo for us.**

   Trust us — you'll understand this one when you try it.

6. **Click the exit sign when you get bored.**

The Trojan Room

URL:

```
http://www.cl.cam.ac.uk/coffee/coffee.html
```

In England, hackers evidently drink coffee rather than Coke, and there's no point in going down the hall if the pot's empty. So in the finest hacker tradition, they pointed a video camera at the coffee pot with some extremely complicated software to digitize the picture once per second and send the image to their Web server. Now people all over the world can tell — if they happen to fly to Cambridge — whether the coffee is ready (see Figure 19-4).

Sometimes the picture is pitch black. Nothing's wrong, but it's probably the middle of the night and they've turned out the lights.

Figure 19-4:
About half
full.

Answers to the Usenet urban folklore quiz

For much, much more information about these and other topics of vital interest, visit the Usenet groups `alt.folklore.urban` and `alt.folklore.suburban`.

1. False
2. True
3. False
4. True
5. True
6. Both false
7. False
8. True, but it was a reporter's prank
9. False
10. True
11. True
12. True
13. False
14. True
15. False
16. True
17. False
18. True; doctors call this the "photic sneeze effect"
19. True
20. False (take that, Mom)
21. True; the student was mathematician George Dantzig
22. False
23. True
24. False
25. False
26. True (*MAD #33*, "The Potrzebie system of weights and measures")
27. False
28. False
29. False
30. True
31. True
32. True
33. True
34. True
35. True
36. True
37. True
38. True
39. True
40. True
41. True [CA Reg. Title 14, Sec. 671 (c)(2)(J) 1]

Glossary

address. Secret code by which the Internet identifies you. It usually looks like username@hostname, where username is your username or login name or account number, and hostname is the Internet's name for the computer or Internet provider you use. The host name can be a few words strung together with periods. The official *MORE Internet For Dummies* address, for example, is midummies@iecc.com because its username is midummies and it's on a computer named iecc.com.

See Chapter 7 in *The Internet For Dummies* for more information about addresses, including yours, and Chapter 9 of the same book to learn how to find out other people's addresses.

alt. Type of newsgroup that discusses alternative-type topics. The alt groups are not official newsgroups, but lots of people read them anyway. We particularly like alt.folklore.urban and alt.folklore.suburban.

See Chapter 12 in *The Internet For Dummies* for lists of interesting newsgroups.

America Online. A public Internet provider. If you have an account on America Online, username@aol.com is your Internet address, where username is your account name. See Chapter 7 to learn how to use America Online to access the Internet.

anonymous FTP. Using the FTP program to log on to another computer to copy files, even though you don't have an account on the other computer. When you log on, you

enter **anonymous** as the username and your address as the password. This gives you access to publicly available files. See Chapter 16 in *The Internet For Dummies* for more information about FTP-ing in general and anonymous FTP in particular.

ANS. Advanced Network Services, which runs one of the large, high-speed networks on the Internet. Run by Merit, MCI, and IBM.

Archie. A system that helps you find files located anywhere on the Internet. After Archie helps you find the file, you can use FTP to get it. Archie is both a program and a system of servers (that is, computers that contain indexes of files). See Chapter 19 in *The Internet For Dummies* for more information. Chapter 14 of this book tells you how to use Mosaic to submit a request to Archie.

archive. File which contains a group of files that have been compressed and glommed together for efficient storage. You have to use an archive program to get the original files back out. Commonly used programs include compress, tar, cpio, and zip (on UNIX systems) and PKZIP (on DOS systems). See Chapter 17 in *The Internet For Dummies* to learn how to use them.

ARPANET. The original ancestor of the Internet, funded by the U.S. Department of Defense.

article. A posting to a newsgroup (that is, a message someone sends to the newsgroup to be readable by everyone who reads the newsgroup). See Chapter 11 to learn how to use Trumpet to read newsgroups if you use a SLIP connection to the Internet; see Chapter 11 in *The Internet For Dummies* for general information about newsgroups.

AT&T Mail. A mail system that connects to the Internet. If you have an AT&T Mail account, your Internet address is `username@attmail.com`, where `username` is your account name.

AUP. *Acceptable Use Policy,* a set of rules describing which sorts of activities are permitted on a network. The most restrictive AUP was the one on the NSFNET, which prohibited most commercial and non-academic use. The NSFNET AUP is no longer in force anywhere, although many people erroneously believe that it still is.

automatic mailing list. A mailing list maintained by a computer program, usually one named LISTSERV or Majordomo (*see also* mailing list). Also see Chapter 10 in *The Internet For Dummies* for information about how to use mailing lists.

bang path address. An old-fashioned method of writing network addresses. UUCP, an old, cruddy mail system used to use addresses that contained bangs (exclamation points!) to string together the parts of the address. Forget about them.

BBS. Bulletin board system (a system that lets people read each other's messages and post new ones). The Usenet system of newsgroups is in effect the world's largest distributed BBS.

binary file. File which contains information that does not consist only of text. A binary file might contain, for example, an archive, a picture, sounds, a spreadsheet, or a word-processing document (which includes formatting codes in addition to characters).

bionet. A type of newsgroup that discusses topics of interest to biologists. If you're not a biologist, don't bother reading them.

bit. A type of newsgroup that is actually a BITNET mailing list in disguise.

BITFTP. The most widely available FTP-by-mail server. *See* FTP-by-mail.

BITNET. A network of mostly IBM mainframes that connects to the Internet. If you have an account on machine `xyzvm3` on the BITNET and your username on the machine is `abc`, your Internet mail address is `abc@xyzvm3.bitnet` or, if your system isn't well-informed about BITNET, `abc%xyzvm3.bitnet@cunyvm.cuny.edu`. See Chapter 9 in *The Internet For Dummies* for more information about BITNET.

BIX. A commercial system formerly run by *Byte* magazine and now run by Delphi. If you have a BIX account, your Internet address is `username@bix.com`, where `username` is your account name.

biz. A type of newsgroup that discusses business and commercial topics. Most other types of newsgroups are supposed to stay away from commercial messages.

bridge. Something that connects two networks so that they appear to be a single larger network. For the fine distinction between a bridge, a router, and a gateway, see Chapter 6 in *The Internet For Dummies*.

Cello. Program that allows you to access the World Wide Web from your PC running Windows. It provides a nifty point-and-click graphics interface to WWW. A similar program is called Mosaic.

CERFnet. One of the regional networks originally set up to work with the NSFNET, headquartered in California.

Chameleon. Software that enables you to connect directly to the Internet by way of a SLIP Internet provider.

chatting. Talking live to other network users from any and all parts of the world. To do this, you use Internet Relay Chat (IRC), described in Chapter 15.

CIX. The *C*ommercial *I*nternet *Ex*change, an association of Internet providers that agree to exchange traffic without regard to AUP rules of academic networks.

ClariNet. Usenet newsgroups that contain various categories of news, including news from the UPI newswire, distributed for a modest fee. The most important one is, of course, clari.feature.dave_barry. Not all systems carry the ClariNet newsgroups (World does). You can also subscribe to them yourself — for information, send mail to info@clarinet.com.

com. When these letters appear at the last part of an address (for example, in middumies@iecc.com), they indicate that the host computer is run by a company rather than by a university or government agency. It also means that the host computer is probably in the United States.

communications program. A program you run on your personal computer that enables you to call up and communicate with another computer. This is a rather broad term, but most people use it to mean a program that makes your computer pretend to be a terminal (that's why they are also known as *terminal programs* or *terminal emulators*). The most commonly used communications programs on PCs are Windows Terminal ('cause it's free with Windows), Crosstalk, and Procomm, although there are many others.

Chapter 4 discusses how to use a communications program to enable your PC to call up public Internet providers.

comp. A type of newsgroup that discusses topics about computers, such as comp.lang.c (which discusses the C programming language) and comp.society.folklore (which covers the folklore and culture of computer users). See Chapter 11 in *The Internet For Dummies* for lists of interesting newsgroups.

CompuServe. An on-line information provider that gives you some Internet access. Jeez, everyone must have heard of it by now. It provides lots of forums, which are like newsgroups, including many that provide excellent technical support for a wide range of PS and Mac software. If your CompuServe account number is 7123,456, for example, your Internet address is 7123.456@compuserve.com (note the period in the account number). See the end of Chapter 7 for information about how CompuServe connects to the Internet.

country code. The last part of a geographic address, which indicates which country the host computer is in. An address that ends in *ca* is Canadian, for example, and one that ends in *us* is in the U.S. For a complete list, see Appendix A in *The Internet For Dummies*, which discusses Internet geographic zones.

Delphi. An on-line information provider that includes access to lots of Internet services. If you have an account on Delphi, your Internet address is username@delphi.com, where username is your account name. See Chapter 5 to learn how to use Delphi to access the Internet.

digest. A compilation of the messages that have been posted to a mailing list during the past few days. Many people find it more convenient to receive one big message than a bunch of individual ones. See Chapter 10 in *The Internet For Dummies* and Chapter 16 in this book.

domain. The official Internet-ese name of a computer on the net. It's the part of an Internet address that comes after the @. Internet For Dummies Central is at midummies@iecc.com, for example, and the domain name of the computer it's on is iecc.com.

domain name server. (Or just *name server,* or abbreviated as *DNS*). A computer on the Internet that translates between Internet domain names, such as xuxa.iecc.com, and Internet numerical addresses, such as 140.186.81.2.

dynamic rerouting. A method of addressing information about the Internet (not just mail messages, but all information) so that if one route is blocked or broken, the information can take an alternate route. Pretty darned clever. The U.S. Department of Defense built this method into the design of the Internet back for the benefit of the military, to resist enemy attack. Also useful when nonmilitary networks are attacked by errant backhoes.

e-mail. *E*lectronic *mail,* also called *email* or just *mail;* messages sent by way of the Internet to a particular person. For the basics of sending and receiving e-mail, see Chapter 7 in *The Internet For Dummies.*

Easylink. An e-mail service formerly run by Western Union and now run by AT&T. If you have an Easylink account, your Internet address is 1234567@eln.attmail.com, where 1234567 is your account number.

edu. When these letters appear in the last part of an address (in info@mit.edu, for example), they indicate that the host computer is run by an educational institution, probably a college or university. It also means that the host computer is probably in the United States.

elm. An easy-to-use UNIX mail reader, which we vastly prefer to mail. Another good one is pine.

Eudora. A nice mail-handling program that runs on the Macintosh and under Windows. Originally a shareware program, it is now sold by Qualcomm. See Chapter 10 to learn how to get and use it.

FAQ. *F*requently *a*sked *q*uestion. This regularly posted newsgroup article answers questions that come up regularly. Before you ask a question in a newsgroup, make sure that you have read its FAQ because it may well contain the answer. People get annoyed if you ask questions that are answered in the newsgroup's FAQ, because they have probably already answered the question 150 times.

FAQs are posted regularly, usually once a month. To read all the regularly posted FAQs for all newsgroups, read the newsgroup news.answers.

FIDONET. A worldwide network of bulletin board systems (BBSs). Each individual BBS is called a *node* on FIDONET and has a three- or four-part numeric address in the form *1:2/3* or *1:2/3.4* (who the heck thought of this?). To send Internet mail to someone on FIDONET, address it to this line (for nodes with four-part names):

firstname.lastname@p4.f3.n2.z1.fidonet.org

or to this line (for nodes with three-part names):

```
firstname.lastname@f3.n2.z1
```

and substitute the addressee's username for `firstname.lastname`.

file-transfer protocol. A method of transferring one or more files from one computer to another on a network or phone line. The idea of using a protocol is that the sending and receiving programs can check that the information has been received correctly. The most commonly used dial-up protocols are XMODEM, YMODEM, ZMODEM, and Kermit. See Chapter 4 for more information.

finger. A program that displays information about someone on the net. On most UNIX systems, this command tells you who is logged on right now. On most Internet hosts, it tells you the name and perhaps some other information, based on the person's Internet address and the last time she logged on. See Chapter 9 in *The Internet For Dummies* to learn how to use it. To install a Windows-based finger program for use with a SLIP connection to the Internet, see Chapter 9. To use it by way of the World Wide Web, see Chapter 14 in this book.

firewall. A system has a *firewall* around it if it lets only certain kind of messages in and out from the rest of the Internet. If an organization wants to exchange mail with the Internet, for example, but doesn't want nosy college students telnetting in and reading everyone's files, its connection to the Internet can be set up to prevent incoming telnets or FTPs.

freenet. A free on-line system. Wow! The first one, created at the University of Cleveland, is called the Cleveland Freenet and offers local community information and limited access to the Internet. Lots of other freenets have sprung up, and because you can telnet from one to another, if you can access one, you can access them all.

For a list of freenets, see Chapter 27 in *The Internet For Dummies*.

FTP. *File-transfer protocol.* Also the name of a program that uses the protocol to transfer files all over the Internet. For instructions on how to use FTP, see Chapter 16 in *The Internet For Dummies*.

FTP-by-mail. A method by which you can send a mail message to a server computer to request that a file be mailed to you by way of e-mail. This is a method of getting files over the net, slowly, if you have access only to e-mail. See Chapter 17 in *The Internet For Dummies* for more information.

gateway. A computer that connects one network with another when the two networks use different protocols. The UUNET computer connects the UUCP network with the Internet, for example, providing a way for mail messages to move between the two networks. For more information about how gateways work, see Chapter 6 in *The Internet For Dummies*.

GEnie. An on-line service run by General Electric. If you have an account on GEnie and your mail name (not your username!) is `ABC`, your Internet address is `ABC@genie.gies.com`.

GIF. A type of graphics file (GIF stands for Graphics Interchange Format). See Chapter 14 to learn how to install a GIF viewer on your Windows computer.

global kill file. A file that tells your news reader which articles you always want to skip. This file applies to all the newsgroups to which you subscribe.

Gopher. A system that lets you find information by using menus (lots of menus). To use Gopher, you usually telnet to a Gopher server and begin browsing the menus. For the straight dope on Gopher, see Chapter 20 in *The Internet For Dummies.*

Gopherspace. The world of Gopher menus. As you move from menu to menu in Gopher, you are said to be moving around in Gopherspace.

gov. When these letters appear in the last part of an address (in cu.nih.gov, for example), they indicate that the host computer is run in some part by a government body rather than by a company or university. Your tax dollars at play! Most gov sites are in the U.S.

HGopher. A cool Microsoft Windows program that helps you view Gopher information, including seeing graphics right on your screen. It's described in Chapter 12.

host. A computer on the Internet you may be able to log in to by using telnet, get files from using FTP, or otherwise make use of.

HHTP. HyperText Transfer Protocol, which is the way World Wide Web pages are transferred over the net. See Chapter 14 to learn how to read the World Wide Web from a PC with Windows. Also see Chapter 22 in *The Internet For Dummies.*

HTML. Hypertext Markup Language, used in writing pages for the World Wide Web. It lets the text include codes that define fonts, layout, embedded graphics, and hypertext links. Don't worry — you don't have to know anything about it to use the World Wide Web. See Chapter 14 to learn how to use the World Wide Web; also see Chapter 22 in *The Internet For Dummies.*

hypermedia. *See* hypertext, except think about all kinds of information, not just text.

hypertext. A system of writing and displaying text that enables the text to be linked in multiple ways, available at several levels of detail. Hypertext documents can also contain links to related documents, such as those referred to in footnotes. Hypermedia can also contain pictures, sounds, video — you name it. The World Wide Web, described in Chapter 14, uses hypertext.

Internet. You still don't know what it is, and you're way back here in the glossary. Yikes — we must have done a terrible job of explaining this stuff. The Internet is an interconnected bunch of networks, including networks in all parts of the world. There are lots of ways to get access to the Internet, many of them explained in Parts II and III of this book. For a complete beginner's explanation, get *The Internet For Dummies.*

Internet Protocol. *See* IP.

Internet Relay Chat (IRC). A system that enables Internet folks to talk to each other in real time (rather than after a delay, as with e-mail messages). Chapter 15 describes how to get in on the action.

Internet Society. An organization dedicated to supporting the growth and evolution of the Internet. You can contact it at isoc@isoc.org.

InterNIC. The *Internet Network Information Center,* a repository of information about the Internet. It is divided into three parts: Information Services run by General Atomics in California, Directory Services run by AT&T in New Jersey, and Registration Services run by Network Solutions in Virginia. It is primarily funded, for now at least, by the National Science Foundation.

To FTP information from InterNIC, try `ftp.internic.net`.

IP. Internet Protocol, a scheme that enables information to be routed from one network to another as necessary (you had to ask). Don't worry — you don't have to know about it. For a long and tedious discussion of IP, see Chapter 2.

IRC. *See* Internet Relay Chat.

Jughead. A program that helps you find information in Gopher by searching Gopher directories for the information you specify. Sort of like Veronica.

JvNCnet. One of the regional networks originally set up to work with the NSFNET, headquartered in New Jersey.

k12. A type of Usenet newsgroup that contains information for elementary through high school students and teachers.

Kermit. A file-transfer protocol developed at Columbia University and available for a wide variety of computers, from PCs to mainframes. See Chapter 4 for more information about file-transfer protocols.

kill file. A file that tells your news reader which newsgroup articles you always want to skip.

LISTSERV. A family of programs that automatically manage mailing lists, by distributing messages posted to the list, adding and deleting members, and so on, without the tedium of someone doing it manually. The names of mailing lists maintained by LISTSERV usually end with `-l` (that's an *el*, not a one).

See Chapter 10 in *The Internet For Dummies* for information about how to get on and off LISTSERV mailing lists. Chapter 16 in this book talks about mailing lists too.

mail. Pieces of paper stuffed in envelopes with stamps on the outside. Actually, this term refers to an old-fashioned type of mail known among Internauts as `snail-mail`, which casts aspersions on your local letter carrier. Other types of mail include *voice mail,* which you probably already know and hate, and *e-mail* (or electronic mail), which is a powerful service the Internet provides.

For an introduction to e-mail, see Chapter 7 in *The Internet For Dummies.*

mail server. A computer on the Internet that provides mail services. A mail server usually sends mail out for you (using a system called SMTP) and may also enable you to download your mail to a PC or Mac by using a protocol called POP. See Chapter 10 to learn how to use Eudora to grab your mail from a mail server.

Majordomo. Like LISTSERV, a program that handles mailing lists (see Chapter 16).

MCI Mail. A commercial e-mail system linked to the Internet. If you have an MCI Mail account, you have both a username and a seven-digit user number. Your Internet address is `1234567@mcimail.com` or `username@mcimail.com`, substituting your username or number.

Watch out when you address mail by name on MCI Mail — more than one person may have the same name! Numbers are safer. If a name is ambiguous, MCI Mail returns a message giving some hints about how to find the user you want.

MERIT. A regional network in Michigan affiliated with ANS.

message. A piece of e-mail or a posting to a newsgroup.

mil. When these letters appear in the last part of an address (for example, in `wsmr-simtel20@army.mil`), they indicate that the host computer is run by some part of the U.S. military rather than by a company or university.

mirror. A FTP server that provides copies of the same files as another server. Some FTP servers are so popular that other servers have been set up to mirror them and spread the FTP load to more than one site.

misc. A type of newsgroup which discusses topics that don't fit under any of the other newsgroups types, such as `misc.forsale`, `misc.jobs.offered`, and `misc.kids`.

See Chapter 12 in *The Internet For Dummies* for lists of interesting newsgroups.

modem. A gizmo that lets your computer talk on the phone. A modem can be internal (a board that lives inside your computer) or external (a box that connects to your computer's serial port). Either way, you need a phone wire to connect the modem to your phone jack. For tons of information about modems and how to use them, get *Modems For Dummies*, by Tina Rathbone (IDG Books Worldwide).

moderated mailing list. A mailing list run by a *moderator* (*q.v.,* or for you non-Latin speakers, go check out the definition of *moderator*).

moderated newsgroup. A newsgroup run by a moderator (go ahead, *see* moderator).

moderator. Someone who looks first at the messages posted to a mailing list or newsgroup before releasing them to the public. The moderator can nix messages that are stupid (in his or her opinion, of course), redundant, or inappropriate for the list or newsgroup (wildly off the topic or offensive, for example). Yes, this is censorship, but the Internet is getting so big and crowded that nonmoderated discussions can generate an amazing number of uninteresting messages. *See* moderated mailing list and moderated newsgroup.

Mosaic. A Windows-based, WinSock-compliant program that lets you read information about the World Wide Web. See Chapter 14 to learn how to get, install, and use it.

MUD. Multi-User Dungeon (that is, a "dungeons and dragons"-type game that many people can play at a time). These games can get so complex and absorbing that players can disappear into their computers for days and weeks at a time. For information about how to join a MUD, consult the newsgroup `rec.games.mud.announce` or mail a message consisting of the word *help* to `mudlist@glia.biostr.washington.edu.`

name server. *See* domain name server.

NEARnet. One of the regional networks originally set up to work with the NSFNET, headquartered in New England.

network. Don't get us started. Many things are called networks, but for our purposes, we are talking about lots of computers connected together. Those in the same or nearby buildings are called *local area networks,* those that are farther away are called *wide area networks,* and when you interconnect a bunch of networks all over the world, you get the Internet!

For more than you want to know about how networks are connected in the Internet, see Chapters 2 and 3 in this book and Chapter 6 in *The Internet For Dummies.*

news. A type of Usenet newsgroup that contains discussions about newsgroups, such as `news.announce.newusers` (announcements of interest to new users).

news reader. A program that lets you read the messages in a Usenet newsgroup and respond if you are absolutely sure that you have something new and interesting to say. See Chapter 11 to learn how to use the Trumpet newsreader on your PC.

news server. A computer on the Internet that not only gets Usenet newsgroups but also lets you read them. Programs such as Trumpet and Cello use a news server to get the articles for the newsgroups you request. See Chapter 12 to learn how to install Trumpet to read the news provided by a news server.

newsgroup. A distributed bulletin board system about a particular topic. Usenet news (also known as *net news*) is a system that distributes thousands of newsgroups to all parts of the Internet.

See Chapter 11 in *The Internet For Dummies* for a description of how to read newsgroups, and Chapter 12 in the same book for lists of interesting newsgroups. While you are at it, check out Chapter 11 in this book to learn how to read newsgroups by using Windows programs.

newsgroup kill file. A file that tells your newsreader which articles you always want to skip. This file applies to only a specific newsgroup (*see also* global kill file).

NIC. Network Information Center. The address of the one for the U.S. part of the Internet is `rs.internic.net`. A NIC is responsible for coordinating a set of networks so that the names, network numbers, and other technical details are consistent from one network to another.

NIS. Formerly known as the *Yellow Pages* (before some trademark lawyer in the U.K. complained), this facility is used on UNIX networks to administer a group of computers (usually workstations and PCs) as though they were one big computer. For Internet purposes, who cares? NIS sorts incoming e-mail on some UNIX systems and can cause peculiar-looking mail addresses. See Chapter 4 in *The Internet For Dummies* if you care about this subject.

NNTP server. *See* news server.

node. A computer on the Internet, also called a *host.* Computers that provide a service, such as FTP sites or places that run Gopher, are also called *servers.*

NSFNET. The National Science Foundation's network, a part of the Internet devoted to research and education and funded by government money. Chronically reported to be going away, to be replaced by pieces of commercial networks.

NYSERnet. One of the regional networks originally set up to work with the NSFNET, headquartered in New York.

OARnet. One of the regional networks originally set up to work with the NSFNET, headquartered in Ohio.

Open Book Repository. A collection of on-line text, including the text of books, journals, and other reference materials, maintained by the On-line Book Initiative at `obi..std.com`.

packet. A chunk of information sent over a network. Each packet contains the address it is going to, the address of who sent it, and some other information. For more than you ever wanted to know about how the Internet handles packets, see Chapters 2 and 3 in this book and Chapter 6 in *The Internet For Dummies.*

page. A document, or hunk of information, available by way of the World Wide Web. To make information available on the World Wide Web, you organize it into one or more pages. Each page can contain text, graphics files, sound files — you name it. Don't worry — you don't have to create WWW pages — you can just read them. See Chapter 14 to learn how to use Mosaic to read WWW pages, and Chapters 17 through 19 for a list of interesting ones.

pine. A UNIX-based mail program based on `elm`. `Pine` is easy to use.

ping. A program that checks to see whether you can communicate with another computer on the Internet. It sends a short message to which the other computer automatically responds. If you can't "ping" another computer, you can't talk to it any other way either.

Chapter 8 describes how to get and use a program called Pingw for Windows systems connected to the Internet by using SLIP.

Pipeline. An Internet provider that works with a special Windows communications program. It uses its own protocol to talk to this program, which enables it to display everything in a nice Windows-y way.

PKZIP. A file-compression program that runs on PCs. PKZIP creates a *ZIP file* that contains compressed versions of one or more files. To restore them to their former size and shape, you use PKUNZIP. PK, by the way, stands for Phil Katz, who wrote the program. PKZIP and PKUNZIP are shareware programs available from many FTP sites. If you use the programs, you are honor-bound to send Mr. Katz a donation (the program tells you the address).

If you use a Windows computer, you will probably prefer WinZip, which has nice Windows-y menus and buttons.

POP. Post Office Protocol, a system by which a mail server on the Internet lets you grab your mail and download it to your PC or Mac. See Chapter 10 to learn how to install and run Eudora, which requires POP.

port number. On a networked computer, an identifying number assigned to each program that is chatting on the Internet. The program that handles incoming telnet sessions uses port 23, for example, and the program that handles some other service has another number. You hardly ever have to know these — the Internet programs work this stuff out among themselves. For more information, see Chapter 6 in *The Internet For Dummies.*

posting. An article in a newsgroup.

PPP. Point-to-Point Protocol, a scheme for connecting two computers over a phone line (or a network link that acts like a phone line). Like *SLIP,* only better (see Chapter 2).

Prodigy. A large on-line system run by IBM and Sears. If you have a Prodigy account, *username*@prodigy.com is your Internet address, substituting your username for *username*.

protocol. A system that two computers agree on. When you use a file-transfer protocol, for example, the two computers involved (the sender and the receiver) agree on a set of signals that mean "go ahead" and "got it" and "didn't get it, please resend" and "all done."

The Internet involves tons of different protocols as the many different types of computers on the net interact.

PSI. Performance Systems International, one of the large, commercial Internet networks.

public service provider. A time-sharing or SLIP service that enables you to use the Internet on a pay-by-the-hour basis. Part II of this book describes a bunch of timesharing-type public-service providers, in which you use your personal computer to log in to the provider's computer as a terminal. Part III tells you how to use SLIP-based programs to access the Internet by using a SLIP provider.

Sorry about all these acronyms — but check out Chapters 4 and 8 for more information about them (and look at the coupons in the back of this book).

RCP. Remote Copy, a UNIX command that lets you copy files from one computer to another. See Chapter 16 in *The Internet For Dummies* for details.

rec. A type of newsgroup that discusses recreational topics, such as `rec.humor.funny` (jokes that are sometimes funny) and `rec.gardens` (guess).

See Chapter 12 in *The Internet For Dummies* for lists of interesting newsgroups.

router. No, this isn't a power tool used for finish work on fine cabinetry (that's pronounced "rowter"). This system, pronounced "rooter," connects two or more networks, including networks that use different types of cables and different communication speeds. The networks all have to use IP (the Internet Protocol), though. If they don't, you need a *gateway* — for info about this stuff, see Chapter 6 in *The Internet For Dummies.*

***Note*:** Our readers Down Under have reported that non-American speakers of English pronounce this word "rowter" no matter what we say, because a *rooter* has a pouch and hops around the Outback.

RTFM. Read The Darned Manual. A suggestion made by people who feel that you have wasted their time asking a question you could have found the answer to in another way.

A well-known and much-used FTP site named `rtfm.mit.edu` contains FAQs for all Usenet newsgroups, by the way. Read The FAQ, Man!

sci. A type of Usenet newsgroup that discusses scientific topics.

server. A computer that provides a service to other computers on a network. An Archie server, for example, lets people on the Internet use Archie.

SIMTEL. A computer that used to contain an amazing archive of programs for MS-DOS in addition to Macintosh and UNIX. It was run by the U.S. Army and was shut down in 1993. Fortunately, its files live on in mirror (duplicate) archives at `oak.oakland.edu` and `wuarchive.wustl.edu`. See Chapter 18 in *The Internet For Dummies* in addition to Chapters 17 through 19 in this book for other top spots for FTP-able files.

SLIP. A software scheme for connecting a computer to the Internet. If you can run SLIP on your personal computer, for example, and you call up an Internet provider that does SLIP, your computer is *on the Internet* — it's not just a terminal, it's right on it. You can telnet and FTP to other computers, and when you get files, they arrive back on your PC, not on the Internet provider's computer. Anyone else on the Internet, in fact, can try to telnet to *your* computer, so watch out!

For instructions on how to run SLIP on your computer, see Chapter 8.

SMTP. Simple Mail Transfer Protocol, the method by which Internet mail is passed around.

soc. A type of newsgroup that discusses social topics, covering subjects from `soc.men` to `soc.religion.buddhist` to `soc.culture.canada`. See Chapter 12 in *The Internet For Dummies* for lists of interesting newsgroups.

socket. When your computer is on the Internet by using a SLIP connection, a *socket* is a conversation your computer is having with a computer elsewhere on the net. You might have one socket for an FTP session, for example, another socket for a telnet session, and another socket in which Eudora is getting your mail.

Spam. Originally a meat-related sandwich-filling product. The word is now used to refer to the act of posting inappropriate commercial messages to a large number of unrelated, uninterested Usenet newsgroups. See the section "I don't like Spam!" in Chapter 18.

Sprintlink. One of the large, commercial networks in the Internet, run by Sprint (the telephone company).

Sprintmail. An e-mail system provided by Sprintnet and formerly named Telemail. Believe it or not, if you have a Sprintmail account, your Internet address is

```
/G=firstname/S=lastname/O=company/
C=countrycode/A=TELEMAIL/
@sprint.com
```

Yuk! Substitute your first name, last name, company name, and country code (*us* for United States folks).

SURAnet. One of the regional networks originally set up to work with the NSFNET, headquartered in Florida.

talk. A type of newsgroup that contains endless arguments about a wide range of issues, such as `talk.abortion` and `talk.rumors`. See Chapter 12 in *The Internet For Dummies* for lists of interesting newsgroups.

TCP/IP. The system networks use to communicate with each other on the Internet. It stands for Transfer Control Protocol/Internet Protocol, if you care. See Chapters 2 and 3 in this book and Chapter 6 in *The Internet For Dummies* for the gory details.

telnet. A program that lets you log in to other computers on the net. See Chapter 14 in *The Internet For Dummies* to learn how to telnet to another computer (that is, log on to it from afar) and Chapter 15 in the same book for a list of interesting computers to telnet to.

terminal. In the olden days, a terminal consisted of a screen, a keyboard, and a cable that connected it to a computer. These days, not many people (well, not many people *we* know) use terminals, because personal computers are so cheap. Why have a brainless screen and keyboard when you can have your own computer on your desk? Of course, there are still lots of times when you want to connect to a big computer somewhere. If you have a personal computer, you can run a program that makes it *pretend* to be a brainless screen and keyboard — the program is called a terminal emulator, terminal program, or communications program.

See Chapter 4 to learn how to use your PC as a terminal to log in to an Internet provider.

terminal program. *See* communications program. Or look at the definition of *terminal,* just above this one.

text file. A file that contains only textual characters, with no special formatting characters, graphical information, sound clips, video, or what-have-you. All computers except some IBM mainframes store their text by using a system of codes named *ASCII,* so these are also known as *ASCII text files.*

The World. A UNIX-based on-line service run by Software Tool and Die. If you have a World account, your Internet address is *username*@world.std.com, substituting your username. The World gives you access to all Internet facilities in addition to the wild and wacky world of UNIX commands. (Yikes!) See Chapter 6 for the complete rundown.

thread. An article posted to a Usenet newsgroup, together with all the follow-up articles, the follow-ups to follow-ups, and so on. Organizing articles into threads makes it easier to choose which articles in a newsgroup you want to read.

threaded news reader. A news reader that enables you to select articles by thread. See Chapter 11 for a description of WinVN, a threaded newsreader for Windows.

Trumpet. A cool news-reader program which runs on computers that run Windows. Chapter 11 tells you all about it.

UNIX. An operating system everyone hates. No, an operating system everyone ought to love. No, it's both! It's an operating system that can be confusing to use, but it sure is powerful. Internet users are likely to run into UNIX if you use the World or another shell provider as your Internet provider or when you telnet to UNIX computers. For the complete truth about UNIX, get a copy of *UNIX For Dummies* (IDG Books Worldwide).

URL. Uniform Resource Locator, a way of linking pages together in the World Wide Web. Luckily, you don't have to know much about them — only the people who *write* WWW pages have to fool with them. See Chapters 14 and 16 to learn how to use the World Wide Web. Also see Chapter 22 in *The Internet For Dummies.*

Usenet. A system of thousands of distributed bulletin boards called *newsgroups.* You read the messages by using a program called a *news reader.* See Chapters 11 and 12 in *The Internet For Dummies* for an introduction to newsgroups and a list of some interesting ones. This book has lots of info about Usenet newsgroups too — Chapter 11 explains how to use Trumpet to read the news on your PC.

UUCP. An elderly and creaky mail system still used by many UNIX systems. UUCP stands for *UNIX-to-UNIX-copy.* UUCP uses mail addresses that contain exclamation points rather than periods between the parts (and they are in reverse order), a method known as *bang path addressing.* Whenever possible, use regular Internet addresses instead.

Uuencode/Uudecode. Programs that encode files to make them suitable for sending as e-mail. Because e-mail messages must be text, not binary information, uuencode can convert nontext files to text so that you can include it in a mail message. When the message is received, the recipient can run uudecode to turn it back into the original file. Pretty clever. For more information, see Chapter 17 in *The Internet For Dummies.*

UUNET. A nonprofit organization that, among other things, runs a large Internet site that links the UUCP mail network with the Internet and has a large and useful FTP file archive. You may encounter it in addresses that contain `uunet.uu.net` at the end. They also run *Alternet,* one of the larger commercial network providers.

V.32. The code word for a nice, fast modem (one that talks at a speed of 9600 baud, or about 960 characters per second). Even faster modems (that talk at 14,400 baud) are called *V.32bis.*

Veronica. A program that helps find things in Gopherspace. See Chapter 7 to find out how to run Veronica from America Online. You can also find Veronica in the World Wide Web.

viewer. A program used by Gopher, WAIS, or World Wide Web client programs to show you files that contain stuff other than text. You might want viewers, for example, to display graphics files, play sound files, or display video files.

VT-100. The part number of a terminal made about 15 years ago by the Digital Equipment Corporation. Why do you care? Because many computers on the Internet expect to talk to VT-100-type terminals, and many communications programs can pretend to be (emulate) VT-100 terminals. See Chapter 5 for more information about communications programs and terminals. The *VT-102* was a cheaper version that for most purposes acted exactly the same.

WAIS. Wide Area Information Servers (pronounced "ways," not "wace"), a system that lets you search for documents which contain the information you are looking for. It's not super easy to use, but it gets there.

See Chapter 21 in *The Internet For Dummies* to learn how to use WAIS, and Chapter 13 in this book for even more about it.

WELL. The WELL (the Whole Earth 'Lectronic Link) is a nationwide public Internet provider. You can contact it at `info@well.sf.ca.us`.

whois. A command on some systems that tells you the actual name of someone based on the person's username. *See also* finger. You can use `whois` by way of the World Wide Web (see Chapter 14).

WinGopher. A Windows program that lets you see Gopher pages. See Chapter 12 to learn how to get, install, and use it.

WinSock. WinSock (short for Windows Sockets) is a standard way for Windows programs to work with TCP/IP. You use it if you use SLIP to connect to the Internet. See Chapter 8 for details. Chapters 9 through 14 describe various WinSock-compliant applications you can run on any Windows computer to use information about the Internet.

WinWAIS. A Windows-based program that lets you use WAIS to search for information about the Internet. See Chapter 13 about both WAIS and WinWAIS.

WinZip. A Windows-based program for zipping and unzipping ZIP files in addition to other standard types of archive files. WinZip is shareware, so you can get it from the net. See Chapter 9 to learn how to get WinZip and install it.

World. See *The World.*

WWW (World Wide Web). A hypermedia system that lets you browse through lots of interesting information. See Chapter 22 in

The Internet For Dummies for an introduction and then check out Chapter 14 in this book for the latest in PC programs that make the WWW even niftier. Chapters 17 through 19 contain information about lots of cool WWW pages.

xarchie. A version of Archie that runs on UNIX under X Windows. If you use a UNIX workstation and Motif (or another windowing system), try typing **xarchie** to see whether you have a copy. If you do, see Chapter 19 in *The Internet For Dummies* to learn how it works.

xgopher. A version of Gopher that runs on UNIX under X Windows. If you use a UNIX workstation and Motif, try running xgopher.

XMODEM. A file-transfer protocol developed ages ago (1981?) by Ward Christianson to check for errors as files are transferred. It has since been superseded by YMODEM and ZMODEM, but many programs (especially Windows Terminal) still use it. See Chapter 4 for information about transferring files.

xwais. A version of WAIS that runs on UNIX under X Windows. If you use a UNIX workstation and Motif, try running xwais.

Yellow Pages. *See* NIS.

YMODEM. A file-transfer protocol that is faster than XMODEM but now as powerful as ZMODEM (see Chapter 4).

ZIP file. A file that has been created by using WinZip, PKZIP, or a compatible program. It contains one or more files that have been compressed and glommed together to save space. To get at the files in a ZIP file, you usually need WinZip, PKUNZIP, or a compatible program. Sometimes you may get a *self-extracting file,* which

is a ZIP file that contains the unzipping program right in it. Just run the file (that is, type the name of the file at the command line) and it unzips itself.

For information about how to get and set up WinZip on a Windows computer, see Chapter 9.

ZMODEM. A fast file-transfer protocol used by many programs. With ZMODEM, you can transfer several files with one command, and the names of the files are sent along with them. Some communications programs (like Procomm) can detect when a ZMODEM transfer has begun and automatically begin receiving the files. Nifty. See Chapter 4 for more info.

Index

● *F* ●

• X •

• Y •

• Z •

Notes

EXPLORE the INTERNET

FREE!

DELPHI is the only major online service to offer you full access to the Internet. And now you can explore this incredible resource with no risk. You get 5 hours of evening and weekend access to try it out for free!

Use electronic mail to exchange messages with over 20 million people throughout the world. Download programs and files using "**FTP**" and connect in real-time to other networks using "**Telnet**." Meet people from around the world with "**Internet Relay Chat**" and check out "**Usenet News**," the world's largest bulletin board with over 4500 topics.

If you're not familiar with these terms, don't worry; DELPHI has expert **online assistants** and a large collection of help files, books, and other resources to help you get started. After the free trial you can choose from two low-cost membership plans. With rates as low as $1 per hour, no other online service offers so much for so little.

5-Hour Free Trial!

Dial by modem, **1-800-365-4636**

Press return a few times. At *Password*, enter DUMMIES

SM

APK Public Access Computer System
Cleveland, Ohio

We've serviced area code 216 — Cleveland, Ohio since 1992

- Full Usenet feed
- IRC Client
- WWW clients; lynx, Mosaic
- WWW Server
- FTP Client
- SL/IP
- POP3 mail services
- MX forwarding

- Shell access
- MUD Clients
- Gopher Clients
- Gopher Server
- anonymous FTP server
- PPP
- domain registration
- Nameservers

Your connection to Internet — easy, reliable, helpful. We offer full range of services, UUCP, shell access, SL/IP and PPP, leased lines, network installation and maintenance.

How to Join:

- send E-mail to — **info@wariat.org**

- call voice — **216/481-9428**

- write to — **APK Public Access Computer System**
  19709 Mohican Ave
  Cleveland, Oh 44119

- telnet to — **wariat.org**

- URL — **http://www.wariat.org**

Include this coupon with registration form to receive free 10 hours of access after you pay for setup fee and first 20 hours of access.

WORLDWIDE ACCESS (SM)

CHICAGOLAND'S PREMIER INTERNET ACCESS SERVICE

The WorldWide Access Advantage Includes:

♦ **Reliability and Technical Excellence**

♦ **Mac and Windows Interfaces**

♦ **Net News, E-Mail, Gopher, IRC, Worldwide Web, and much more**

♦ **Competitive Rates**

♦ **Support, Training, and System Integration**

♦ **Consulting Services**

MAIL THIS COUPON TO WWA AND RECEIVE
15% OFF A YEARLY INTERNET ACCOUNT!

Send Mail To:
Computing Engineers
WorldWide Access
P.O. Box 285
Vernon Hills IL, 60061-0285

Contact Us At:
Phone: +1 708 367-1870
Fax: +1 708 367-1872
E-Mail: support@wwa.com
Sign Up Online: (312) 282-8605 or
(708) 367-1871

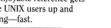

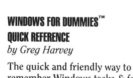

Order Form

Order Center: (800) 762-2974 (8 a.m.-5 p.m., PST, weekdays) or (415) 312-0650

For Fastest Service: Photocopy This Order Form and FAX it to: (415) 358-1260

Quantity	ISBN	Title	Price	Total

Shipping & Handling Charges

Subtotal	U.S.	Canada & International	International Air Mail
Up to $20.00	Add $3.00	Add $4.00	Add $10.00
$20.01-40.00	$4.00	$5.00	$20.00
$40.01-60.00	$5.00	$6.00	$25.00
$60.01-80.00	$6.00	$8.00	$35.00
Over $80.00	$7.00	$10.00	$50.00

In U.S. and Canada, shipping is UPS ground or equivalent.
For Rush shipping call (800) 762-2974.

Subtotal _____

CA residents add applicable sales tax _____

IN and MA residents add 5% sales tax _____

IL residents add 6.25% sales tax _____

RI residents add 7% sales tax _____

Shipping _____

Total _____

Ship to:

Name _____

Company _____

Address _____

City/State/Zip_____

Daytime Phone _____

Payment: ❑ Check to IDG Books (US Funds Only)   ❑ Visa   ❑ Mastercard   ❑ American Express

Card# _____ Exp._____ Signature_____

Please send this order form to: IDG Books, 155 Bovet Road, Suite 310, San Mateo, CA 94402.

Allow up to 3 weeks for delivery. Thank you!

IDG BOOKS WORLDWIDE REGISTRATION CARD

RETURN THIS REGISTRATION CARD FOR FREE CATALOG

Title of this book: **MORE Internet For Dummies**

My overall rating of this book: ❑ Very good [1] ❑ Good [2] ❑ Satisfactory [3] ❑ Fair [4] ❑ Poor [5]

How I first heard about this book:

❑ Found in bookstore; name: [6]

❑ Advertisement: [8]

❑ Word of mouth; heard about book from friend, co-worker, etc.: [10]

❑ Book review: [7]

❑ Catalog: [9]

❑ Other: [11]

What I liked most about this book:

What I would change, add, delete, etc., in future editions of this book:

Other comments:

Number of computer books I purchase in a year: ❑ 1 [12] ❑ 2-5 [13] ❑ 6-10 [14] ❑ More than 10 [15]

I would characterize my computer skills as: ❑ Beginner [16] ❑ Intermediate [17] ❑ Advanced [18] ❑ Professional [19]

I use ❑ DOS [20] ❑ Windows [21] ❑ OS/2 [22] ❑ Unix [23] ❑ Macintosh [24] ❑ Other: [25]_____
(please specify)

I would be interested in new books on the following subjects:
(please check all that apply, and use the spaces provided to identify specific software)

❑ Word processing: [26]

❑ Data bases: [28]

❑ File Utilities: [30]

❑ Networking: [32]

❑ Other: [34]

❑ Spreadsheets: [27]

❑ Desktop publishing: [29]

❑ Money management: [31]

❑ Programming languages: [33]

I use a PC at (please check all that apply): ❑ home [35] ❑ work [36] ❑ school [37] ❑ other: [38] _____

The disks I prefer to use are ❑ 5.25 [39] ❑ 3.5 [40] ❑ other: [41]_____

I have a CD ROM: ❑ yes [42] ❑ no [43]

I plan to buy or upgrade computer hardware this year: ❑ yes [44] ❑ no [45]

I plan to buy or upgrade computer software this year: ❑ yes [46] ❑ no [47]

Name: _____ Business title: [48] _____ Type of Business: [49]

Address (❑ home [50] ❑ work [51]/Company name: _____)

Street/Suite#

City [52]/State [53]/Zipcode [54]: _____ Country [55]

❑ **I liked this book!** You may quote me by name in future
IDG Books Worldwide promotional materials.

My daytime phone number is _____

IDG BOOKS

THE WORLD OF COMPUTER KNOWLEDGE